DEVOLUTION AND THE SCOTLAND BILL

Devolution and the Scotland Bill

By

C.M.G. Himsworth

Solicitor and Reader in Law at the University of Edinburgh

and

C.R. Munro

Professor of Constitutional Law at the University of Edinburgh

EDINBURGH
W. GREEN
1998

First published 1998

Published in 1998 by W. Green & Son Ltd of
21 Alva Street
Edinburgh EH2 4PS

Printed in Great Britain by
The Cromwell Press
Trowbridge, Wiltshire

A CIP catalogue record for this book is available from the British Library

ISBN 0 414 01253 4

© 1998
W. GREEN & SON LTD

PREFACE

Many people in Scotland and south of the border will want to keep abreast of developments as the new Scottish Parliament is established, and many people in other countries are taking an interest in the United Kingdom's constitutional reforms. For these reasons, the publishers decided that readers would welcome a concise account of the details of the proposals on devolution affecting Scotland.

Since its publication in December 1997, the Scotland Bill has provided the main focus of discussion. The Bill advances the proposals which were contained in the Government's best-selling White Paper, *Scotland's Parliament*, which were so convincingly endorsed by voters in the referendum of September 1997. In the course of the second reading debate in the House of Commons on January 12, 1998, Mr James Wallace MP said that he had found parts of the Bill "almost pleasurable reading". Another MP, however, was sure that reading the Bill would remain a minority sport.

It may be too much to say that we aim to pleasure readers, but there is a great deal to be said for the encouragement of minority sports. The purpose of this book is to make the Bill accessible to a wider readership. It contains the full text of the Scotland Bill itself, along with an account of the Bill's prehistory and the constitutional setting in which it was introduced; and includes examination of the rules which provide for the Parliament and its law-making powers; the new Executive; financial arrangements; and relations with local authorities, other public bodies, and the European Union. The explanation and commentary draw on the White Paper's proposals, where appropriate, and there is full reference to the Bill, signalled in our text by the italicisation of clauses and Schedules, when they are cited as relevant. Our aim has been to provide a description of the Bill in a clear and straightforward manner. This task has required some simplification of complex material, but the complete text of the Bill is available for those who seek the full detail. For those starting from the text of the Bill, the Table of Bill Provisions at the end of this book provides cross-references, to point the reader back into the relevant sections of the descriptive account.

Our thanks are due to colleagues who provided assistance and information on some points, and to Philip Munro for suggestions on some draft chapters. The staff of the University of Edinburgh Law Library were helpful as ever, and Margaret Lindley processed our words with her usual efficiency and cheerfulness. We relied on W. Green & Son Ltd. for the efficient production of a book within a space of time which a few years ago would have been inconceivable.

C.M.G.H.   Edinburgh, January 22, 1998
C.R.M.

CONTENTS

Contents

CHAPTER 1
SCOTLAND BEFORE AND AFTER THE UNION

"There's ane end of ane auld sang." The "sang" was Scotland's Parliament, and the Earl of Seafield, Scotland's Lord Chancellor who made the remark, had supported the union with England and Wales in 1707, and seems to have marked the passing of the Parliament in a tone of wry acceptance rather than with any conspicuous regret.

Nearly 300 years later, the song is to be played again. A Scottish Parliament will be elected in 1999 and will be fully operational in the year 2000. Unlike its ancient forebear, however, it will not be the legislature of a sovereign state. The union of states which was agreed in 1707 (and extended to union with Ireland in 1800) remains in place, at least for the time being. Scotland remains part of the United Kingdom of Great Britain and Northern Ireland, to give the state its proper name. But within the setting of that union there is to be a significant further measure of *devolution*, by which is meant the delegation of governmental powers without the relinquishment of sovereignty. The Scotland Bill will, when it is enacted as law, provide for a directly elected Scottish Parliament, from which an Executive, accountable to it, will be formed. In the following chapters of this book, we explain and comment on this constitutional reform and what it will mean, in the light of the provisions of the Bill. In this and the next chapter, we describe the historical background and relate how the Bill has come about.

SCOTLAND BEFORE THE UNION

There had been four kingdoms in the country we call Scotland between the fifth and the ninth centuries. In the ninth century Kenneth MacAlpin, the King of the Scots in Dalriada, became King of the Picts too. In 1018 one of his successors, Malcolm II, conquered Lothian when he defeated the Angles at the battle of Carham, and in the same year succeeded to the Kingdom of the Britons in Strathclyde. He and his grandson Duncan I, who followed him, thus became Kings of all Scotland. From that date onwards, Scotland was a recognisable country with, two or three interregnal periods apart, a continuous line of succession to the throne.

Unlike Wales and Ireland, Scotland was able to maintain its independence. The overlordship of Edward I of England was briefly acknowledged when he was invited to adjudge upon rival claims to the Scottish throne in 1292. But within two years his chosen man, John Balliol, and his counsellors were rebelling. Edward defeated the Scots at Dunbar, but if he thought that he had subdued them, was soon disabused of that notion by the patriot William Wallace. Wallace routed the English army at Stirling Bridge (1297), was defeated at Falkirk (1298), but continued to harry the English forces until his betrayal and death. Robert Bruce, who was crowned King in 1306, carried on where Wallace left off, and his campaigns culminated in a brilliant victory over Edward II at Bannockburn in 1314. The liberation of the country was complete, and its independence was recognised by Edward III in the Treaty of Northampton (1328).

Thereafter, English kings tried more subtle means. Henry VII thought to bring peace to the two kingdoms by the marriage of his daughter Margaret Tudor to Scotland's King James IV in 1503. It was exactly a hundred years before his plan came to successful fruition. In the interim, Henry VIII's armies punished Scottish aggression at Flodden (1513) and he retaliated with invasions in 1544 and 1545 after the Scottish Parliament repudiated a marriage treaty by which his son Edward would have married Mary, the infant Queen of Scots. It was the conversion of Scotland to Protestantism, which that unhappy Queen had been powerless to prevent, that began to bring Scotland closer to England. Then in 1603, when Elizabeth I died, James VI of Scotland became King James I of England too. He was the son of Mary, Queen of Scots and the great-great-grandson of Henry VII.

What occurred in 1603 was merely a personal union of the Crowns, contingent on the different laws of succession to the throne in Scotland and in England. Following the personal union, some trade restrictions between the two countries were abolished, and a common citizenship was introduced. But there was no union of the countries or their laws, and the English Parliament could no more make laws for Scotland than could the Scottish Parliament or Estates (as it was more commonly known) legislate for England. In fact, the circumstance of personal union was not very popular in Scotland, because the seat of royal government had been removed to London. When discontents arose during the reign of Charles I, they were felt all the more keenly in Scotland. The Scottish Presbyterian force of Covenanters took up arms against the King before the English parliamentary forces and, for the rest of the seventeenth century, events were to follow a broadly similar pattern in both countries. Indeed, when Cromwell's forces had succeeded in both, under the constitutions of the Commonwealth and the Protectorate, there was a single Parliament for Scotland, England and Ireland. But the brief experiment of a united Parliament was premature, and separate Parliaments met again following the Restoration, which in this respect as in others signified a deliberate return to the principles and practice of government under law which had been developing in the sixteenth and early seventeenth centuries.

Unfortunately, the restored Stuart kings proved to be unworthy recipients of the authority given them, not least because they seemed to pervert principles of legality by their exercise of the powers of suspending or dispensing with laws. In 1688, James VII of Scotland and II of England fled into exile from a land which would tolerate no longer the abuse of his powers in furtherance of his fellow Catholics' cause.

So in 1688 there was a need for a new constitutional settlement in England. A monarchy was thought desirable, but it had to be a Protestant monarchy. It had also to be a limited monarchy, subordinate in its powers to the Parliament. These points were taken for granted when an informal group of Lords, past members of the Commons (which had not been summoned since 1685), and authorities of the City of London invited William, Prince of Orange (who was married to James's daughter, Mary) to summon a convention. This irregular assembly met, declared the throne vacant, and offered it to William and Mary jointly. The gift was not absolute, but conditional, and the terms were embodied in a constitutional document enacted by the newly constituted Parliament as the Bill of Rights.

The peaceful revolution in England was rather less peacefully and more uncertainly followed, but followed nonetheless, in Scotland, where in 1689 the Scottish Crown too was offered to William and Mary, upon terms that established a limited monarchy, governing with Parliament's consent. The constitutional document which realised the arrangement was called the Claim of Right.

THE UNION

In the 17 years that followed, the Scottish Parliament displayed a greater authority than it had ever before evinced.[1] The greater assertiveness of the body, and the enhanced importance of both Parliaments as against the Crown, were amongst the causes of the progress to a more complete union. There were other underlying trends conducive to harmony, and perhaps unity, such as the geographical factor of sharing an island off the continent of Europe, common dynastic and religious influences, and economic interests.[2]

There had in fact been several earlier attempts to bring about union. Commissioners representing the Scottish and English Parliaments had been appointed in 1604 and again in 1670 in order to negotiate on the matter, but on these as on other occasions the efforts did not bear fruit.

However, after 1688, when it became clearer that the monarchy was to be a limited monarchy, constitutionally responsible to a Parliament, it was not easy to see how the monarchy could be responsible at one and the same time to two Parliaments, each pursuing its own policies. These contradictions were exposed, and perhaps exploited, when in the midst of war against Louis XIV the Scottish Parliament passed an Act (the Act anent Peace and War of 1703) to the effect that no future sovereign should have power to make war or peace without its consent.

By that time, feelings were running high on both sides of the border. There was resentment in Scotland of the Acts passed by the English Parliament which excluded them from trading with the English colonies. The attempt by Scots to found a trading colony of their own, the Darien scheme, had been a disastrous failure, for which the English were also blamed. In England, fearful of a Jacobite restoration, the Parliament had passed in 1700 the Act of Settlement, which declared that after Queen Anne's death the Crown would go to the Hanoverian line. But Scotland had not been consulted, and the Scottish Parliament responded with the Act of Security in 1704. Under its terms, the successor to the Scottish Crown was to be chosen by the Parliament "provided always that the same be

---

[1]   See C.S. Terry, *The Scottish Parliament: its Constitution and Procedure 1603-1707* (1905); R.S. Rait, *The Parliaments of Scotland* (1924). Revisionist historians in recent years have regarded these works as flawed by preconceptions, but have not disputed that the institution was relatively weak until the seventeenth century.

[2]   See R.H. Campbell, "A Historical Perspective on the Union" and J. Morrill, "The English, the Scots and the British" in *Scotland and the Union* (P.S. Hodge, ed., 1994).

not successor to the Crown of England", unless in the meantime some conditions such as freedom of trade had been established between the two countries. The English Parliament retaliated with the Aliens Act of 1705, which threatened to prohibit trade and to treat native Scots as aliens. When a Scottish ship was seized on the Thames, and an English ship captured in the Firth of Forth, the two countries seemed to be on the brink of war.

Perhaps it was that which brought them to their senses. The two Parliaments asked the Queen to appoint commissioners on their behalf, with a view to negotiating a treaty of union. The commissioners met in Whitehall and reached early agreement on the three main points: an incorporating union, guarantees by the English of complete freedom of trade, and acceptance by the Scots of the descent of the Crown according to the Act of Settlement. With a compromise on Scottish representation in the new Parliament, the endeavour was completed in nine weeks.

Critics of the union sometimes observe that the Scottish people did not agree to it. Neither, of course, did the English. Universal adult suffrage was still some 200 years away, and in the early eighteenth century representative democracy was very imperfectly realised. Daniel Defoe, who was sent to Edinburgh as a government agent in 1706, later wrote in his *History of the Union of Great Britain* (1709) that the Scottish people were "generally very desirous of the union" until pamphlets attacking it were circulated. As the terms of the union became known, some sections of the populace, such as the Jacobites, were more easily stirred to disaffection, and there were riots in Edinburgh and Glasgow.

However, in the Scottish Parliament, after clause-by-clause debate, the division on the ratification of the treaty was carried by 110 votes to 69. The scholar David Daiches has concluded that there was no outright bribery to secure the result, although its likelihood was enhanced by a successful exercise in political jobbery.[3] That is a plausible judgment, because the Crown was not entirely inept in the black arts of political "management". Yet the Crown had not been very successful either. The failures and difficulties in the "management" of Scotland after 1688 had made it virtually ungovernable, which at one and the same time suggests another motive for union and suggests the insufficiency of venality as an explanation for the majority vote.

Perhaps the best distillation of the Scottish parliamentarians' motives is still the summary which was offered by the Earl of Roxburgh to Jerviswood, his ally in the colourfully named Squadrone Volante group in the Estates (whose support for the union, when added to the Court Party's votes, was decisive): "Trade with most, Hanover with some, ease and security with others, together with a generall aversion at civil discords, intollerable poverty, and the constant oppression of a bad Ministry."[4]

---

[3] D. Daiches, *Scotland and the Union* (1977). See also P.W.J. Riley, *The Union of Scotland and England* (1978); P.H. Scott, *1707: The Union of Scotland and England* (1979).

[4] George Baillie of Jerviswood, *Correspondence, 1702-1708* (1842), p.138.

In England, the motives were primarily political. Louis XIV was maintaining James Stewart, the legitimist King of England and Scotland, at the French court. Through union, the threat of a Jacobite succession north of the border, with its destabilising consequences, could be averted. If in Scotland motives were mixed, as the historian Hume Brown observed, "it is difficult to escape the conclusion that the men who were chiefly responsible for carrying the Treaty ..... were sincerely convinced that union was the only possible solution of the relations between the two kingdoms."[5]

The commissioners on both sides made concessions, and the provisions of the union legislation which resulted are not such as to suggest a shotgun marriage. The position of Scotland's established church had, for example, been kept outside the commissioners' remit, as being non-negotiable. The English commissioners were obliged not only to concede freedom of trade and navigation, but to grant tax exemptions and payments in compensation. The Scottish commissioners had to agree to the Hanoverian succession.

The Scottish commissioners also had to settle for an "incorporating" union, by which was meant that both countries merged their legislatures and identity. Such an arrangement was naturally seen by the statesmen of the time as offering the most suitable form of government. Some of the Scottish commissioners, notably Andrew Fletcher of Saltoun, were attracted to a more "federal" conception of union. What they seem to have had in mind was rather what we should call a confederation, a league of states without a supreme, central legislature, on the model of the Dutch United Provinces. But an arrangement like that would have been open to the same dangers as the status quo. A truly federal solution would have been a different matter, but that was scarcely in the commissioners' contemplation, as there was not, until the American example in 1787, an obvious model for such a form.

Therefore, what was established was a full political and economic union. As the Crowns were to become one in law, the new state could justifiably be called a "United Kingdom", and it was to be called "the United Kingdom of Great Britain". Yet the union was not designed to effect a complete assimilation. As one historian puts it: "The men who negotiated the Treaty had no interest in creating a united British nation and therefore enabled the Scots to preserve their own national identity within the Union."[6] The Scottish commissioners' proposals concerning their distinct legal system and courts, the royal burghs, and the heritable jurisdictions, engendered no difficulties, while the place of the Kirk had been assured from the outset. These were institutions more strongly rooted in the national affection than was the Parliament which was disappearing.

The union legislation consisted of a principal Act composed of 25 Articles, and three associated Acts which provided for the continuance of the different

---

[5] P.H. Brown, *The Legislative Union of England and Scotland* (1914), p.126; see also T.C. Smout, "The Road to Union" in *Britain after the Glorious Revolution* (G.S. Holmes ed., 1969).
[6] B.P. Levack, *The Formation of the British State* (1987), p.212.

established churches in Scotland and England and the precise manner of electing the Scottish representatives to the House of Commons and the House of
Lords. These Acts of Union were separately enacted first by the Scottish Parliament, then by the English, which were legislating for their own demise, to
be succeeded by the Parliament of Great Britain. The legislation is in Scotland
often referred to as "the Treaty".

Some lawyers have argued that (in the law of Scotland, if not in English
law) the union legislation enjoys a special legal status, so that the United Kingdom Parliament is unable to alter it or at least unable to alter some of its more
important terms.[7] The argument was encouraged by some comments from Lord
President Cooper in the "Royal Numeral" case[8] in 1953, when a challenge to
the Queen's designation as "Elizabeth II" was dismissed.

However, the argument is difficult to sustain, since numerous alterations
have in fact occurred and the courts, if they are not powerless to intervene to
prevent them, have never actually done so. Many repeals and amendments
have been made because specific economic and political arrangements which
were thought appropriate in 1707 were seen as inappropriate or unnecessary at
a later date. Some provisions simply became spent with the passage of time.
Thus items relating to ship registration, customs and excise duties for specified goods, the Equivalents (transfers of money agreed in the terms), the Scottish mint, weights and measures, the Court of Exchequer, Privy Council and
parliamentary elections became otiose or were superseded, and Statute Law
Revision Acts of 1867, 1871, 1906 and 1948 repealed nine Articles wholly and
five others in part.

Far from being unpopular "breaches", many of these repeals and reforms
were either beneficial for Scotland or were uncontroversial. It could not seriously be argued that the corrupt electoral system which existed before the 1832
Reform Act should have been maintained, or that the heritable jurisdictions,
which were the main prop of feudal society in rural Scotland, should have been
preserved. And had not the Act securing the Protestant Religion been amended,
then the appointment of university professors would still be subject to a religious test.

Thus it may be seen that there is ample precedent for alterations when
changing conditions justify them. The evolution of society since 1707 has been
reflected in the evolution of the union, notwithstanding the precise terms of the
provisions as they were enacted then, which can evidently be repealed expressly or by implication. The creation of a devolved Scottish Parliament does
not as such, it may be noticed, involve any alteration or breach of the Articles
of the union legislation (which provided for representation in the new Parliament of Great Britain, but did not in terms abolish the Scottish Parliament or

---

[7]   Professor T.B. Smith and Professor J.D.B. Mitchell were prominent proponents of the argu-
      ment. For a fuller discussion, see C.R. Munro, "The Union of 1707 and the British Constitu-
      tion" in *Scotland and the Union* (P.S. Hodge ed., 1994).

[8]   *MacCormick v Lord Advocate*, 1953 S.C. 396. There were also equivocal comments in some
      later cases: see N. Walker and C.M.G. Himsworth, "The Poll Tax and Fundamental Law"
      (1991) 36 J.R. 45.

the English). By contrast, it is easy to conceive that the Scottish Parliament, in exercise of its powers, might legislate inconsistently with provisions of the union legislation, such as Article VI, providing for "all parts of the United Kingdom for ever from and after the Union" to "have the same Allowances Encouragements and Drawbacks." An argument of legal impediment, to the effect that the union legislation should be regarded as a kind of "fundamental law" which was unalterable, might have been expected to be raised in connection with legislation of the new Scottish Parliament, even if we would expect it to be defeated. However, the prospect has induced the draftsmen of the Scotland Bill to insert a specific provision in the hope of precluding the advancement of such arguments. It is provided that the union legislation shall "have effect subject to this Act" (*clause 35*). This provision purportedly gives primacy to the Scotland Act and anything done under the terms of the Act *vis-à-vis* the union legislation and will, it is submitted, be given effect to (whereas, if the union legislation were really unalterable, the provision would be ineffective).

SCOTLAND IN THE UNION

In the years immediately following 1707, the union was not popular on either side of the border. In Scotland particularly, there were grievances over taxation policies and over actions of the British Parliament such as its legislating for toleration in the Scottish Episcopalians Act 1711 and for the restoration of lay patronage in the Church Patronage (Scotland) Act 1711. These measures were regarded as violations of the spirit of the union agreement, and arguably of its letter as well. In 1713, when a proposal for dissolution of the union was introduced in the House of Lords, it was defeated by only four votes.

However, by the later eighteenth century, the benefits of the union were more generally appreciated. Home and colonial markets had been opened to Scottish traders and venturers as well as English, and the advances brought by the agrarian and industrial revolutions were enabling the people of northern and southern Britain to take full advantage of them. The industrial success of Scotland, initially as part of the customs union of Great Britain and then increasingly in an international free trade economy in the nineteenth century, in which Glasgow became "the second city of the Empire" could hardly be gainsaid. There was, too, a degree of social and cultural assimilation within Great Britain.

Remember, however, that the terms of the union legislation were not designed to effect a complete assimilation. The legislation afforded recognition to the importance of Scottish institutions and traditions in law and religion especially. Even if - as the instances in 1711 seemed to demonstrate - there was ultimately no *legal* impediment to alteration of the union legislation, a frontal assault on the totems of Scottish nationhood would not lightly be undertaken by any British Parliament, if it were against the will of the Scottish people. Thus, it may reasonably be claimed that, aside from any legal impediment, there is at least a *political* inhibition which militates against certain changes being made without consent.

If the separateness of the Scottish legal system owes something to the moral force of these considerations which were in mind in 1707, when some thought was given to maintaining its identity, there are other spheres such as education and aspects of arts and culture (such as architecture, or the press) and social and economic practice (such as patterns of domestic housing) where Scottish distinctiveness owes little or nothing to the union legislation as such.

So, for a variety of reasons, elements of distinctive traditions, characteristics, and culture have survived in Scotland, and contribute to feelings of separate national identity.[9] Indeed, it has been persuasively argued that the forces which shaped British political identity in the eighteenth century, namely Protestantism, the external threat posed by France and the commercial opportunities of Empire, were beginning to wane in the nineteenth century, and more ancient alignments and loyalties began to re-emerge.[10]

ADMINISTRATIVE DEVOLUTION

Be that as it may, when the "Irish question" dominated Westminster politics in the second half of the nineteenth century, more serious consideration began to be given to the Scottish question as well. After the union of 1707, there was no reason of principle why special arrangements should be made for Scotland in the matter of executive government. Yet there were always differences. In the eighteenth century, political management made of Scotland virtually a separate satrapy, as in the long period from the 1760s to the start of the nineteenth century when the influence of Henry Dundas (later Viscount Melville) was paramount. In the nineteenth century government functions were often carried out separately in Scotland through agencies and boards such as the Fisheries Board and the Prison Board or, like schools and public health and policing, were essentially organised at local levels.

In 1885, at a time when the Irish home rule question had become particularly acute, it was decided to differentiate the handling of Scottish affairs more clearly. So a Scottish Office was created as a department of government, whose Minister, the Secretary of State for Scotland, was to be responsible for law and order, education, and a few other matters.

These moves marked the start of an arrangement which may be called administrative devolution,[11] where the central government, without creating legislatures and executive governments in different parts of the state, arranges for aspects of its work to be conducted by a department which is defined *territorially* rather than *functionally*. What was devised in this fashion for Scotland was later to be followed (more slowly, and in a rather more limited way) for Wales, and (in rather different circumstances) for Northern Ireland.[12]

[9]   See L. Paterson, *The Autonomy of Modern Scotland* (1994).
[10] L. Colley, *Britons: Forging the Nation 1707-1837* (1992).
[11] The phrase was employed in the report of the Royal Commission on the Constitution 1969-1973, Cmnd. 5460 (1973). Although commonly used, it has been criticised as something of a misnomer: see A.W. Bradley, "Devolution of Government in Britain - Some Scottish Aspects" in *Devolution* (H. Calvert ed., 1975).
[12] V. Bogdanor, *Devolution* (1979).

As for the Scottish Minister, it became the practice to allocate a place in the cabinet to that person from 1892, and in 1926 the holder's office was raised in status to that of a Secretary of State. Since 1939, the principal base of the Scottish Office has been in Edinburgh, first at St Andrew's House on Calton Hill, and later in more modern, less pleasing buildings.

Over the years, the functions and importance of the Scottish Office have gradually increased.[13] On the recommendation of the Gilmour Committee on Scottish Administration in 1937,[14] a number of statutory boards with particular functions were abolished, and their powers vested in the Secretary of State. Some more functions were allocated to the minister as a result of recommendations made by the Royal Commission on Scottish Affairs which reported in 1954,[15] and others from time to time. Today the minister, with five junior ministers and a Scottish Office organised in five departments, is responsible for agriculture and fisheries, the arts, crofting, education, the environment, the fire service, forestry, health, housing, industrial assistance, some legal matters,[16] local government, police, prisons, roads, rural and urban development, social work, sport, transport, tourism and town planning, as well as some minor departments and some public corporations operating in Scotland.

Even that, however, is only part of the story. There are some other matters for which the Scottish Secretary is jointly responsible with an "English" colleague. More importantly, it is recognised that in a more general sense he is "Scotland's Minister" and has an interest in all matters affecting Scotland. As the Gilmour Committee put it, "there is a wide and undefined area in which he is expected to be the mouthpiece of Scottish opinion in the cabinet and elsewhere."[17]

Scotland has probably profited from the Secretary of State system. Certainly, it has enjoyed a higher expenditure per head of population than other parts of Great Britain,[18] and it is reasonable to attribute this in part to the advantage of having a spokesman at cabinet level. Administration has probably been better by reason of the Scottish Office civil servants being closer to the country's concerns and its people. Policies formulated in areas such as social work services and education have often compared favourably with the English equivalents. Policies which apply to the whole kingdom may be applied with

---

[13] A.G. Donaldson, "Administrative and Legislative Devolution" in *Independence and Devolution: The Legal Implications for Scotland* (J.P. Grant ed., 1976); A. Midwinter, M. Keating and J. Mitchell, *Politics and Public Policy in Scotland* (1991), Chaps. 3 and 4.

[14] Report of the Committee on Scottish Administration, Cmd. 5563 (1937).

[15] Report of the Royal Commission on Scottish Affairs, Cmd. 9212 (1954).

[16] Other functions in connection with the Scottish legal system fall to the Lord Advocate's Department and the Crown Office, for which the Lord Advocate is responsible.

[17] para. 37.

[18] However, this is not to say that the higher spending is undeserved, because it may for example reflect a poorer infrastructure and a higher level of social need. The arguments are complicated by the deficiencies of official statistics, different methods of calculation, and disagreement about what to include or exclude from the figures. See A. Midwinter, M. Keating and J. Mitchell, *Politics and Public Policy in Scotland* (1991), Chap. 5; A. Brown, D. McCrone and L. Paterson, *Politics and Society in Scotland* (1996), Chap. 4.

Scottish conditions in mind, and tailored or tempered accordingly. For example, the Conservative government which carried through the privatisation of water companies in England and Wales was persuaded to modify its policy for Scotland, nonetheless insisting on a reorganisation. The scope for administrative initiative has increased since 1978, when a change in the method of allocating funds enabled the Secretary of State to have greater freedom of action within the total budget.

At the same time, it is difficult to form an accurate picture. The collective responsibility of governments, and the secrecy surrounding British government, prevent us from knowing when, for example, the Secretary of State has been instrumental in winning something for Scotland or when he has been frustrated or defeated by a cabinet majority. It can be argued that, although the system has eased access to local officials, it has only produced marginal gains.[19]

More fundamentally, there is a weakness at the heart of the system, in that the executive and administrative powers are not properly matched by a legislature or political base. In this sense there is something of a "democratic deficit". The Secretary of State is a member of the United Kingdom government. When the majority in the House of Commons and the majority of Scottish MPs come from different parties (as they did between 1959 and 1964, between 1970 and 1974, and from 1979 to 1997), then the Secretary of State has less of the appearance of being Scotland's Minister and more of the appearance of being a colonial governor. The problem was exacerbated (and quite naturally exploited in the rhetoric of the other parties), when the Conservatives won only 10 of Scotland's 72 seats in the 1987 general election.

The system of administrative devolution involves problems of accountability as well as of legitimacy. Scottish Ministers' appearance on the rota for question time in the House of Commons once every three weeks is hardly commensurate with the scale of Scottish Office activities. The establishment of a Select Committee on Scottish Affairs as part of the departmental select committee system instituted in 1979 improved matters to a degree, although difficulties in agreeing on composition prevented the formation of the committee from 1987 to 1992. In any event, it was still obvious that the House of Commons had insufficient time for effective scrutiny of Scottish government.

With regard to legislation, the United Kingdom Parliament is the supreme legislature for all three of the legal systems in the United Kingdom, and might legislate for any or all of them. However, the numerical predominance of members for England and Wales constituencies in the House of Commons might explain, if not excuse, a tendency to "Anglocentricity". A look at the statute book might confirm that such a tendency has existed. Its symptoms, so far as Scotland is concerned, might be seen either in the failure to find sufficient parliamentary time for distinctive legislation or sometimes in an insensitivity to different legal traditions, when the law is amended by means of an Act applying throughout Great Britain or throughout the United Kingdom.

---

[19]   See J.P. Mackintosh, "Regional Administration: Has it Worked in Scotland?" (1964) 42 *Public Administration* 253.

Some minor variations in the usual parliamentary processes are available for Bills (or parts of Bills) which are exclusively Scottish in application. Procedural rules of the House of Commons allow for such proposals to be debated by the Scottish Grand Committee (a body consisting of all 72 Scottish MPs) at the second reading stage, which is the main opportunity for debate on the principle of the Bill, instead of in the House itself. Then the committee stage of such Bills (which is the occasion for debate on matters of detail) may be referred to a Scottish Standing Committee, composed of some 16 or 20 MPs. Another reform in 1980 allowed the Scottish Grand Committee to meet in Scotland. These arrangements permit Scottish legislative business to be dealt with in the main by Scottish members, but are arguably more symbolic than real, because within the Westminster system they are allowed to operate only within the presumption that the will of the United Kingdom government (which can use its Commons majority to enforce it, if necessary) should prevail.

Enough has been said to explain the essentials of the system of administrative devolution which has operated from 1885 up to the present day. The system has not been without merits. Scotland, in acknowledgment of its nationhood, has received some special consideration which is denied, for example, to regions of England. Along with the preservation of some of Scotland's institutions and distinctive practices, the devolution of administrative powers and the special arrangements for Scottish legislation, have combined to appease some of the demands for separate treatment. But the system has also been something of an untidy compromise, and since the 1960s its deficiencies have come under more vigorous challenge.

CHAPTER 2

UNFINISHED BUSINESS

If the nationhood of Scotland (and, to a lesser degree, Wales) had received constitutional recognition within the United Kingdom in a number of ways, these differences were not enough to satisfy everyone. Nationalists wanted nothing less than independence, and others wanted something more in the nature of "home rule", under which there would be substantial autonomy in domestic matters, but without separate statehood.

The Scottish National Party (SNP) and Plaid Cymru, the Welsh Nationalist Party, had roots in home rule movements in the 1880s, but were slow to develop as effective political parties. As late as 1959, the SNP was winning a mere 21,738 votes across the five seats it contested in the general election of that year, about the same as in 1931. But in the 1960s, the nationalist parties began to attract more significant support, as economic grievances were felt more keenly, and dissatisfaction increased with what were seen as remote and unsympathetic governments in London. By-election victories for Gwynfor Evans at Carmarthen in 1966 and Winifred Ewing at Hamilton in 1967 heralded spectacular advances over the following 10 years. In the 1970 general election, the SNP took 11 per cent of Scottish votes (306,802); at the February 1974 election, it more than doubled its votes and won seven seats; and in the general election of October 1974, with 30 per cent of the Scottish vote, won 11 seats.

The two largest British political parties were diffident, and rather defensive, in their response to the threat posed by these nationalistic stirrings. The Conservatives, in opposition, set up in 1968 a committee chaired by Sir Alec Douglas-Home, which reported two years later in favour of the creation of an elected Scottish Convention, which would deal with some stages of the Scottish Bills initiated at Westminster, but would not have its own legislative powers.[20] The Labour Party, with more seats to lose in Scotland and Wales, was more concerned. However, in 1969 Wilson's Government resorted to a favourite method of sidelining troublesome issues: it set up a Royal Commission.

THE ROYAL COMMISSION
The Royal Commission on the Constitution had unusually wide terms of reference. It was asked "to examine the present functions of the central legislature and government in relation to the several countries, nations and regions of the United Kingdom; and to consider ..... whether any changes are desirable ..... in the present constitutional and economic relationships". Under that remit, almost any constitutional question could have been considered, but the majority of the Commissioners largely confined themselves to issues of the geographical distribution of power.

The Commission was singularly ill-starred in its fortunes, and its report did

[20]   *Scotland's Government* (1970).

not appear until October 1973, four and a half years after its appointment.[21] Its first chairman, Lord Crowther, and another member died, and no fewer than three others resigned during its deliberations. Lord Kilbrandon, who took over the chairmanship, was unable to deliver anything approaching unanimity. Two members, Lord Crowther-Hunt and Professor Alan Peacock, regarded their disagreement with the others as so fundamental that they did not sign the majority report, and wrote a substantial Memorandum of Dissent. The eleven others signed, but were far from agreed on the course to follow.

On two points there was agreement. Independence for Scotland and Wales, or "separatism", as it was perhaps more pejoratively described, was flatly rejected, because "the political and economic unity of the United Kingdom should be preserved",[22] and "the vast majority of people simply do not want it to happen".[23] Surprisingly, there was an equally quick dismissal of federalism. It was considered that "the United Kingdom is not an appropriate place for federalism",[24] and noted that "there was very little demand for federalism in Scotland and Wales, and practically none at all in England".[25] It was asserted that "only within the general ambit of one supreme elected authority is it likely that there will emerge the degree of unity, co-operation and flexibility which common sense suggests is desirable".[26]

Beyond that, the Commissioners found it difficult to agree. It was accepted that the administrative devolution of the Secretary of State system had been carried about as far, or at least almost as far, as it could reasonably go, and that something different was needed. Eight of the Commissioners supported a scheme of legislative devolution to Scotland, with a directly elected assembly having power to legislate on subjects largely co-extensive with those for which the Scottish Office already had responsibility, and an Executive drawn from the assembly. Six of the eight also favoured legislative devolution to Wales, but the other two recommended only an elected Advisory Council for Wales, with scrutinising and advisory functions. A ninth member would have given Scotland and Wales a council of that sort, with the Scottish one having additional functions in relation to Parliament's Scottish Bills.

Two Commissioners signing the majority report favoured a scheme of executive devolution, under which directly elected assemblies, not only in Scotland and Wales, but also in eight regions of England, would have responsibility for subordinate policy-making and administration within the framework set by Parliament and the central government. Eight other Commissioners would

---

[21] Report of the Royal Commission on the Constitution 1969-1973, Cmnd. 5460 (1973). For a useful account, see J.P. Mackintosh, "The Report of the Royal Commission on the Constitution" (1974) 27 *Parliamentary Affairs* 115; for further discussion, see T.C. Daintith, "The Kilbrandon Report: Some Comments" and other essays in *Devolution* (H. Calvert ed., 1975).

[22] Report of the Royal Commission on the Constitution 1969-1973, Cmnd. 5460 (1973), para. 431 and Chaps. 11 and 12.

[23] para. 497 of the report.

[24] para. 539 of the report.

[25] para. 498 of the report.

[26] para. 539 of the report.

have established regional councils, with lesser responsibilities, for those eight regions.

Lord Crowther-Hunt and Professor Peacock also advocated a form of executive devolution. They believed that the causes of dissatisfaction with government were common to all parts of Great Britain, and in their view the claims of Scotland and Wales to nationhood did not "entitle the people in Scotland and Wales to be better governed or to have more participation in their own affairs than is offered to the people of Yorkshire or Lancashire".[27] Their concern for equality of rights led them to propose in their Memorandum of Dissent a scheme of "intermediate level government", allowing for seven directly elected assemblies and governments, for Scotland, Wales, and five regions of England. They also interpreted the terms of reference more widely, and made a number of other suggestions, including reform of the House of Lords, a new system of specialised parliamentary committees, and the creation of a strengthened Prime Minister's Department.

Perhaps the most conspicuous characteristic of the Commissioners' work was their diversity of views, and it was small wonder that it was initially received with disappointment and some bafflement. Besides, the Heath Government which was in office at the time of publication had more pressing problems, and within four months there was a general election, in February 1974.

In that election the SNP gained six more seats and Plaid Cymru won two. When Wilson took office at the head of a minority Labour Government, it was announced in the Queen's speech that proposals on devolution would be brought forward in the light of consideration of the report. Labour continued in government with a tiny majority after the October 1974 election, and, after a succession of White Papers, the Scotland and Wales Bill 1976 was introduced. The Bill was unpopular with MPs and poorly drafted. It was progressing so slowly that the Government proposed a guillotine motion to limit the time spent on it. That was defeated, and the Government was ignominiously obliged to shelve its intended enactment.

In 1977, the Government made a parliamentary pact with the Liberals, and tried again. This time there were two Bills, which after protracted proceedings in both Houses became law as the Scotland Act 1978 and the Wales Act 1978. These would have given directly elected assemblies to Scotland and Wales, the Scottish one having legislative powers, and the Welsh only executive powers. However, amongst the amendments which the Government had been forced to accept was one which proved fatal. The Government planned to hold referendums in Scotland and Wales, so as to give electors an opportunity to say whether they wanted the proposals to come into effect. George Cunningham, a backbench Labour opponent of devolution, successfully proposed that if less than 40 per cent of those entitled to vote were to vote "Yes", then orders for the repeal of the legislation would have to be laid before Parliament.[28] The polls took place

---

[27] Report of the Royal Commission on the Constitution 1969-1973, Vol. 2, Memorandum of Dissent, Cmnd. 5460-1 (1973), para. 129.

[28] Scotland Act 1978, s.85; Wales Act 1978, s.80.

on March 1, 1979. In Wales, only 11.9 per cent of the electorate voted "Yes". There was insufficient enthusiasm for further devolution, or at least for the degree of it on offer. In Scotland, the result was more equivocal and, from any perspective, more unsatisfactory. A majority of those who voted were in favour of the Scotland Act proposals, because 32.9 per cent of the electorate said "Yes" and only 30.8 per cent said "No". However, 36.3 per cent of the registered electorate did not vote, and so the threshold requirement set by the Cunningham provision was not satisfied.

The results led indirectly to a change of government because, when the SNP withdrew its support from the Labour Government in reaction to its response to them, the Government was shortly defeated on a vote of confidence, and so was obliged to resign. It may be said that the Government was morally bound by the terms of the Cunningham amendment although, in view of the supremacy of Parliament, referendum results can only be advisory, rather than mandatory, in the United Kingdom. Thus, the obligation to repeal the Act rather than to bring its provisions into effect, could itself have been repealed. However, a Conservative Government, with Margaret Thatcher as Prime Minister, took office as a result of the ensuing general election, and repealing orders were laid before Parliament and approved.

THE SCOTLAND ACT 1978

Although, therefore, the Scotland Act 1978 was never brought into effect, it is of some interest to notice the main features of the devolution scheme which was on offer at that time. Some of the work which was done by politicians and by civil servants at that time provided a basis for later schemes of devolution, including the proposals contained in what will be enacted as the Scotland Act 1998. Equally, it may be said that experience of some of the more problematic or controversial aspects of the 1978-79 scheme contributed to redesigns in the aftermath of its failure.

The following were some of the main features of the scheme.

(1) Some powers were devolved to a Scottish Assembly, but the Act did not purport to limit in any way the legislative sovereignty of the United Kingdom Parliament over the whole of the United Kingdom. Thus Parliament would not have been restrained by law from legislating on matters within the legislative competence of the Scottish Assembly, but only by expectations of its inhibiting itself, which might develop to become a constitutional convention to that effect.

(2) There was to be a single chamber Assembly, elected initially in multimember constituencies with each parliamentary constituency returning two or three members according to size, except that Orkney and Shetland would return one member each. For subsequent elections, the Boundary Commission for Scotland was to divide parliamentary constituencies into single member Assembly constituencies. Members would have been elected under the familiar "first past the post" method: the Labour Government of the time resisted the Liberals' preference for elections under proportional representation.

(3)   The standard term of the Assembly was to be four years, although an Assembly could be dissolved within that period by order of the Secretary of State if two-thirds of the Assembly members so resolved.

(4)   The Assembly was not granted any tax raising powers at all, nor permitted to raise loans. Finance for the devolved functions was to be provided by a block grant voted by the Westminster Parliament. This system would have maintained the supremacy of the Treasury, and emphasised the dependence of the Assembly and Executive. As there was concern, however, that annual discussions of the level of block grant might be inappropriate and would tend to provoke acrimony, the Government suggested that the total of devolved spending in Scotland should be related to comparable expenditure elsewhere in the United Kingdom on the basis of population and relative needs, and then expressed as a percentage. The resultant equation came to be known (after the Chief Secretary to the Treasury at the time) as "the Barnett formula" and came into use as a practically convenient way to determine Scottish Office allocations, notwithstanding the failure to set up an Assembly.

(5)   The United Kingdom Government kept in its own hands powers of economic management and industrial policy for the whole United Kingdom. The Scottish Assembly would have lacked the means to control Scotland's economic development.

(6)   In allocating legislative competence, the 1978 Act adopted a rather complex and opaque method. It neither defined the subjects to be devolved, leaving the residue to the centre, nor defined the subjects to be retained, all others being devolved. What it did was to list the devolved matters in general terms, while specifying in another list matters which were to be excluded from the Assembly's competence. Demarcation difficulties would certainly have arisen.

(7)   If it was doubtful whether a Scottish Assembly Bill was within the competence of the Assembly, there was provision for judicial scrutiny. The Secretary of State for Scotland was to refer such Bills to the Judicial Committee of the Privy Council, and if that court ruled them to be beyond the powers of the assembly, they would not be submitted for the Royal Assent. After enactment, too, the validity of Scottish Assembly Acts would have been challengeable in the courts, with final appeal to the Judicial Committee of the Privy Council.

(8)   The Secretary of State for Scotland could also reserve for consideration by Parliament any Bill passed by the Scottish Assembly which, in his view, would or might affect a non-devolved matter (such as the economy or defence) and was not in the public interest. Then the Houses of Parliament could by resolution prevent submission of the Bill for the Royal Assent.

(9)   There was to be a Scottish Executive consisting of a First Secretary and other ministers called "Scottish Secretaries" and assistants, drawn from the membership of the Assembly. The First Secretary would have been appointed on the nomination of the Assembly, by the Secretary of State,

and subsequent appointments would be on the advice of the First Secretary. They would have had executive powers over devolved matters (including the making of subordinate legislation). The Secretary of State would have had powers of veto or direction, subject to parliamentary approval, in respect of executive actions affecting non-devolved matters.

(10) The Secretary of State for Scotland was to remain as a Cabinet minister's office in the central government. What the role would have involved under the new dispensation was not entirely clear.

(11) There was no alteration of the level of Scottish representation in the Westminster Parliament, and so the notorious "West Lothian question" was left largely unresolved. Tam Dalyell, then the Labour MP for West Lothian, had repeatedly protested about the anomaly whereby, since the representation of Scotland in Parliament was maintained, Scottish MPs might have a decisive say over legislation in a matter only concerning England, whereas English MPs would have forfeited their right to a say in legislation devolved to the Scottish Assembly. An amendment carried against the wishes of the Government, which described it as a "constitutional imbecility", provided for a delayed second vote (at which it was hoped that Scottish MPs would be persuaded to abstain) when the second reading of an "English" Bill was approved only because of the support of Scottish MPs.

THE ROAD TO REFORM

Following the 1979 referendum results in Scotland and Wales, there was naturally some loss of enthusiasm for further devolution amongst the uncommitted, both in the general population and in political circles. The subject had claimed a lion's share of parliamentary time; it had provoked jealousies between different parts of the United Kingdom, and caused divisions within as well as between the parties; and, in the end, it had come to nothing. Legislation on the subject was not likely to be attempted again for some time.

In any event, as we have noticed, the referendum results led indirectly to a change of government, with the Conservatives' success in the general election of 1979. The administrations led by Margaret Thatcher and John Major showed no interest in reviving any proposals for legislative devolution. On the whole, their disinclination towards substantial reform was to be expected, for the reason of principle that the party's philosophy was historically opposed to it - between 1912 and 1965 the party in Scotland was officially the Scottish Unionist Party - and perhaps for the practical reason that the party enjoyed its strongest support in England, especially south of a line from the Severn to the Wash.

In the 1992 general election campaign, John Major robustly defended the union, while simultaneously hinting at possible changes when he addressed Scottish voters, with the promise that "after the election we will take stock".[29]

---

[29]   *The Scotsman*, February 24, 1992.

However, he was apt to have seen in the election result (perhaps even in the Scottish results, with a marginal gain in share of the vote and in seats won, as compared with 1987) a vindication of his general approach, and so the impetus for change was reduced. There was a review,[30] followed by some minor reforms in the handling of parliamentary business in 1994 and 1995, including greater use of the Scottish Grand Committee, which was encouraged to meet in other Scottish cities and towns as well as Edinburgh.[31] However, as the Government itself virtually admitted, the tinkering had about reached its limit. Nothing could much alter the democratic deficit, unless it was conceded that Scottish voters should be entitled to a measure of home rule.

The Liberals have long advocated home rule for Scotland, generally as part of "home rule all round", with assemblies in Wales and England (or regions of England) as well. Usually they have favoured a full-blown federal system, under which national or regional assemblies would be co-ordinate with a central assembly, each body having exclusive competence in different spheres. The Liberals, before and through their years of alliance with the SDP, to their present incarnation as the Liberal Democrats, can claim to have been the most consistent proponents of home rule.

The Labour Party could not be entirely absolved from the suspicion that its actions in government from 1974 to 1979 had been driven by political expediency rather than clear principle. Historically, the party's leanings had been more centralist. But for a party which held (after the 1987 general election) 50 seats in Scotland, there were obvious electoral advantages to be garnered from espousing the cause of a Scottish Parliament, if it were popular, and losses to be risked if it did not. Moreover, especially after John Smith became the party's leader in 1992, there could be no doubt over the party's commitment to that cause. For John Smith, who had piloted the Scotland Act 1978 through the Commons, the project of Scottish home rule was, quite simply, "unfinished business".

Political parties' policies were important, because only a party (or coalition of parties) in government could deliver constitutional reforms. But some pressure groups were formed in the wake of the 1979 referendum or later, which were influential in keeping the issue of reform in front of the public and the parties during the long period of Conservative governments.

One such group was the Campaign for a Scottish Assembly, a gathering of notables which through a committee in 1988 produced a report entitled *A Claim of Right for Scotland*, which asserted the right of the people of Scotland to decide on their own constitution. The document also recommended that a convention should be brought into being to draw up a scheme for a Scottish assembly or parliamentary body.

Accordingly, a body calling itself the Scottish Constitutional Convention was set up and held its first meeting in March 1989. The Conservatives refused

---

[30] *Scotland in the Union: A Partnership for Good*, Cm. 2225 (1993).
[31] See C.M.G. Himsworth, "The Scottish Grand Committee as an Instrument of Government" (1996) 1 *Edinburgh Law Review* 79.

to join the body, and the SNP withdrew before meetings began, having formed the view that the option of independence was not likely to be seriously pursued under the *modus operandi* of proceeding by consensus. The Labour Party and the Liberal Democrats participated in the Convention, however, along with the Greens and a few other minor parties, and representatives or delegates of local authorities, trade unions, churches and some other organisations. Although it had no official status, the body did contain 59 of the 72 MPs and six Scottish MEPs. The joint chairs of the Convention were drawn from Labour (Lord Ewing of Kirkford) and the Liberal Democrats (Sir David Steel, the former leader of the party), and its Executive was chaired by Canon Kenyon Wright.

In November 1990 the Convention published a report, *Towards Scotland's Parliament*, with the central proposal of a directly elected Scottish Parliament which would have a defined range of powers and responsibilities, including exclusive responsibility on many matters. It was envisioned that the powers of the Scottish Parliament and Executive should not be alterable by the Westminster Parliament without the consent of the Scottish Parliament. Whether such a form of entrenchment or protection is competent under the British constitution is contestable, however.[32]

Through collaboration in the Convention, Labour and the Liberal Democrats entered the 1992 general election with a broad measure of agreement on Scottish constitutional reform, although there were some matters, including the method of election for the Parliament and the method of funding Scottish government, on which agreement had not been secured or there were differences between the parties. After the 1992 election, the Convention appointed a commission to tackle some of the outstanding disagreements and problems, which was chaired by the journalist Joyce McMillan and included amongst its members Professor John Sewel (who was made an Under Secretary of State in the Scottish Office team, after Labour won the election in 1997). The commission's work was incorporated in the Convention's final report, *Scotland's Parliament. Scotland's Right*, which was presented on St. Andrew's Day, 1995.

The scheme contained in the final report accepted that legal entrenchment should not be attempted, but proposed instead that there be a solemn declaration of intent by the United Kingdom Parliament to the effect that there would be no repeal or alteration of the Act founding the Scottish Parliament, without the consent of the Scottish Parliament and of the people of Scotland. In this and a few other respects, there is a hint of naivety, or an impression of pious aspirations, about the proposals.

However, the substance of the report commanded respect for its thoroughness and attention to detail as well as principle. The proposals were for a Parliament of 129 members, elected under an additional member system; a power to increase or decrease the basic rate of income tax by a maximum of 3p in the pound to be given to the Scottish Parliament, but with funding chiefly through

---

[32] On the general question of entrenchment, see C.R. Munro, *Studies in Constitutional Law*, (1987) Chap. 5; A.W. Bradley, "The Sovereignty of Parliament - in Perpetuity?" in *The Changing Constitution* (J. Jowell and D. Oliver ed., 3rd ed., 1994).

an assigned budget from central government; and substantial devolution of legislative and executive functions to a Scottish Parliament and an Executive formed from it.

The Scottish Constitutional Convention must be counted as an effective pressure group and a significant force for change. Its particular importance is evident in two ways especially. First, its work over a period of years in progressively developing a scheme for constitutional reform meant that a sympathetic government could import the proposals more or less wholesale. With other proposals on more technical matters[33] that could be added as appropriate, a government could avail itself of a reform package which was "off the peg" to the extent that it was willing to do so.

A second feature to note is that the cross-party collaboration which was involved was a relatively unusual phenomenon in British or Scottish politics, at the national level. The experience of co-operation between Labour and the Liberal Democrats was not consigned afterwards to the dustbin of history, but was taken as a model and encouragement to further collaboration in plotting constitutional reforms, both before and after the general election of May 1997.

THE WHITE PAPER AND THE REFERENDUM

The Labour Party had for some years expounded the view that victory at a general election would afford a sufficient mandate for the creation of a Scottish Parliament along the lines presented in their election manifesto. However, in the summer of 1996, after Tony Blair had become leader following the death of John Smith, it changed its mind. Perhaps the leadership was worried that the Conservatives' attacks were having effect. Michael Forsyth, who had become the Secretary of State for Scotland in 1995, was a clever politician who had coined the term "tartan tax" to focus the minds of the electorate on the costs which a tax-raising Parliament could involve, both immediate and personal, and longer term and more general.

In order both to undermine the Conservatives' campaign and to test and secure the commitment of Scottish voters, the idea of a referendum was conceived and commended itself to the Labour leadership, which determined on a tactical shift. Lord Ewing, a former Labour minister, resigned as joint chair of the Scottish Constitutional Convention in disgust, and the party also lost a front bench spokesman when John McAllion MP, who had not been consulted on the change, resigned in protest. Otherwise the Scottish Labour Party reluctantly succumbed. There was a period of some disarray, when decisions about how many referendums were desirable were switched and switched again, but the eventual policy was to hold votes on two questions (the principle of support for a Parliament, and the principle of its possessing tax-varying powers) on one occasion only, in advance of legislating.

[33] For example, under the auspices of the John Wheatley Centre, work has been done on parliamentary procedures: B. Crick and D. Millar, *To Make the Parliament of Scotland a Model for Democracy* (1995). A substantial report on the implementation of proposals was produced by the Constitution Unit, entitled *Scotland's Parliament: Fundamentals for a New Scotland Act* (1996).

Labour, therefore, entered the general election with a commitment to subject its devolution proposals for Scotland (and Wales) to referendums, as well as a commitment that, given affirmative results, it would legislate for a Scottish Parliament within a year of taking office. In one respect, at least, its policy was quite consistent, for referendums were also being proposed by Labour for a number of other choices which the incoming government would face, including the single currency, a political settlement for Northern Ireland, and a new strategic authority for London. This form of direct democracy, traditionally viewed with some suspicion in Britain, seemed to be becoming almost *de rigueur.*[34]

When the general election held on May 1, 1997 brought Labour to power with a huge overall majority (of 179 seats), the new Government was true to its promise to act quickly on devolution. White Papers regarding Scottish and Welsh devolution were published in July. The White Paper on Scottish devolution, *Scotland's Parliament*,[35] was written in a clear, readable style and attracted sufficient interest to enter the bookshops' best-selling charts. Work was already proceeding in the Scottish Office on the details of the Scotland Bill, and the Bill, which is explained in this book, transforms into the language of legislation those parts of the White Paper which require legislative form.

First, a referendum campaign had to be fought, and on the basis of the White Paper. So one difference from 1979, when electors were voting on whether the provisions of the Scotland Act 1978 and Wales Act 1978 should come into effect, was that the 1997 referendums were pre-legislative. Objection might be taken to this, especially if there were significant differences between the White Paper proposals and the eventual Act. However, given their fortuitously large majority as well as fidelity to their professions of policy, it seems probable that we shall be able to acquit the Government on that count. Besides, it is arguable that the proposals in White Paper form were more user-friendly and more accessible to the electorate than provisions in a Bill or Act. Another practical advantage for the Government in moving earlier was that clear indications of electoral support in advance could be used in order to ease the passage of the Bill through Parliament. Tony Blair had described this as a "principled, tactical policy",[36] and on another occasion had warned that the Government's tolerance of "game-playing"[37] would be limited. The measure providing for the referendums, the Referendums (Scotland and Wales) Act 1997, had itself been guillotined. There is, as a committee recently confirmed, a convention that "Bills of first class constitutional importance should have all their stages on the floor of the House",[38] and if this were adhered to and opponents were persistent, the Commons stages could have been difficult and protracted.

[34] See C.R. Munro, "Power to the People" [1997] P.L. 579.
[35] Cm. 3658 (1997). Hereafter, references in this book to "the White Paper" are references to *Scotland's Parliament.*
[36] *New Statesman*, July 5, 1996.
[37] *Hansard*, H.C. Vol. 294, col. 68 (May 14, 1997).
[38] Select Committee on Modernisation of the House of Commons, *First Report: The Legislative Process*, (1997-98), H.C. 190, para. 74.

The attitude of the House of Lords, arguably but not certainly inhibited by the "Salisbury doctrine",[39] was also unpredictable.

Another difference from 1979 was the absence of a threshold requirement. In theory, there is something to be said for thresholds, as a kind of equivalent to the entrenchments generally found in written constitutions, on the principle that constitutional amendments ought to command substantial support. However, there was some bitterness and a degree of disillusion in the aftermath of the 1979 Scottish result, and the Government would have considered the setting of a threshold for the 1997 referendums to be politically impossible, even if otherwise persuaded of its merits. A simple majority of those voting was held to be sufficient, if it could be achieved.

A relatively short period was allowed for referendum campaigning in 1997, with only seven weeks separating the publication of the White Paper and the Scottish polling day (on September 11), much of it overlapping with the holiday season, and further contracted when campaigning was virtually suspended for seven days, in the extraordinary atmosphere which followed the death of Diana, Princess of Wales, on the last day of August.

Perhaps, however, it might be argued that the issue of constitutional reform had already become quite familiar to the Scottish electorate, through repeated airings. If, as the Labour leader John Smith had maintained, the demand for a Scottish Parliament was "the settled will" of the people of Scotland, neither the length nor the events of the campaign would matter much.

In fact, for probably a mixture of reasons, the campaign was rather lacklustre.[40] Predictably, Labour and the Liberal Democrats, partners in the Scottish Constitutional Convention, co-operated to press for a double "Yes" vote. Significantly, so did the SNP, once satisfied that there was nothing in the Government's plans which would formally prevent a Scottish Parliament in the future from debating on or voting for independence. Umbrella groups were formed for the purpose of the campaign, "Scotland FORward" on one side, and "Think Twice" on the other. However, the effectiveness and vigour of the "No" campaigners were reduced because Scottish Conservatives, who would have been expected to figure most prominently in their campaign, could display neither good morale nor much cohesion in the wake of a general election result which had left the party with no Scottish seats.

On September 11, voters were given two ballot papers.[41] On the first, 1,775,045 voters (or 74.3 per cent of those voting) said "I agree that there should be a Scottish Parliament", while 614,400 (or 25.7 per cent) disagreed.

---

[39] The "Salisbury doctrine" is a doctrine of self-restraint, under which the House should not reject Bills considered to have been approved by the electorate. However, Colin Turpin concludes that "it may be doubted whether these principles have a sufficient clarity, or are supported by a sufficient agreement, to give them the status of a convention": *British Government and the Constitution* (3rd ed., 1995), p.412.

[40] See P. Jones, "A Start to a New Song: The 1997 Devolution Referendum Campaign" (1997) *Scottish Affairs*, No. 21, 1.

[41] As two separate ballot papers were used, figures are unavailable to reveal the numbers of persons who split their vote along "Yes"/"No" or even "No"/"Yes" lines.

There was a "Yes" majority in all 32 of the local authority areas. Incidentally, with a turnout figure of 60 per cent, the "Yes" vote represented 45 per cent of the electorate, and so would also have been easily sufficient to pass the 40 per cent hurdle set by the Cunningham amendment in 1979.[42]

As expected, voting on the second question was less positive. But there was still a majority in 30 of the 32 local areas (Orkney and Dumfries and Galloway being the exceptions) for the proposition, "I agree that a Scottish Parliament should have tax-varying powers". The overall voting was in favour by 1,512,889 to 870,263 (or 63.5 per cent to 36.5 per cent).

There could no longer be any real dispute about "the settled will" of the Scottish people. The Government had secured a specific mandate to complete the unfinished business of legislative devolution, and three months later, on December 18, it published the Scotland Bill.

---

[42] The electoral register is quite liable to be inaccurate by about 10 per cent, due to deaths and omissions: R. Blackburn, *The Electoral System in Britain* (1995), pp.83-88. If the conventional discount for deaths were made, the vote on the second question would also have satisfied a threshold of 40 per cent of the electorate. The inaccuracy of the registers provides an argument against employing thresholds which are based on them.

CHAPTER 3
SCOTLAND WITHIN THE UNITED KINGDOM

The Conservative Party's opposition to the creation of a Scottish Parliament could be explained on various grounds, but was to some extent a natural implication of their unionist principles. A commitment to preserving the United Kingdom may sit more easily with a common approach to its constituent parts, although a willingness to regard Northern Ireland differently did not go unnoticed. For most of the last 20 years, the Conservatives have argued that devolution of legislative powers to an assembly in Scotland was a step too far, and warned that the effect of taking such a step would be to destabilise and threaten the continuance of the union. What the Conservatives decried as a "slippery slope to independence" was for that arch-sceptic of devolution in the Labour Party, Tam Dalyell, a "motorway without exit to a destination that may not have been intended".[43] The plausibility of such judgments was apt to be increased when some, at least, of the members of the Scottish National Party, supported the establishment of a devolved assembly because (by their more gradualist travel metaphor) it would be a stepping-stone to independence.

However, the Labour Party and the Liberal Democrats are (in this sense) unionist parties too. Since the early 1970s, opinion polls have consistently shown that legislative devolution (rather than independence or no change) was the most preferred constitutional option amongst Scottish electors.[44] It is that preferred aspiration which the Labour Government now aims to satisfy, and it does so under a calculation that maintaining the status quo, when it fails to please, would be more destabilising and threatening, while providing a new constitutional settlement could help to strengthen the union.

These sentiments find prominent expression in the White Paper. Donald Dewar, the Secretary of State for Scotland, begins his prefatory message with the sentence: "The Government's aim is a fair and just settlement for Scotland within the framework of the United Kingdom - a settlement which will be good both for Scotland and the United Kingdom".[45] Later, the credo is expanded: "The Union will be strengthened by recognising the claims of Scotland, Wales and the regions with strong identities of their own. The Government's devolution proposals, by meeting these aspirations, will not only safeguard but also enhance the Union".[46]

If sentiments of this kind are rather less apparent in the Scotland Bill, it has to be remembered that the emphasis of a Bill is naturally on what will change rather than what remains the same. Likewise, most of the remainder of this book will be concerned with what is new or being altered. It is important, however, to bear in mind also what is not changing, and to consider the ways in

---

[43] *Hansard*, H.C. Vol. 299, col. 486 (July 31, 1997).
[44] *Scottish Election Surveys* (1974, 1979, 1992); MORI poll results (various dates).
[45] Foreword.
[46] para. 3.1.

which, further devolution notwithstanding, governmental arrangements for Scotland are still located within the framework of the United Kingdom's constitution.

SOVEREIGNTY

A good deal of nonsense has been said and written about issues of sovereignty. However, those responsible for it may plead mitigating circumstances in extenuation, because the term "sovereignty" is one of the most treacherous to be encountered in political and legal discourse. The word is redolent of ancient conceptions of kingship and overlordship, but when its associations and our attitudes are stripped away, there remains a need to analyse the ways in which power is exercised in society. There is not even a single usage found in legal terminology. In public international law, sovereignty is an attribute of states, which have an independent and plenary capacity to conduct relations with other states. In municipal law the monarch, king or queen, may be referred to as the sovereign.

Another use, familiar to constitutional lawyers, is that the English jurist A.V. Dicey described what is perhaps better referred to as the legislative supremacy of the UK Parliament as "the sovereignty of Parliament".[47] In this umbrella concept, he brought together several propositions, notably that Parliament might pass any law as it liked, might repeal any law as it chose, and that no other body could countermand it.

Even Dicey, however, acknowledged that moral considerations and practical politics meant that there were restraints on what Parliament would actually do. He also recognised that the word "sovereignty" was employed in different senses and appreciated that in another and ultimate sense, in a democracy, it was the electorate who were sovereign.

Some notion of "popular sovereignty" has often been boasted as a characteristic of the Scottish polity, said to be evinced, for example, in the Declaration of Arbroath (1320) and the Claim of Right in 1689. The Scottish Constitutional Convention adopted popular sovereignty as "the fundamental tenet of ..... faith"[48] and looked to "a constitutional settlement in which the Scottish people, being sovereign, agree to the exercise of specified powers by Westminster but retain their sovereignty over all other matters".[49]

The idea of popular sovereignty should not be dismissed out of hand because it captures something of the notion that government should (and perhaps must) rest on consent. However, when people use the notion to distinguish Scotland from England, they betray an ignorance of history because English kings who lost popular support (such as Richard II) were displaced more often than Scottish, and the subordination of English monarchs to the law goes back to Magna Carta. More generally, the error lies in the confusion of different

[47] A.V. Dicey, *Introduction to the Study of the Law of the Constitution* (10th ed., 1959), Chap.1.
[48] Scottish Constitutional Convention, *Towards a Scottish Parliament* (1989), p.17.
[49] Scottish Constitutional Convention, *A Constitutional Framework for Scotland* (1989), para. 10.3.

senses of sovereignty. An interpretation of political history which is not entirely free from romantic myth cannot justifiably be treated as legal principle.

At the level of legal analysis, the characteristics which Dicey attributed to the UK Parliament are not necessarily true of the principal legislature of every state. Indeed, they are not indisputably true of the United Kingdom any more, as Parliament's ability to legislate in disregard of EC law has become qualified, at least.

However, devolution is another matter. The question which arises is whether the Scotland Act will detract from whatever legislative supremacy the Westminster Parliament enjoys. A related question is whether there is any attempt to "entrench" the position of the Scottish Parliament, so that it would have some form of constitutional or special protection against the repeal or alteration of the relevant provisions.

Under a written constitution, which almost every state in the world has, it is entirely conceivable that the principal legislature will be subject to limitations. Under a federal system, which is found in roughly one-sixth of the states in the world, "the powers of government are divided between a government for the whole country and governments for parts of the country in such a way that each government is legally independent within its own sphere",[50] so there are by definition limitations on the central legislature, and there is by definition some protection of the position of the legislatures for the various provinces or parts.

In the United Kingdom, of course, there is no written constitution with a higher law status which establishes and regulates the institutions of government. In its absence, constitutional changes are necessarily effected by Acts of Parliament. Orthodox theory would deny that a Parliament can limit its successors. At the least, as was noted in the last chapter, its capacity to do so is doubtful. Besides, the Westminster Parliament, conscious of its position and powers, might be loth to contemplate any attempt at restriction.

In the event, there is no attempt. The White Paper states that "the UK Parliament is, and will remain sovereign in all matters" and "Westminster will be choosing to exercise that sovereignty by devolving legislative responsibilities to a Scottish Parliament without in any way diminishing its own powers. The Government recognise that no UK Parliament can bind its successors."[51] In the light of this, devolution is not expressed to be permanent or irrevocable in the Scotland Bill. For the avoidance of doubt - because legally it is otiose - the continuing competence of the UK Parliament to legislate for Scotland is restated (*clause 27(7)*). It follows that the provisions of the Scotland Act itself will be open to amendment by the Westminster Parliament, whereas they are generally not open to amendment by the Scottish Parliament (*clause 28(2)*). It follows too that there is no reason, legally, why the Scottish Parliament could not be abolished by a later Act of the Parliament at Westminster, and in this

[50] K.C. Wheare, *Modern Constitutions* (2nd ed., 1966), p.19.
[51] para. 4.2.

respect the abolition of the devolved Northern Ireland Parliament by the Northern Ireland Constitution Act 1973 could be cited as a precedent.

However, probability is another matter entirely. The White Paper sought to reassure: "The Government ..... believe that the popular support for the Scottish Parliament, once established, will make sure that its future in the UK constitution will be secure."[52] Arguably, the holding of a referendum also helps to provide a kind of moral and political entrenchment, especially when it results in a clear expression of will, and it could be contended that if the creation of a democratic institution merited a referendum vote, any abolition in contemplation should too. The reality is that abolition is not foreseeable, politically, albeit that it is possible, legally.

RESERVED MATTERS

When the Scotland Act comes into operation, therefore, there will be a Parliament at Westminster with legislative supremacy, and a Parliament in Edinburgh with the powers conferred on it by the Act.

The Scottish Parliament's powers are limited in various ways, and an important limit is that some matters will continue to be dealt with at the UK level. Even in a federal system, matters such as foreign affairs, defence and macroeconomic policy will typically be dealt with at the federal or central level. In a system of devolution there is a more contingent delegation from the centre of power to act in some areas but not in others. Some powers are delegated or devolved, others are retained or reserved. In the Scotland Bill, the terms used are "devolved" and "reserved" (*clause 29*). So far as the devolved matters are concerned, remember that the powers of the Scottish Parliament to legislate are not exclusive, because the UK Parliament's competence is expressly restated (*clause 27(7)*). No doubt it is hoped, and perhaps it is intended, that Westminster will not choose to exercise its competence freely on matters which also lie within the competence of the Scottish Parliament. However, this may be to put the point too emotionally. Just as at present there are occasions when it is convenient for Parliament to legislate in the same Act for Scotland and England (perhaps because some reforms are to apply to both, while in other respects there will be differences, as with the Defamation Act 1996, for example), there will be occasions after 2000 when pragmatic considerations argue for action by the Westminster Parliament. There is notice of this in the White Paper: "There may be instances (for example, international obligations which touch on devolved as well as reserved matters) where it will be more convenient for legislation to be passed by the UK Parliament."[53]

When it comes to reserved matters, there is no sharing of competence. The Scottish Parliament does not have competence to legislate on subjects such as defence or international relations, which will be solely within the competence of the UK Parliament. The general rule is that the matters defined as reserved matters lie outside the Scottish Parliament's competence (*clause 28(2)(c)*). There

[52]   para. 4.2.
[53]   para. 4.4.

are a few caveats to the general rule, as explained in Chapter 5. Subject to these limited exceptions, if the Scottish Parliament were to legislate on a reserved matter, it would be acting beyond its powers. There are procedures for pre-legislative scrutiny (*clauses 30, 31*) and for pre-assent reference of Bills to the Judicial Committee of the Privy Council (*clause 32*), designed to prevent such an occurrence, and issues of competence arising subsequently may be determined in the courts (*clause 91, Schedule 6*). These possibilities are also explained more fully in Chapter 5, after the competence of the Scottish Parliament is described and illustrated.

It is reasonable to claim, as the White Paper did, that the Parliament's legislative competence is "wide-ranging".[54] In this chapter, because the subject is "Scotland within the United Kingdom", it is appropriate first to describe the reserved matters at some length, in order to indicate the scale and importance of matters which will continue to be dealt with at the UK level (where Scotland will still be represented) and are not being devolved. It should also perhaps be stressed that the provisions under consideration here are about legislative competence. There is nothing to prevent the Scottish Parliament, as a debating chamber, considering and discussing matters which are "reserved",[55] although legislation is ruled out.

The reserved matters are specified in *Schedule 5*. As a general summary, the matters reserved for the competence of the UK Parliament (in so far as they are within domestic, rather than European Community competence, at all) are as follows:

1. The constitution of the United Kingdom, including the Crown and succession to the Crown, the UK Parliament, electoral law regarding the House of Commons and the European Parliament, and the franchise for all elections, the civil service, the award of dignities and titles of honour, and the law of treason.

2. International relations and foreign policy, including the ability to conclude agreements in the European Union and its institutions (which may cover devolved as well as reserved areas) or with other territories or international organisations; regulation of international trade, and international development assistance and co-operation.

3. Defence and national security, including responsibility for the armed forces of the Crown and visiting forces; the security services; powers and provisions for dealing with terrorism or subversion; the subject-matter of the Official Secrets Acts and the Interception of Communications Act 1985 (except so far as they relate to criminal investigation); and emergency powers.

4. The protection of borders and certain matters subject to border controls, including designation of the United Kingdom's land and maritime borders and fisheries limits, immigration and nationality, passports, extradition, and

---

[54] para. 2.2.
[55] The White Paper affirmed that there might be debate on matters "whether devolved or reserved": para. 2.5.

asylum; the criminal law in relation to firearms and drugs, and the regulation of misuse of drugs.

5. Fiscal, economic and monetary policy, including the issue and circulation of money, the currency, taxes and excise duties, government borrowing and lending, control over United Kingdom public expenditure, the exchange rate and the Bank of England. However, the tax-varying powers given to the Scottish Parliament in *clauses 69-75* constitute an exception to the reservation, and another exception is for provision on local taxation to fund local authority expenditure in Scotland.

6. Matters relevant to common markets for UK goods and services at home and abroad, including the law on companies and business associations, insurance, corporate insolvency, competition policy, intellectual property, regulation of financial markets and financial services, consumer protection laws and product safety and labelling, regulation of the energy supply industries, and international trade policy and Export Credit Guarantee Department matters; also under this heading, wireless telegraphy and telecommunications regulation and licensing, regulation of pharmaceutical prices, postal services, weights and measures and technical standards of goods, and the regulation of time zones.

7. Employment legislation, including industrial relations and trade union law, equal opportunities law, health and safety and the matters for which the Employment Service is responsible.

8. Social security policy and administration, including benefits and the matters for which the Benefits Agency is responsible, contributions, and child support maintenance; occupational and personal pension scheme regulation and related employment policy, services and assistance; and war pensions.

9. Regulation of the medical, dental, nursing and other health professions, including veterinary surgeons; regulation of the professions of architect, and of auditor, of insolvency practitioners and insurance intermediaries; regulation of the conduct of estate agency business.

10. Transport safety and regulation, including regulation of aviation and shipping, marine and air safety, rail safety and provision and regulation of rail services, and some aspects of road traffic regulation, including driver and vehicle licensing and some offences; transport of radioactive material.

11. Miscellaneous matters currently subject to regulation or operation at British or UK level, including nuclear safety, the control and supply of medicines, the UK Research Councils, the designation of assisted areas, the Ordnance Survey, the BBC and the regulation of broadcasting, the licensing of theatres and cinemas and film classification arrangements, the regulation of video recordings, data protection, anti-discrimination legislation (covering race, gender and disability), judicial salaries, and betting, gaming and lotteries; also, in the field of health, matters including abortion, human fertilisation and embryology, surrogacy, human genetics, xenotransplantation, and scientific procedures on live animals.

Having seen what appears on the reserved list, we may be curious about the rationale behind it. The Government's general justification, which spokes-men have repeated almost as a mantra, appears in the White Paper: "There are many matters which can be more effectively and beneficially handled on a United Kingdom basis."[56] There is also reference to "strong and effective de-fence and foreign policies" and "participation in an economic unit which ben-efits business and provides access to wider markets and investment and in-creases prosperity for all."[57]

In fact, the placing of some matters such as defence and foreign affairs on the reserved list would probably command general assent, within the context of either a federal or a devolved system. However, there are many others which are more debatable. It is not self-evident that the laws of Scotland and England should not differ on abortion or firearms or broadcasting, when they may ap-parently differ on contraception or offensive weapons or newspapers, and a bland assertion in the White Paper about "the benefits of a consistent and inte-grated approach"[58] hardly provides a complete answer. This is not to deny that commonality may be desirable on many matters - although when so-called anomalies are highlighted, they are often merely consequences of there being different legal systems - but is rather just to observe that, when particular mat-ters are brought into question, justifications will have to be better than bland generalities.

There may be resistance to trimming the reserved list, but the borders of reserved and devolved will not be set in stone when the Scotland Act becomes law. There is provision for transferring matters from - or to - the reserved list by statutory instrument (*clause 29(2), (3)*). Such an instrument will require the affirmative approval of both Houses at Westminster and the Scottish Parlia-ment (*clause 101*), and has to be made by the UK Government (*clause 102*). The Scottish Parliament, therefore, cannot extend its legislative competence except with the concurrence of Westminster and Whitehall. There is much which it can do, but under the Scotland Bill, it is unmistakably a subordinate legisla-ture within the United Kingdom.

WESTMINSTER ARRANGEMENTS

Important matters like foreign affairs and defence, which affect Scotland as well as the rest of the United Kingdom, will as reserved matters continue to be within the responsibilities of the UK Parliament. For this and other reasons - including the principle of no taxation without representation - the continuing involvement of Scottish members at Westminster after 2000 is appropriate and necessary.

However, the creation of a Scottish Parliament to deal with domestic mat-ters does raise issues of a consequential kind in regard to Westminster, notably the issue of appropriate Scottish representation and the related matter of the "West Lothian question".

[56] para. 3.2.
[57] para. 3.2.
[58] para. 3.4.

Representation at Westminster

The electorate of Scotland is at present represented by 72 MPs in the House of Commons, amongst the 659 who sit there. The number may seem to constitute a small minority of the total, but in fact it may plausibly be argued that Scotland is over-represented. If electoral area apportionment in the United Kingdom were carried out on a basis of strict arithmetical equality, as in the United States is constitutionally required, Scotland would have 58 or 59 constituencies rather than 72. Generous representation for Scotland (and for Wales, which similarly profits) can be viewed as another instance of differential treatment in acknowledgment of nationhood. Indeed, on one review of the issue, any diminution of the numbers of Scottish and Welsh seats was rejected because it "might give rise to a good deal of political feeling and would lend support to the separatist movement in both countries".[59]

However, with the creation of a devolved Parliament, the case is altered. Some of the Westminster Parliament's business, on matters such as foreign policy which are not being devolved, remains of legitimate concern to Scottish MPs, but given the devolution of other matters, there is less need (and perhaps less entitlement) for the same level of Scottish representation. Moreover, there is a precedent because, when there was devolution of legislative powers to the Northern Ireland Parliament at Stormont, the number of Northern Ireland seats was reduced to 12, being raised to 17 after the reimposition of direct rule in the 1970s. The Scottish Liberal Democrats have conceded for some years that, in fairness, the creation of a devolved Parliament with substantial competence and the diminished interest of Scottish MPs in Westminster's business would justify a reduction in the number of Scottish seats in the Commons, at least to the extent of preventing over-representation. Labour's attitude, when in Opposition, was more neutral or at any rate more uncertain.

However, if the proposals had not included any provision for change in this respect, it was entirely foreseeable that objections would have been raised during the parliamentary passage of the Scotland Bill. The Labour Government, in anticipation, has tried to defuse the issue, by a subtle act of referral, which was heralded in the White Paper:

"The distribution of seats in the House of Commons will be reviewed by the Parliamentary Boundary Commissions which follow criteria defined in statute. At present, special statutory provisions stipulate a minimum number of Scottish seats. The Government have decided that in the next review this requirement will no longer apply. Other statutory requirements, notably the need to give due weight to geographical considerations and local ties, will continue to apply to reviews for Scotland in the same way as they will apply to reviews for other parts of the UK."[60]

These decisions are translated into the provisions of *clause 81*. The rule which required the Boundary Commission for Scotland to propose that there

[59]   Minutes of Speaker's Conference, 1944, cited in I. McLean, "Are Scotland and Wales Overrepresented in the House of Commons?" (1995) 66 *Political Quarterly* 250.
[60]   para. 4.5.

be not less than 71 constituencies in Scotland is removed (*clause 81(2)*). A specific instruction added is that the Orkney Islands and the Shetland Islands are not to be joined to the whole or part of any other local government area to form a constituency (*clause 81(3)*). The guideline to the effect that constituency electorates should approximate to equal size (which has previously been framed to apply not *across* England, Scotland, Wales and Northern Ireland, but to each of the four separately) is modified so as to apply to Scotland on the same basis as England (*clause 81(4)*).

However, a careful reading of the White Paper in conjunction with the Parliamentary Constituencies Act 1986 (which is amended by these provisions) suggests that the effect will not be too drastic a reduction in the number of Scottish seats. The statutory guidance to the Boundary Commissions allows departure from strict arithmetical equalisation when it is justified by "special geographical considerations, including in particular the size, shape and accessibility of a constituency",[61] and although there is no further elucidation of this criterion, it seems apt to refer to parts of rural Scotland. In considering alterations, the Commissions are also required to take account of "any local ties which would be broken by such alterations".[62] When discretion is applied to these guidelines, the resultant reduction will probably not be too severe.

The provision about equalising sizes of Scottish and English constituencies only applies expressly to the next report of the Boundary Commission for Scotland (which as things stand will be due between 2002 and 2006). However, as there are larger issues in the background which will require consideration, including the size of membership of the House of Commons (which a growing body of opinion considers to be too large) and the electoral system, this may not be inappropriate.

The West Lothian Question

Another matter is what has become known as the "West Lothian question". Its naming has been attributed to Enoch Powell, but the undisputed champion of the question is Tam Dalyell, now MP for Linlithgow, whose tenaciousness alternatively provokes irritation or admiration.[63]

The central problem which he returns to is the anomaly of Scottish MPs debating and voting on English affairs at Westminster, after there is devolution of corresponding Scottish affairs, and MPs will have no say in what happens at Edinburgh. There are other facets and corollaries, such as doubts over the appropriateness of a "Scottish" member of the UK Government being responsible for distinctly English matters, and uncertainties over whether Scottish (or other) MPs should be able to raise at Westminster matters which have been devolved as the business of members of the Edinburgh Parliament.

In fact, there is nothing new under the sun. The failure to resolve satisfactorily questions concerning the numbers, powers and duties of Irish MPs at

[61] Parliamentary Constituencies Act 1986, Sched. 2, rule 6.
[62] Parliamentary Constituencies Act 1986, Sched. 2, rule 7.
[63] For a polemic on the subject, see T. Dalyell, *Devolution: The End of Britain?* (1977).

Westminster, contributed substantially to the difficulties of the Irish Home Rule Bills of 1886, 1893 and 1912. As with that other conundrum of the nineteenth century, the Schleswig-Holstein question, the complexity of the problem seemed to defy solution.

The devolution of legislative powers to the Northern Ireland Parliament raised the same issue, if less acutely.[64] After the 1951 general election, the Conservative Government depended for its majority on the support of Ulster MPs, so that measures on, for example, education in England and Wales were passed in that way, although education in Northern Ireland was devolved to Stormont.

The UK Government is formed so as to have a majority in the House of Commons. A potentially aggravating factor in the West Lothian question is the possible dependence, for a majority, on the inclusion of MPs from certain parts of the United Kingdom. For example, if the 1997 general election had (with the same outcomes in Scotland) resulted in a slender overall Labour majority, then a Labour government would have depended on Scottish MPs for the safe passage of its legislation for England. With its actual majority, of course, this twist in the problem does not arise, at least until 2002.

How can Tam Dalyell's question be answered? The elimination of Scottish representation at Westminster would resolve it in a way, but would not be justifiable (and is not in contemplation). A reduction in the numbers of Scottish MPs, as considered above, does not address the question in principle, but it does tend to alleviate the effects of the problem.

Another way of tackling the problem, sometimes called the "in and out" approach, involves special parliamentary procedures so as to allow Scottish MPs to participate in other business while preventing them from speaking or voting on "English" matters corresponding to the devolved matters. This approach would create different majorities in the Commons for different issues, and some members have suggested that it would be damaging to the House's corporate spirit. The difficulties of definition and demarcation and practical arrangements which it would create are also very considerable, and so the approach has not commended itself to most politicians. A weaker form of the same approach would rely on a constitutional convention or expectations of non-participation, but the difficulties would remain. As was noticed in Chapter 2, the Scotland Act 1978 included, against the Government's wishes, a rather clumsy provision along these lines.[65]

The West Lothian question would not arise if there were an independent Scotland, nor if there were a federal system or even "home rule all round". It arises under an asymmetrical or partially devolved system. Another response is to accept that asymmetry will involve anomalies, which may be a price worth paying, and to observe that anomalies are no strangers to our constitution, with

[64] See H. Calvert, *Constitutional Law in Northern Ireland* (1968); B. Hadfield, *"Scotland's Parliament:* A Northern Ireland Perspective on the White Paper" [1997] P.L. 660.
[65] Scotland Act 1978, s.66.

its unelected second chamber, ancient prerogatives, and over-reliance on constitutional conventions.

INTERLOCKING

Scotland will, according to the White Paper, "of course remain an integral part of the United Kingdom", and "the Queen will continue to be head of state of the United Kingdom".[66] The position of the Crown is preserved (as well as reserved). The UK Parliament, Scottish representatives included, will retain its supremacy and retain importance for many Scottish interests. The central institutions of the UK Government will still play a significant part in the government of Scotland after the year 2000, not least in determining the assigned budget for the Scottish Parliament (see Chapter 7), and the unity of the Home Civil Service will be maintained (*clause 47*). In reserved matters, the UK institutions will have full responsibility, and more generally they will shape and condition what it is possible and practical for the Scottish institutions to do. In real as well as symbolic ways, the Government's proposals reinforce the policy of keeping Scotland in the union. One of the more symbolic decisions is to have the two most senior judges of the Scottish courts, the Lord President of the Court of Session and the Lord Justice-Clerk, appointed by Her Majesty on the advice of the Prime Minister (*clause 89*). With the appellate functions of the House of Lords, there is already some linkage of the court systems, and the new functions of the Judicial Committee of the Privy Council under the Bill (see Chapter 5) might be regarded in this light.

In these ways, and through (it is hoped) the satisfaction of many of the demands for reform, it is intended to lock Scotland into an enduring framework of union. However, the interlocking of the new institutions into the framework is also required. The Scottish Parliament and the Executive which will be formed from it under the provisions of the Scotland Act will not operate in a vacuum. The strength and quality of devolved government in Scotland will depend significantly upon relations between the Scottish institutions and their UK level counterparts. The practical operation of this partnership will no doubt be affected by the political conditions of the time including, in particular, the balance of power between political parties in all of them. Some of the Government's intentions with regard to these relationships do emerge in the White Paper, and a few of the ground rules are found in the Scotland Bill, but much will evolve with its own dynamic in the years to come.

Here, it may be useful to comment on the role of the Secretary of State and then, more generally, on liaison. The particular powers and functions of different kinds which fall to the Secretary of State under the Bill are described when relevant in Chapters 4, 5, 6 and 7.

The Secretary of State

The point should perhaps be made that while we in Scotland tend to interpret "the Secretary of State" as being "the Secretary of State for Scotland", legal

[66]   para.4.2.

powers are generally reposed in "the Secretary of State" *simpliciter*, as indeed they are in the Scotland Bill (e.g. *clauses 2, 11, 61*). When that practice is employed, the powers in question are in law exercisable by any of Her Majesty's ministers holding such a designation (of whom there are normally about a dozen).[67] Thus if, in a future UK Government, there were no office of Secretary of State for Scotland, other persons could exercise the powers.

Whether, following legislative devolution, it is necessary or desirable to retain such a ministerial office in the UK Government has in fact been a subject of debate. The Liberal Democrats came to the view that the office would be redundant, while Labour's preference was for retaining it, so in the absence of agreement the Scottish Constitutional Convention skirted the issue. Labour has maintained its position in office, and the White Paper explains their conception of the role:

> "The role of the Secretary of State for Scotland will be to secure the passage and implementation of the legislation to establish the Scottish Parliament; and then to support its initial development. Once the Scottish Parliament is in being, and the Scottish Executive established, the responsibilities of the Secretary of State for Scotland will change. The focus will be on promoting communication between the Scottish Parliament and Executive and between the UK Parliament and Government on matters of mutual interest; and on representing Scottish interests in reserved areas."[68]

The Secretary of State will, it seems, be something of a midwife for the birth of a Scottish Parliament, and for a while afterwards will be the health visitor who passes on folk wisdom and ensures healthy bonding. These services should be welcome, when performed by a minister of the UK Government which has delivered the Parliament, especially if the same political party predominates there. Over a longer timescale, some commentators consider that the Scottish arm of the UK Government, being less able to claim to represent Scotland than representatives of the directly elected Parliament, will wither and die.[69] Certainly, when different parties are in government in London and Edinburgh, the position of Secretary of State is likely to be distinctly less comfortable.

Liaison

Liaison is amongst the Secretary of State's functions as currently foreseen, then, but the nature of these functions may alter, even if the office survives. In any event, there will be a need for much wider liaison and co-operation between different institutions.

The Scotland Bill makes no particular provision for communications between Edinburgh and London, but the White Paper had this to say:

> "The Scottish Executive will need to keep in close touch with Departments

---

[67] Interpretation Act 1978, Sched. 1; *London and Clydeside Estates Ltd. v. Secretary of State for Scotland*, 1987 S.L.T. 459.

[68] para. 4.12.

[69] See J. Kellas, "The Policy Process" in *Scotland: The Framework for Change* (D. Mackay ed., 1979).

of the UK Government. Good communication systems will be vital. Departments in both administrations will develop mutual understandings covering the appropriate exchange of information, advance notification and joint working. The principles will be as follows:

- the vast majority of matters should be capable of being handled routinely among officials of the departments in question;
- if further discussion is needed on any issue, the Cabinet office and its Scottish Executive counterpart will mediate, again at official level;
- on some issues there will need to be discussions between the Scottish Executive and ministers in the UK Government.

Representatives of the UK Government (usually the Secretary of State for Scotland) and the Scottish Executive will meet from time to time, to discuss particular issues or simply to take stock of relations. These arrangements will be updated regularly to reflect the evolution of administrative conventions of co-operation and joint working."[70]

In some matters, it is particularly important for the United Kingdom to speak with one voice, and for those representing the United Kingdom to take proper account of the interests of all parts of the Kingdom. So close liaison is particularly appropriate and necessary when international relations or negotiations are involved,[71] and negotiations within the European Union provide a special example of that (on which, see Chapter 9).

A particular need which was identified was for the appointment of a new Scottish law officer to advise the UK Government on Scots law, whether reserved or devolved, because the Lord Advocate and Solicitor General for Scotland will be transferred to the Scottish institutions. The new ministerial office is called the Advocate General for Scotland (*clause 82*).

[70] paras. 4.13, 4.14.
[71] paras. 4.18, 4.19.

CHAPTER 4

THE SCOTTISH PARLIAMENT: ELECTIONS, MEMBERS AND PROCEDURE

"There shall be a Scottish Parliament" (*clause 1(1)*). With these words the Scotland Bill begins, and the auxiliary verb is used not to make a prediction but to express a legal imperative.

Parliaments, however, vary considerably in their status, composition and functions, depending on the laws which affect them and the constitutional framework and context within which they operate. In this chapter, we shall consider the composition of the Scottish Parliament and see what the legislation says about its members and how it should operate. In the next chapter, we consider its powers. It is a Parliament from which an Executive headed by a First Minister will be formed, and the Executive is dealt with in Chapter 6.

First of all, before explaining the electoral arrangements for the composition of the Scottish Parliament, we might notice the framework provisions for its creation and operation.

THE PARLIAMENTARY TERM

The United Kingdom Parliament may not run for a term of more than five years, by the Parliament Act 1911. However, subject to that maximum, its lifespan is indeterminate. It is summoned and dissolved by the Crown under royal prerogative powers. A dissolution may follow when a government loses a vote of confidence, as the minority Labour Government did in 1979. Otherwise, since the sovereign, at least normally, is by constitutional convention bound to act on the Prime Minister's advice in the matter, it follows that the Prime Minister effectively chooses, within the maximum, the date of the general election which is consequential on a dissolution. A Prime Minister may well be influenced by considerations of party advantage, and indeed may have taken other decisions with an eye on the choice of election date. One constitutional lawyer described this as "the least creditable aspect of the British Constitution".[72]

The Scottish Parliament will have a fixed term of four years, normally (*clause 2(2)*), and its meeting and dissolution will be statutorily determined. Polling day for the first general election for the Parliament will be on a day appointed by the Secretary of State (*clause 2(1)*). It is expected that the date will be May 6, 1999, but the United Kingdom Government retains discretion on timing. If, as is also anticipated, the Parliament is not completely up and running until (probably) January 2000, then it would appear that the new Parliament will be sitting in its first term for a duration closer to three years than four.

This outcome follows because polling day for subsequent "ordinary general elections" will normally take place on the first Thursday in May in the fourth calendar year following the previous ordinary general election (*clause*

---

[72]   O. Hood Phillips, *Reform of the Constitution* (1970), p.52.

2(2)). There is provision to vary the date by up to a month in either direction, on the proposal of the Parliament's Presiding Officer, with Her Majesty empowered to so arrange in that situation by means of a proclamation (*clause 2(5)*). Thus the second general election date should be on May 1, 2003, but if that day were unsuitable for some reason, another date within a month of it could be proposed.

When parliamentary bodies have a fixed term, it may be necessary or desirable to have a safety valve, in case of problems. For that reason, the legislation also provides for "extraordinary general elections" in *clause 3*. These will be proposed by the Parliament's Presiding Officer and may then be sanctioned by Her Majesty in two different situations. First, if no nomination of a First Minister has been made within the period prescribed under *clause 43* (normally 28 days) for the Parliament to make one. Secondly, when the Parliament resolves that it should be dissolved with the necessary support on a division for that purpose, which is put at "not less than two-thirds of the total number of seats for members of the Parliament" (and would therefore require the votes of 86 or more members in a Parliament of 129). So these provisions cater, for example, for the occasions where the Executive loses the support of most of the Parliament (perhaps because a coalition between parties has foundered) and no new administration can be formed from the composition as it stands which would have sufficient support. If an extraordinary general election is held within six months before an ordinary general election would be due, it replaces the ordinary general election (*clause 3(3)*). Otherwise, however, it does not affect the normal quadrennial cycle (*clause 3(4)*); so if, for example, there had to be an extraordinary general election in September 2002, the Parliament elected would be only of seven or eight months' duration.

ELECTIONS

One or two persons who have not been elected as members may participate in the proceedings of the Scottish Parliament (although they may not vote), under *clause 26*. These persons are the Scottish Law Officers, namely the Lord Advocate and the Solicitor General for Scotland, office holders appointed by royal warrant who need not be elected members. They will act as legal advisers to the Parliament and the Executive, over and above other functions.

With that slight qualification, the Scottish Parliament, like the House of Commons but unlike the House of Lords, will be an elected body. To describe its composition, therefore, essentially involves explaining the electoral law. The issues which merit attention are as follows: (i) the electoral system; (ii) eligibility to vote; (iii) eligibility to stand for election; (iv) gender balance; and (v) the rules about conduct of election campaigns.

The Electoral System

The Scottish Parliament is to be elected under an additional member system (AMS). The electoral system used for elections to the House of Commons is a relative majority system involving single member constituencies, popularly "first past the post". That system broadly tends to favour the larger parties at the expense of the smaller and to exaggerate the effects of a movement of support as between the larger parties. The first past the post system has generally produced a decisive result in so far as one party has won an overall majority of seats in the House of Commons (for example, in all bar one of the last 15 general elections, since 1945). However, the system does not ensure proportionality between votes cast for parties and seats won, and so may be perceived, by that yardstick, as unfair.

Reform of the electoral system for the House of Commons is under active consideration, and it is already proposed that elections of British members of the European Parliament will take place in 1999 under a system of proportional representation, a regionally based party list system. Another proportional system, the Single Transferable Vote (STV), has been used for various kinds of elections in Northern Ireland.

The Government seems to believe in different horses for different courses. The Scottish Parliament (and the National Assembly for Wales) are to be elected under an additional member system. The additional member system is actually a mixed system, which combines single member representation based on constituencies with an element of "topping up" from a party list system. As explained in the White Paper:

"A constituency link will be the essential foundation of the new Scottish Parliament. However, it is also important to provide for greater proportionality to build stability into the overall settlement. It is therefore proposed that there be a significant number of additional members elected on a wider and proportional basis, in order to bring a closer relationship between votes cast and seats won."[73]

Under this system, an elector has two votes to cast. The first is for a candidate to represent the constituency, while the second is for a party. When the constituency seats are filled, the other seats available are allocated to candidates on the party lists so as to arrive at or at least approach toward a directly proportional end result. Within this broad account of the system, there are several choices to be made and possible variations. For example, the method of electing the constituency members might be first past the post or might be under the alternative vote system (a preferential system used to elect the Australian House of Representatives). The constituency members and list members might be in 50:50 or in other proportions. And a "threshold" might be set so that parties would have to secure a minimum percentage of the vote before qualifying for any representation. In Germany, where the additional member system is used in electing the Bundestag, the proportions are 50:50, and a party must poll a minimum of five per cent of the total second votes in the country or else win at least three constituency seats by first votes.

The provisions in the Scotland Bill follow closely the proposals of the Scottish Constitutional Convention in its final report.[74] They provide for a Parliament which will have 129 members, consisting of 73 members elected in sin-

---

[73] para. 8.1.
[74] *Scotland's Parliament. Scotland's Right* (1995), p.21.

gle member constituencies and 56 additional members elected under the system of proportional representation laid down, which is a regional list system (*clause 1(2), (3), (5)*). One respect in which the Government has had second thoughts is in allowing for the possibility of additional members to be independents, who would not feature on a political party's list. There is a healthy tradition of independent candidates standing, at least in local government, in some parts of Scotland. By accommodating the possibility of electing such persons, the Government both acknowledges that tradition and helps to meet one of the criticisms levelled at electoral systems which put more power in the hands of parties.

The "constituency members" will be elected under the familiar first past the post system, and the 73 constituencies correspond to those defined and used for elections to the House of Commons, except that the Orkney Islands and the Shetland Islands (which form one Westminster constituency) become two constituencies for Scottish Parliament purposes. Casual vacancies arising in constituency seats will be filled by by-elections held within three months (*clause 8*).

The provisions for election of the additional "regional members" are naturally more complex. For this purpose, Scotland is divided into the eight regions which are already European Parliament constituencies (under the European Parliamentary Constituencies (Scotland) Order 1996), and seven members will be returned from each. Persons may stand as "individual candidates", who are independent, or may appear on a political party's list of candidates for the region (*clause 4(1), (3)*). A candidate of either sort may stand as a regional member and also as a constituency member within the same region, but other forms of double candidature are barred (*clause 4(2), (6), (7)*). Political parties will have to be registered in order to submit a list (*clause 4(4), (8)*), and legislation will be introduced for the registration of political parties.[75] Parties may have not more than twelve persons on their list (*clause 4(5)*), and will rank them in order.

Voters, having exercised one vote for the constituency election, may cast a second vote, either for a political party which has submitted a list or for an individual candidate (*clause 5(2), (3)*). The determination of winning constituency members is carried out first (*clause 6(1)*), and the numbers of seats won by parties in the constituency elections which fall within the region are taken account of in the calculations for allocation of seats to regional members. The calculations involve a formula which is recalculated after each of the regional seats is awarded to a party (allocating it to the highest name on the list, unless already successful), and the process carries on until the right number is reached. An individual candidate with a high enough number of votes could also be successful (*clauses 6, 7*).

One problem for the system is to cater for casual vacancies arising in the regional members' seats, by-elections not being appropriate for the purpose. The solution proposed is to leave any individual member's seat vacant until

---

[75]   White Paper, Annex C.4.

the next general election, but to fill a party list member's seat with the person who was next highest on that party's list and is available (*clause* 9).

The basic design of this electoral system is to seek to ensure that if a party's candidates in the constituencies have won disproportionately few seats, considering its overall level of electoral support, then it will be compensated by being allocated more or "additional" seats from the party lists of candidates than another party which gained a disproportionately high number of constituency seats.

The system as devised for Scotland has the advantage of building on the electoral system with which voters are familiar and retaining the territorial link between members and constituencies, which is often thought to be important and valuable, while at the same time providing a result which approximates to party proportionality. The approximation to proportionality would be even higher if the system were applied nationally rather than regionally, but something would be lost in so far as the regional members too may be expected to have a territorial connection with electors, albeit a weaker one.

The system thus has considerable merits. One argument against it (or the list part of it) is that by promoting to membership of the Parliament persons who were not voted for as such, it to some extent transfers power from the electors to political parties (and within the parties tends to move power from the local level to the national party organisation). There may be reservations on this count, but it can be viewed as the price to be paid for achieving a high degree of party proportionality.

A more general feature of any proportional representation system is that it is less likely that any single party will have an overall majority of seats, and so in a system of parliamentary government it is likely that coalitions or pacts will be necessary for the formation of effective governments. It is therefore to the credit of the Labour Party, which might hope to be dominant under other electoral systems, that it was prepared to legislate for a system which will probably mean that no single party is dominant. Coalition governments, if they tend to be less stable, can be supported on the ground that the more consensual style of politics which they foster is preferable to the more adversarial style which has been prevalent at Westminster. An argument on the other side is that coalitions typically come about after deals between party leaders in "smoke-filled rooms", which again in a way transfers power to the parties at the expense of the electors.

However, this is not the place for a full discussion of electoral systems.[76] What we should notice is that, while the present system persists for the House of Commons, the likelihood is that a government with an absolute majority at Westminster will be dealing with a Scottish Parliament and Executive which (because there is no absolute majority) has a different complexion.

[76] Readers interested in further discussion of a general kind might consult D. Oliver, *Government in the United Kingdom* (1991), Chap.8; C. Turpin, *British Government and the Constitution* (3rd ed., 1995), pp.439-449; R. Blackburn, *The Electoral System in Britain* (1995), Chap. 8.

Incidentally, the expectation is that the number of members of the Parliament will be revised downwards. As was noticed in the last chapter, the provision stipulating a minimum number of Scottish constituencies in the House of Commons is being removed for the next review of electoral areas carried out by the Boundary Commission for Scotland (*clause 81*). By *Schedule 1*, any alteration to the UK parliamentary constituencies will automatically involve a corresponding alteration in the constituency member representation in the Scottish Parliament, and the Commission's reports should make such recommendations as are appropriate for consequential alteration of the regional member representation to satisfy the principle that, so far as reasonably practicable, the ratio of constituency member seats to regional member seats is to remain the same. So, for example, if after review the number of Scottish constituencies were reduced to 60, the number of regional members should fall to 46 or thereabouts.

Eligibility to Vote

The provisions in *clause 10* concerning the franchise or eligibility to vote in elections for the Scottish Parliament follow the proposals of the White Paper, and are relatively uncontroversial. The basic principle underlying the provisions is that of universal adult suffrage (although persons subject to a legal incapacity, such as convicted criminals serving sentences of imprisonment, are barred from voting).

As with elections to the Westminster Parliament, the inclusion of a person's name on the relevant electoral register will be a condition precedent for voting, and the electoral register is based on residence. Thus persons who are resident within an electoral area in the Edinburgh West constituency and are qualified to vote, may do so in that area, provided that their names appear on the register. If, however, their names are not included on the register, they will be unable to vote, even if they would otherwise have been entitled to.

In case law, the courts have taken a broad, matter-of-fact approach to the concept of residence. It is recognised that a person may have more than one place of residence: university students who are living away from home for part of the year provide an obvious example.[77] It has also been recognised that the quality of accommodation is irrelevant, so that somebody sleeping in a tent is just as entitled to be registered as someone inhabiting a mansion.[78] However, the nature and purpose of occupation of accommodation may be taken into consideration: in one Scottish case, an Edinburgh family's use of a holiday cottage in Polwarth for three and a half months of each year was held to be insufficient to qualify as "residence".[79] In any event, no particular *period* of residence is required. The only question is whether, on the qualifying date for the register, a person is regarded as resident, in a sufficient sense, in the constituency. Those persons who, like many university students, are registered in

[77] *Fox v. Stirk* [1970] 2 Q.B. 463.
[78] *Hipperson v. Electoral Registration Officer for Newbury* [1985] Q.B. 1060.
[79] *Scott v. Phillips*, 1974 S.L.T. 32.

more than one place, may choose where to vote (but may not vote twice, or would commit a criminal offence).

The criterion of residence does, of course, have the effect of disqualifying most expatriate Scots, while it allows non-Scots who reside in Scotland to vote. The same rule applied to the referendum vote in 1997, and the issue was personified in footballing terms as "the Gary McAllister question" and "the Paul Gascoigne question". Scotland's sometime captain, McAllister, who has played for Leeds United and Coventry City in recent years and has his home in England, is disenfranchised, while the English player Gascoigne, with a home in Scotland and a Glasgow Rangers player, could vote. While, with regard to the referendum, there may have been wider grounds on which to criticise the limited franchise, the question becomes rather different where voting for constituency representatives is concerned, and few would find the rules unacceptable in this regard.

Eligibility to vote for the Scottish Parliament will actually correspond to the franchise for local government elections, rather than that for UK Parliament elections. This decision means that two categories of person who may not vote in elections for the House of Commons are included: first, peers eligible to sit in the House of Lords; second, nationals of other European Community states resident in Scotland. Commonwealth citizens and citizens of the Republic of Ireland will be able to vote, as they are in UK Parliament elections. One category of persons enabled to vote in Westminster elections will not be able to vote in Scottish Parliament elections, however: by legislation in the 1980s, the normal rule of residence was waived for UK citizens who had taken up residence outside the UK but who had been registered electors in a constituency in the UK within the last 20 years.[80] For Scottish Parliament elections, British expatriates are not being accorded the same generosity.

Eligibility to Stand
Eligibility to stand for election to the Scottish Parliament will, with one or two exceptions, be similar to the corresponding eligibility to stand for election to the UK Parliament.

There is, it may be noticed, no residence rule for UK parliamentary candidates (although candidates who lack association with a constituency in which they are standing are liable to be attacked as "carpetbaggers" by their opponents), and this will generally be the case the Scottish Parliament too. There is, however, a nationality qualification. For the UK Parliament, UK citizenship, citizenship of a Commonwealth country, or citizenship of the Republic of Ireland is required. For Scottish Parliament candidature, any of these citizenships will suffice, as will additionally citizenship of another EC state, but only when the person concerned is resident in the United Kingdom (*clause 15(2)*).

One other variation which is noteworthy is that there will be no disqualification of priests or ministers of religion (*clause 15(1)*). Some categories of

---

[80] Representation of the People Act 1989 (replacing a less generous provision in the Representation of the People Act 1985).

clergy are disqualified from membership of the House of Commons, under ancient provisions which were motivated by prejudice or malice. These anachronistic and discriminatory exclusions are not to apply to the Scottish Parliament.

Peers and peeresses who, as has been noted, may vote in elections for the Scottish Parliament (assuming that they satisfy other requirements such as residence) may also stand for election to the Scottish Parliament (*clause 15(1)*). Two or three, including the Earl of Mar and Kellie (whose ancestor favoured union in 1707) and Lord Sempill (whose ancestor was opposed in 1707) are reported as having expressed interest in doing so. Such persons, if elected, would of course simply rank as ordinary members within the unicameral Scottish Parliament.

In other respects, too, dual mandates are not prohibited. The legislation does not prohibit a Member of the Scottish Parliament from being a member of the House of Commons or of the European Parliament, or a member of the National Assembly of Wales or of a local authority. There may indeed be arguments that dual membership is advantageous, for cross-fertilisation. However, given the extremely heavy workload involved in a dual mandate, and perhaps also given public expectations of their representatives, it is not likely to be a common or durable phenomenon, except perhaps where Scottish Parliament membership and local authority membership are combined. Political parties, in the absence of legislative prohibition, may themselves seek to exclude or discourage dual mandates in the longer term, although some of them may tolerate and will perhaps even encourage them during the Scottish Parliament's infancy.

The requirement, arguably anomalous, that members of the Commons must be over 21 years of age is retained in connection with standing for the Scottish Parliament. Other disqualifications for membership of the Commons - for mentally ill persons, undischarged bankrupts, and convicted prisoners serving a sentence of imprisonment which is of more than one year, or indefinite - will apply equally to the Scottish Parliament. So will the disqualification of categories of office-holders whose offices or employments are deemed to be incompatible with membership of Parliament on constitutional grounds, such as judges, civil servants, full-time police officers, members of the regular armed forces, members of foreign legislatures, and members of various bodies performing public functions (as regards which, by *clause 14(2)*, there is provision for a list of disqualifying offices to be included in a new Order in Council).

If a person who is disqualified is returned as a member, the return is void and the seat is vacated (*clause 16(1)*), and if a sitting member becomes disqualified, likewise the seat is vacated (*clause 16(2)*). A complaint that a person who has been elected is disqualified may be instigated by an election petition under the provisions of the Representation of the People Acts (*clause 11(4)*), while a claim that a person returned as a member is or has become disqualified may otherwise be brought before the Court of Session, which can make a declarator to that effect (*clause 17*).

Gender Balance

Women have been persistently under-represented in public life in Scotland. Besides, it is often argued that attracting the greater participation of women would change the ethos and style of conducting politics in ways that are beneficial. For these reasons, one of the more radical strands in the thinking of the Scottish Constitutional Convention was an acceptance that the new Parliament should reflect a new style of politics in which men and women would be equal participants.[81] While the leadership of the Convention itself scarcely exemplified the principle, it was the Convention's adoption of the principle, effectively promoted by the Scottish Trades Union Congress and women activists in the political parties and other groupings, which was significant. The Scottish Labour Party was sufficiently persuaded to favour statutory quotas which would ensure equal gender numbers. The Liberal Democrats shared the aim but were more uneasy about state intervention and preferred a strategy of encouraging selection of women candidates.

In the Convention, a compromise was arrived at which relied on an "Electoral Agreement". In November 1995 at Inverness, the leaders of the Labour Party and the Liberal Democrats in Scotland agreed to "select and field an equal number of male and female candidates for election, taking into account both the constituency and additional member list candidates; ensure that these candidates are equally distributed with a view to the winnability of seats; use an additional member system (AMS) for elections; ensure that the size of the Scottish Parliament is large enough to facilitate effective democratic representative government." In its final report, the Convention called on other parties to implement the principle as well.[82]

However, between the aspiration to gender balance and its achievement, there could lie legal obstacles. When the Labour Party implemented a policy of women-only shortlists, its legality was challenged, and an industrial tribunal held that it was contrary to the requirements of the Sex Discrimination Act 1975 (which does not generally permit "positive discrimination" or affirmative action).[83] The ruling is not necessarily authoritative, because it was made at the lowest rung of the judicial ladder and not appealed, and it remains contestable whether the Act was meant to apply to political parties' selection of candidates. Nevertheless, it signalled a possible difficulty with harder-edged quota policies.

By contrast, softer-edged policies of hopes and targets are likely to be permissible, even if the Act is applicable to the situation. The Labour Party is considering "twinning", which would work in the constituency part of the vote by pairing seats by winnability and location and then choosing a man and a woman to fight the two paired seats in one selection process.

In any event, the matter will depend on the parties' decisions, unordained

---

[81] A. Brown, D. McCrone and L. Paterson, *Politics and Society in Scotland* (1996), Chap.8.
[82] *Scotland's Parliament. Scotland's Right* (1995), p.22.
[83] *Jepson and Dyas-Elliott v. The Labour Party* [1996] I.R.L.R. 116.

by and unassisted by the law. The White Paper did retain something of the Scottish Constitutional Convention's vision in the form of an exhortation:

"The Government are keen to see people with standing in their communities and who represent the widest possible range of interests in Scotland putting themselves forward for election to the Scottish Parliament. In particular the Government attach great importance to equal opportunities for all - including women, members of ethnic minorities and disabled people. The Government urge all political parties offering candidates for election to the Scottish Parliament to have this in mind in their internal candidate selection processes."[84]

It remains as exhortation. The Scotland Bill has no provisions on gender (or ethnicity) in the membership of the Parliament, and nor does it exempt candidate selection from the operation of the Sex Discrimination Act.

Conduct of Election Campaigns

For the United Kingdom Parliament, there is an intricate body of rules about the conduct of elections (and what is permitted or not in campaigns) in the Representation of the People Act 1983, as amended. With due modifications, many of the same rules apply to local authority elections and European Parliament elections.

The technique used in the Scotland Bill is simply and similarly to allow the UK Government (the Secretary of State) to make provision by statutory instrument for the conduct of elections to the Scottish Parliament, which may include the application with or without modifications of the rules in the Representation of the People Acts or other enactments relating to other categories of election (*clause 11*).

This is a convenient technique in some ways, but it allows considerable discretion to the government of the day in London, and it means that some quite controversial aspects of campaign rules (for example, on expenditure limits) will be dealt with only in a statutory instrument made by a minister within the approval of the two Houses at Westminster (*clause 101*). It also means that it is impossible for us to comment on the substance of any such rules, because they have yet to be made.

MEMBERS

The men and women who are successful in elections become members of the Scottish Parliament, as will those persons who are deemed to be returned under the provision for filling regional vacancies (in *clause 9*). All will be members of the Scottish Parliament or MSPs (as distinguished from MPs, who are members of the House of Commons, and MEPs, who are members of the European Parliament). Given the electoral system which has been adopted, there are two classes of member, namely "constituency members" and "regional

---

[84] para. 8.5.

members". However, if somewhat different political responsibilities may accrue to members depending on their route to membership, they will have precisely the same status and privileges in law.

Term of Office

The duration of a member's term of office is precisely specified in the Scotland Bill. The term of office begins "on the day on which the member is declared to be returned" and ends "with the dissolution of the Parliament" (*clause 12*). Otherwise, a term of office may be terminated by death or resignation. In the House of Commons, there is no ordinary procedure for resignation as such, and so the traditional device employed to engineer one has been an MP's appointment to a disqualifying office, with a few Crown sinecures (such as Bailiff and Steward of the Chiltern Hundreds) maintained for that purpose. Dispensing with anachronistic curiosities, the Scotland Bill provides that a member "may at any time resign his seat by giving notice in writing to the Presiding Officer" (*clause 13*).

Remuneration

The Bill makes provision for remuneration of members of the Scottish Parliament and the Scottish Executive, by specifying means rather than by specifying amounts. As with the salaries at Westminster, it may seem that parliamentarians are judges in their own cause, for it is the Scottish Parliament which is required, whether by an Act or by a resolution, to provide for the salaries (*clause 76*). However, what is intended to happen is set out in the White Paper: "The Government will invite the independent Senior Salaries Review Body to set the salaries of MSPs in the first instance. Thereafter, the Government will expect movements to be linked to changes in the salaries received by MPs".[85] The Scottish Parliament is also empowered to provide for the payment of allowances to members of the Parliament and members of the Executive (*clause 76(2)*), and to provide for the payment of pensions, gratuities or allowances to former members (*clause 76(3)*). There is a duty of disclosure, so that the public will be informed: the Parliament has to ensure that information concerning sums paid as salaries, allowances, pensions or gratuities is published for each financial year (*clause 78(1)*).

As we have noticed, dual mandates are not prohibited. But double salaries are. If an MSP receives a salary as a member of the Westminster Parliament or as a United Kingdom MEP, then the Scottish Parliament is required to ensure that there is a reduction in the salary payable as MSP, by such proportion or amount as it determines (*clause 77*).

Oath

Members of the Parliament are required to take the oath of allegiance on being returned to the Parliament. An elected member may not take part in proceedings of the Parliament until he or she has done so (*clause 79(2)*) and is not

---

[85] para. 9.3.

entitled to payment of salary or allowances without having done so (*clause 78(2)*). The member's seat is vacated if an oath has not been taken within two months of the member's being returned, unless the Parliament allows an extension (for example, on account of illness) (*clause 79(3)*).

An oath involves religious commitment. The standard form of the oath of allegiance (prescribed in the Promissory Oaths Act 1868) would be as follows:

"I, John Brown, do swear that I will be faithful and bear true allegiance to Her Majesty Queen Elizabeth, Her Heirs and Successors, according to Law. So help me GOD."

However, gradually, in nineteenth century legislation, provision was made for Quakers, Jews, and atheists to be able to make an equivalent affirmation consistently with their principles. By the Oaths Act 1978, the alternative form is available for anyone "who objects to being sworn". The alternative form is:

"I, Mary Brown, do solemnly, sincerely, and truly declare and affirm that I will be faithful and bear true allegiance to Her Majesty Queen Elizabeth, Her Heirs and Successors, according to Law."

If differences in (or absence of) religious faith have been catered for, the oath of allegiance may still present difficulties of other kinds. For example, currently two persons elected to the House of Commons, Sinn Fein MPs Gerry Adams and Martin McGuinness, have refused to take the oath, and in consequence have been unable to participate in proceedings of the House and have been barred from using the House's facilities. More generally, the form of the oath or affirmation could pose a dilemma to persons of republican sentiment, and the Scottish National Party has proposed its replacement. However, Roseanna Cunningham, the SNP MP for Perth, who has republican views, felt able to take the oath of allegiance at Westminster.

Members of the Scottish Executive are additionally required to take the official oath (or equivalent affirmation), which (as prescribed in the Promissory Oaths Act 1868) involves an undertaking to serve Her Majesty in that office (*clause 79(4)*).

PROCEDURE AND PRIVILEGES

The procedures and privileges of the United Kingdom Parliament are sufficiently extensive as to merit lengthy and detailed exposition in the treatise which has become known as "the parliamentary Bible".[86]

For the new Scottish Parliament, a less encrusted regime is appropriate. In the White Paper, the Government said that it would "provide a framework for the Scottish Parliament, but it will be left open to that Parliament itself to develop procedures which best meet its purposes".[87] In accord with those intentions, the Scotland Bill deals with a few matters only. Beyond these, the Parliament is given authority to regulate proceedings by standing orders (*clause 21*). Some minimum requirements as to the content of standing orders are insisted

[86]   *Erskine May's Treatise on the Law, Privileges, Proceedings and Usage of Parliament* (21st ed. by C.J. Boulton, 1989).
[87]   para. 9.11.

on, and there are other provisions indicating what standing orders "may" do, but there is a wide area of discretion left, within which the Parliament will be able to decide on how its business is arranged and conducted.

Procedure

One important procedural matter provided for is the election of a Presiding Officer and two deputies. The Presiding Officer's role will be roughly equivalent to the Speaker's in the House of Commons: according to the White Paper, the Presiding Officer "will ensure the efficient conduct and administration of Scottish parliamentary business and chair sessions of that Parliament".[88] The Presiding Officer and two deputies are elected by the Parliament from among its members (*clause 18(1)*). Normally, they will be elected at the first meeting of the Parliament following a general election and will hold office until the next such occasion (*clause 18(1), (2)*), but a vacancy arising may also be filled by an election at the time (*clause 18(3)*). Standing orders will provide for occasions when the Presiding Officer is unable to act or that office is vacant (*clause 18(4)*), although generally the Presiding Officer may authorise a deputy to act in his or her stead (*clause 18(5)*). Standing orders may also provide rules on the participation and voting of these three officers, who are also members, in the proceedings of the Parliament (*clause 18(6)*).

Clause 20 and *Schedule 2* provide for the establishment of the Scottish Parliamentary Corporate Body. It is convenient, and indeed necessary, for there to be a body with legal powers to hold property, make contracts and handle money, and bring or defend legal proceedings by or against the Parliament. Its principal function is to ensure that the Parliament is provided with the property, staff and services required. The corporation will consist of the Presiding Officer (who will preside at its meetings) and four members of the Parliament appointed in accordance with standing orders. This body will be responsible for the appointment of the staff of the Parliament, including a Clerk of the Parliament (*clause 19*), Assistant Clerks and others (*Schedule 2, paragraph 3*), and will determine the terms and conditions of their employment. The financial arrangements for the corporation are linked to the financial provisions in *Part III* (*clauses 61-68*) of the Bill, so that they are within Treasury or central government control.

As noticed above, there are some mandatory requirements for the procedural rules which will be adopted as standing orders. *Schedule 3* includes mandatory requirements on five matters. First, the rules must include "provision for preserving order in the proceedings of the Parliament, including provision for preventing conduct which would constitute a criminal offence or contempt of court". Secondly, proceedings must be held in public, except when standing orders otherwise provide, but there may be provision as to the conditions to be complied with by members of the public who attend. Thirdly, the rules must include provision for reporting the proceedings of the Parliament and for publishing the reports. Fourthly, the rules must ensure that appointments to

---

[88] para. 9.5.

committees and sub-committees are made with regard to the balance of parties in the Parliament. Fifthly, it is required that royal consent should be signified before the Parliament can pass any Bill affecting the Crown's interests (a procedure which is also applicable to the Westminster Parliament).

Particular provision is also made for standing orders in connection with legislative procedure. Given that the Parliament is unicameral, it must have been thought desirable to ensure that there would be adequate opportunities for the proper scrutiny of proposed legislation. Accordingly *clause 34* stipulates that, except in so far as modified by standing orders, there must be stages, first, affording opportunity for general debate, second, for consideration of detail, and third, for a final decision to pass or reject a Bill.

There are some other provisions in the Scotland Bill which include mandatory requirements or permissive options for standing orders, which will be referred to when appropriate. However, it is fair to say that much is being left for the Parliament itself to decide, including important matters such as the dates and times of sitting, the general disposition of functions, and the committee structure.

Privileges

The Houses of Parliament at Westminster enjoy some privileges, powers and immunities at law in order to enable them to act freely, protect their proceedings, and preserve their authority and dignity. This part of the law is called parliamentary privilege.[89] Much of it is derived from a customary basis, but recognised as part of the common law. In part it is statutory, being found in the Bill of Rights and the Claim of Right from 1688-89. The rules in those enactments about "Parliament" were taken to apply to the United Kingdom Parliament after 1707.

As the new, devolved Scottish Parliament will not benefit from any customary privileges, it is necessary to provide in legislation for any privileges which, it is felt, ought to be enjoyed by it.

Members of the Westminster Parliament enjoy the privilege of exemption from jury service as of right (under the Juries Act 1974), and this privilege has been extended to members of the Scottish Parliament, members of the Scottish Executive and junior Scottish Ministers (*clause 80*). An archaic and anomalous remnant of a rule, which affords members of the Westminster Parliament an immunity from arrest in civil proceedings, is sensibly not extended to the new Parliament.

Privileges are conferred for the benefit of the Parliament in the public interest, even if they may incidentally be of advantage to members. Thus the privilege of freedom of speech enjoyed by members of the Houses at Westminster affords them an immunity from being prosecuted or sued in legal proceedings in connection with the business of the Houses, but its real purpose is to ensure that the members of the legislature are able to perform their duties fully and freely, without fear of penalty.

---

[89] See C.R. Munro, *Studies in Constitutional Law* (1987), Chap.7.

A more restricted immunity will apply to the Scottish Parliament's members, because the provision made is limited to two specific legal wrongs. First, it is provided that any statement made "in proceedings of the Parliament" is absolutely privileged, for the purpose of the law of defamation (*clause 37*). What this entails in practice is that any person defamed, let us say by an MSP speaking in the course of a debate in the Edinburgh Parliament, will have no legal remedy, because any action would be met by the complete defence of absolute privilege. "Statement", incidentally, is defined so as to mean "words, pictures, visual images, gestures or any other method of signifying meaning" (by *clause 37(2)*). However, "proceedings of the Parliament" is a (perhaps deliberately) vague term, and a similar phrase in the Bill of Rights has caused difficulties of interpretation and application, for example with relation to members' correspondence. Admittedly, other defences might be available to members as part of the general law. The defence of qualified privilege should apply to anything done by members in carrying out their duties, provided there is an absence of malice.[90]

The defence of absolute privilege is also to cover any statement in a "publication under the authority of the Parliament" (*clause 37*), so that official papers and reports will be clothed with protection against defamation actions as well. Unofficial reports (such as reporting in newspapers or on television) will be subject to the general law.

The second specified immunity is for contempt of court, but is more limited (as well as more unclear). The law of contempt of court has a variety of forms and purposes, but its most important role is to prevent or penalise potentially prejudicial comment on legal proceedings which are *sub judice* as being before (or shortly to be before) the courts. The Scotland Bill provides that things said or written in "proceedings of the Parliament in relation to a Bill or subordinate legislation" (or to the extent that they are in a report of such proceedings) will not be subject to the strict liability form of contempt (*clause 38*). The strict liability form of contempt is defined in the Contempt of Court Act 1981. However, as the provisions of the 1981 Act are untidily grafted on to the common law (which was not entirely superseded), disapplication of the offence is less than total, even for the restricted category of parliamentary business to which it is intended to apply.

The Westminster Parliament has developed its own rule in order generally to avoid comments on proceedings which are *sub judice*, and it seems to be intended that the Scottish Parliament will do the same because, as already noticed, it is required in standing orders to provide for "preventing conduct which would constitute ..... contempt of court" (*Schedule 3, paragraph 1*). So instances should be infrequent, anyway.

In practice, defamation is the legal wrong most likely to be committed in the course of Scottish parliamentary proceedings (and indirectly in their reporting). However, it is worth remarking that there are other criminal and civil wrongs which may be committed by words, for example incitement to racial

[90] As in *Beach v. Freeson* [1972] 1 Q.B. 14.

hatred or breach of confidence. In the absence of a more general provision for privilege, no special immunity will protect MSPs (or usually those reporting them[91]) from the consequences.

Another matter connected to freedom of speech is the problem of influence on members' actions. Some influences, such as the party system and the ordinary processes of communication, are regarded as proper or acceptable, but other influences or pressures may be regarded as improper or unacceptable. Often the difficulty arises because parliamentarians choose to augment their salaries by accepting payments for services rendered to outside organisations, companies or persons. In recent years, and especially during the 1992-97 Parliament, the dignity and reputation of the House of Commons have suffered through frequent allegations of "sleaze". In response, John Major's Government established a Committee on Standards in Public Life (chaired by Lord Nolan until 1997, and subsequently by Lord Neill), which has undertaken a series of inquiries and recommended reforms.

The Nolan Committee's first subject was the House of Commons,[92] and their approach and recommendations have in turn shaped the provisions on members' interests for the Scottish Parliament. The fact that there are statutory provisions is symptomatic: self-regulation is not sufficiently trustworthy. Following Nolan too, there is a specific ban on paid advocacy: members will be prohibited from advocating or initiating any cause or matter on behalf of any person for payment or benefit (or urging another member to do so), as will be specified in standing orders (*clause 22(4)*). This restriction will be alongside the operation of the ordinary criminal law, because *clause 39* provides that the Parliament will count as a public body for the purpose of the Prevention of Corruption Acts 1889 to 1916, which penalise the corrupt making or accepting of payments, in money or kind, for activity (or forbearance) in connection with a public body's business. Less specific arrangements - such as when a member for a fee acts as a parliamentary consultant to a company or a trade union or an organisation - are not prohibited. However, depending on the details of the provisions to be made in standing orders, they will probably fall to be registered, and the register of members' interests will be published and available for inspection (*clause 22(1)*). A financial interest or an interest of any other kind (as defined and specified in standing orders to be made) in any matter must also be declared by a member before participating in proceedings relating to the matter (*clause 22(2)*), and (depending upon standing orders) may prevent or restrict participation in such proceedings (*clause 22(3)*). A member who fails to comply with or contravenes any of these requirements is liable to be excluded from proceedings under standing orders (*clause 22(5)*) and is also guilty of a summary offence punishable by fine (*clause 22(6), (7)*).

---

[91] However, an amending provision in *Schedule 7* precludes the reporting of proceedings of the Scottish Parliament (as distinct from the proceedings themselves) from being the subject of prosecution for incitement to racial hatred under the Public Order Act 1986.

[92] Committee on Standards in Public Life, First Report, Standards in Public Life, Cm. 2850 (1995).

The Houses of Parliament have the privilege of regulating their own composition, within the requirements of statute law. Some remaining aspects of this privilege in regard to Westminster, such as settling disputes about entitlement to membership and determining when casual vacancies will be filled through by-elections, do not arise in regard to the Scottish Parliament because the matters are entirely statutorily governed. Another aspect of the privilege is the Houses' right to expel members whom they judge to be unfit to continue in that capacity (for example, because they are convicted of a criminal offence involving turpitude). The Scottish Parliament is given authority to exclude a member from proceedings not only for breaches of the rules on members' interests (*clause 22(5)*) but also for the purpose of preserving order in the proceedings (*Schedule 3, paragraph 1*). The Parliament is not expressly given a power to expel members, and in its absence probably cannot lawfully assert such a power within its procedures, against the argument that a member's term of office is statutory.

The Houses of Parliament also have exclusive cognisance of internal affairs, which (subject to any statutory restrictions) makes them masters of their own procedure, and precludes outside bodies such as courts from interfering. The position of the Scottish Parliament is broadly similar in this respect because, as we have seen above, it is free to decide on its own procedures, subject to the specific requirements included in the legislation. In part reflection of the Westminster Houses' privilege, it is also provided that "the validity of any proceedings leading to the enactment of an Act of the Scottish Parliament shall not be called into question in any legal proceedings" (*clause 27(5)*). Whether an ouster clause of this sort would necessarily be effective in all circumstances may be doubted, however, as the courts will not easily accept that they can be deprived of jurisdiction to adjudicate,[93] and some aspects of the proceedings (for example, on stages of a Bill, in *clause 34*) are statutorily enjoined.

More generally, the Houses of Parliament, as the High Court of Parliament, have similar powers to ordinary courts of law and have an inherent jurisdiction to deal with breaches of privilege or any offences to their authority, dignity or functioning which they classify as contempt of Parliament, whether committed by members or outside persons. How far the Scottish Parliament could competently assert similar powers within its authority to make procedural rules is doubtful, but as the Houses tend to exercise their penal jurisdiction only sparingly, caution would be appropriate in any event. There are specific provisions for summoning witnesses: the Scottish Parliament is given power to require persons to attend to give evidence or to produce documents in their custody or control, in relation to devolved matters or matters in relation to which statutory functions are exercisable by the Scottish Ministers (*clause 23*). Persons competently summoned commit a summary offence (for which they may be fined or imprisoned for up to three months) if they refuse or fail without reasonable excuse to attend or co-operate, or refuse to take an oath which may be required of them (*clauses 24, 25*). The creation of offences dealt with in the

[93] See *Anisminic Ltd v. Foreign Compensation Commission* [1969] 2 A.C. 147.

ordinary courts would tend to suggest that the Scottish Parliament is not expected to ape Westminster in exercising an independent penal jurisdiction to any significant extent, certainly where outsiders are concerned.

CHAPTER 5
THE SCOTTISH PARLIAMENT: LAW-MAKING POWERS

The Scottish Parliament will have a number of important functions. One of its principal responsibilities will be to increase democratic control over Scottish government by holding Scottish Ministers to account for the performance of their functions and much of the energy of MSPs will doubtless be devoted to this task. Above all, however, the Parliament is to have wide powers to make new laws for Scotland, the feature which most clearly distinguishes it from the Welsh Assembly proposed in the Government of Wales Bill. The legislative competence of the Parliament forms the subject-matter of this chapter. There are three main elements. First we discuss the method proposed in the White Paper and adopted in the Bill for the devolution of legislative power, and notice the limits on the Parliament's competence. Then, more particularly, the extent of devolved powers, *vis-à-vis* reserved matters, is examined. Thirdly, because any system for the allocation of law-making power will inevitably produce questions in practice about whether a law (proposed or actually made) of the Scottish Parliament is within the area of competence allocated to it, there have to be procedures for handling such questions. These are addressed in the final two sections of the chapter.

DEVOLUTION OF LEGISLATIVE POWER: METHOD AND LIMITS
The point of devolution is to confer a range of law-making powers on the Scottish Parliament and what the devolution scheme must do is to define with reasonable precision those law-making powers. This is, at one level, quite a simple thing to do. It requires a listing of all the different areas of law-making activity of the Westminster Parliament and then a division of that list into two sublists of (a) powers proposed to be devolved and (b) those proposed to remain not devolved. It is not, however, essential that both sublists of powers be set out in the devolution legislation. Instead, one model would be that the legislation sets out the list of powers to be devolved whilst at the same time making clear that all powers not mentioned are not devolved but retained by the Westminster Parliament alone; on another model the legislation lists the powers which are to be retained, on the assumption this time that powers not mentioned are passed to the devolved Parliament.

The Scotland Act 1978 did not conform to either model, although it was closer to the first. The Act set out at very great length and with meticulously detailed reference to then-existing statutes the powers to be devolved to the proposed Scottish Assembly. The scheme was extremely complex; it would probably have required frequent adjustment; it would have been a constant cause of dispute in the courts; it would have caused friction in the Assembly; and would have contributed to the general instability of the devolution arrangements as a whole.

Now, the Government's White Paper proposals[94] and the Scotland Bill it-

---

[94]   See also the Constitution Unit, *Scotland's Parliament: Fundamentals for a New Scotland Act* (1996) Chaps. 3, 4.

self have adopted a different approach to the allocation of devolved legislative (and also executive) powers. Not only are the powers to be devolved broader than those under the 1978 Act, but the method adopted is that of listing the powers retained to the Westminster Parliament - the "reserved matters" - and leaving all else devolved.

Thus, in terms of *clause 27(1)*, the Scottish Parliament is given the power "to make laws, to be known as Acts of the Scottish Parliament". The power, as observed in the last chapter, is not exclusive, as Westminster's competence is restated (*clause 27(7)*). More importantly, the power to make laws conferred by *clause 27(1)* has to be read subject to the terms of *clause 28* in which the limits of the legislative powers of the Parliament are laid down. One point of interest is that neither *clause 27* nor *clause 28* provides any general definition of the scope of the laws that may be made. There is not, for instance, as there was in the case of the Government of Ireland Act 1920, any use of a formula such as one empowering the making of laws for "the peace, order and government" of Scotland. There is simply the power to make laws, subject only to the limitation in *clause 28(1)* that "[a]n Act of the Scottish Parliament is not law so far as any provision of the Act is outside the legislative competence of the Parliament."

Then, in *clause 28(2)*, there are set out the five grounds (*(a)* - *(e)*) upon which a provision of an Act of the Parliament of Scotland is to be treated as *outside* its legislative competence. Of these much the most complex is ground *(c)* which, along with other clauses in the Bill, deals with the "reserved matters" themselves. These will be discussed in the next section (with certain other important rules which affect competence in general) but first let us consider the other four limitations on the Parliament's legislative competence:

1. A provision is outside the legislative competence of the Parliament if "it would form part of the law of a country or territory other than Scotland" (*clause 28(2)(a)*). In other words, the Parliament will have no power to legislate extraterritorially, or furth of Scotland. "Scotland" is defined to include "so much of the internal waters and territorial sea of the United Kingdom as are adjacent to Scotland".[95]

2. With certain limited exceptions set out in *Schedule 4* to the Bill, the Parliament will be unable to modify any provision of the Scotland Act itself (*clause 28(2)(b)* and *(3)*). The Scottish Parliament will not in general be able to vary the terms of the Act which creates it, although there will be no legal restraint on such a variation being made by the UK Parliament.

3. The Scottish Parliament may make no provision which is "incompatible with any of the Convention rights or with Community law" (*clause 28(2)(d)*). This restriction on competence reaffirms two principles which would, in any event, have operated to place limits around the Parliament's legislative

---

[95] *Clause 111(1). Clause 111(2)* enables the boundaries to be determined. See also *clause 99* (Tweed and Esk) and certain "reservations" e.g. at *Sched. 5, Head 4, S. 2* (Scots law and jurisdiction of Scottish courts in relation to offshore activities).

powers. The United Kingdom is a party to both the European Convention on Human Rights (ECHR) and to the European Community Treaties and the opportunity is taken here to make explicit the obligation of the Scottish Parliament not to enact legislation incompatible with the United Kingdom's own obligations.

In the case of the Convention rights (i.e. the rights and fundamental freedoms set out in the ECHR and its First Protocol[96]), the Scottish Parliament's obligations have to be read alongside the Government's broader proposals for the strengthening of human rights protection as set out in their White Paper *Rights Brought Home: The Human Rights Bill*[97] and the Human Rights Bill itself. These proposals provide new mechanisms for the enforcement of Convention rights in domestic courts, where hitherto the status of the ECHR has been marginal at best. Up to the present, the United Kingdom's obligation to observe the Convention has only been enforceable indirectly, by using the machinery of the European Commission and Court of Human Rights at Strasbourg. Once the Human Rights Act is enacted and brought into effect, domestic courts will be able to strike down as invalid the decisions of public authorities which are incompatible with the Convention rights. Special rules are to apply in relation to Acts of the UK Parliament but Acts of the Scottish Parliament (and the actions including subordinate legislation of the Scottish Ministers) will be treated in much the same way as other public decision-making. If a provision in a Scottish Act is held to be incompatible with a right guaranteed under the Convention, it will not be valid. One important consequence, however, of making this explicit in the Scotland Act as an issue of legislative competence is that compatibility with Convention rights will become subject to pre-Assent challenge in the Judicial Committee of the Privy Council (see below). It will also become a "devolution issue" and will be subject to the special procedural provisions in *Schedule 6* to the Bill, including special access to and decision by the Judicial Committee rather than standard treatment by the appellate process in the courts. This will have the probable advantage of keeping all issues of legislative competence together and ensuring a relatively rapid response on crucial questions affecting the validity of Scottish legislation. It will also, however, create a curious division in the Scottish legal system between, on the one hand, the handling of Convention rights which raise "devolution issues" (including quite low level decision-making by members of the Scottish Executive) and which may, therefore, be decided finally by the Judicial Committee and, on the other hand, other Convention rights issues.

The other limb of *clause 28(2)(d)* which requires provisions in Acts of the Scottish Parliament to be compatible with Community law[98] also reflects wider obligations bearing upon public bodies in the United Kingdom

---

[96] See *clause 111(1)* and clause 1 of the current Human Rights Bill.

[97] Cm. 3782 (1997).

[98] For the Bill's definition, see *clause 111(6)*.

and other member states of the European Community.[99] Although the jurisprudential basis for the two sets of rules differs greatly, the obligation of the Scottish Parliament to behave in ways compatible with Community law, irrespective of the duty imposed by *clause 28(2)(d)*, will be similar to its position under the new Human Rights Act. Community legislation (including the Treaties and regulations and directives enacted under them) now covers very broad areas and, as supported by the doctrines of supremacy and direct effect developed by the European Court of Justice, serves to restrict the competence of all other legislative bodies, including national Parliaments. The Scottish Parliament would be similarly restricted and its Acts open to challenge in the courts on grounds of incompatibility even if this were not explicitly stated in the Scotland Act itself. The effect of defining the matter as one of "legislative competence" is, however, to render issues of Community law, like issues of Convention rights, subject to the special forms of review in the courts.

4. Finally, a very specific restriction is imposed on the Parliament by *clause 28(2)(e)* which places beyond its competence a provision which "would remove the Lord Advocate from his position as head of the systems of criminal prosecution and investigation of deaths in Scotland". This is an important part of a package of provisions in the Bill designed to protect the independent role of the Lord Advocate. It is discussed further in Chapter 6.

DEVOLVED AND RESERVED

As explained in the White Paper, the Government's intention is to establish a Parliament for Scotland with wide law-making powers. The actual powers to be devolved were set out in Chapter 2 of the White Paper and may be listed in summary form as follows:

Health	School education
Further and higher education	Aspects of science and research funding
Training policy and lifelong learning	Vocational qualifications
Careers advice and guidance	Local government
Social work	Voluntary sector issues
Housing	Area regeneration
Land-use planning and building control	Economic development
Aspects of financial assistance to industry	Inward investment
Promotion of trade and exports	Tourism
Passenger and road transport	Aspects of air and sea transport
Inland waterways	Criminal law (with exceptions)
Civil law (with exceptions)	Electoral law (local government only)
Most judicial appointments	Criminal justice and prosecution

[99] For further treatment of EC relations, see Chap. 9.

Civil and criminal courts	Tribunals (in relation to devolved matters)
Legal aid	Parole
Prisons	Police and fire services
Civil defence and emergency planning	Some functions under international legal agreements
Liquor licensing	Protection of animals
Environmental protection	The natural heritage
The built heritage	Flood prevention, coast protection and reservoir safety
Agriculture (subject to co-ordination)	Food standards (subject to co-ordination)
Forestry	Fisheries
Sport	The arts
Statistics, public registers and records	

This is a long list of powers but, as already explained above, it is not a list which is repeated in the Bill itself. Instead the Bill lists the areas of potential law-making activity which are *not* to be devolved. This is achieved (subject to certain qualifications considered below) by means of *clause 28(2)(c), (4), (5), (6)*; *clause 29* and *Schedule 5*.

Clause 28(2)(c) provides simply that any provision of an Act of the Scottish Parliament is outside the legislative competence of the Parliament if "it relates to reserved matters". Then *clause 29* of the Bill gives effect to *Schedule 5* which actually lists the "reserved matters" and defines as "devolved matters" all matters which are not reserved. A summary of the list of reserved matters has already been set out in Chapter 3 where it was also pointed out that the listing of reserved matters in *Schedule 5* has to be read subject to further important provisions in *clauses 28* and *29* of the Bill. First, the Schedule can itself be amended - not only by an Act of the UK Parliament but also by subordinate legislation made by a UK minister. This "may make any modifications of that Schedule which the person making the legislation considers necessary or expedient" (*clause 29(2)*). It is further stated that such "subordinate legislation may modify any enactment (including any other provision of this [Scotland] Act, instrument or other document" (*clause 29(3)*). The power could presumably be used either to make marginal adjustments to the list of reserved matters or to make substantial changes. The power is, at any event, exercisable only with the assent of both Houses of the UK Parliament as well as of the Scottish Parliament.[100]

Secondly, there are in *clause 28* of the Bill further provisions which affect the way in which the law-making power of the Scottish Parliament will be interpreted and applied. It is, for instance, made clear in the Bill that an Act of

[100]   *Clause 101(1), (3)*.
[101]   A term to be interpreted to include re-enactment and codification (*clause 28(10)*).

59

the Scottish Parliament may be used to modify[101] a provision made by or under an Act of the UK Parliament, provided that the modification is otherwise within the Scottish Parliament's legislative competence (*clause 28(8)*). It seems likely that much of the legislation made by the Scottish Parliament will be by reference to existing legislation of the UK Parliament. Such existing legislation might, in relation to Scotland and to devolved matters, be amended or repealed or replaced by a consolidation Act. It might be re-enacted as part of a wider programme of codification of statutory and common law rules.

Then three related subclauses make further provision for the handling of the boundary line between reserved and devolved matters. *Clause 28(6)* recognises a general difficulty inherent in the operation of any system of allocating legislative powers. What does one do about a provision in an Act of the Scottish Parliament which appears to have both a devolved and a reserved aspect?[102] In principle, it must be invalid because "it relates to reserved matters", at least to the extent that it does so relate. There may be a question about whether the enacted provision can survive as valid - except as far as it relates to reserved matters - or whether its validity is completely lost. But what *clause 28(6)* usefully provides, subject to an important qualification, is that a provision does not relate to reserved matters (at all) "merely because it makes provision for purposes relating to devolved matters which incidentally affects reserved matters". If a provision satisfies this test of affecting reserved matters but only "incidentally", it is simply deemed not to relate to reserved matters and is, therefore, competent. It may be that problems will arise in the interpretation of "incidentally" - but see also the guidance given by *clause 28(9)* mentioned below.

The important qualification to the general rule in *clause 28(6)* is that it does not apply to a provision of an Act of the Scottish Parliament which "makes modifications of Scots private law or Scots criminal law, or of any enactment, as it applies to reserved matters". Definitions of the terms "Scots private law" (to mean the civil law of persons, obligations, property and actions) and "Scots criminal law" (to include "criminal offences, evidence, procedure and penalties and the treatment of offenders") are to be found in *clause 111(3), (4)*. What this exception recognises is a rather difficult cross-current in the overall scheme of division between devolved and reserved matters. The definition of reserved matters (and, therefore, of devolved matters) is mainly done by subject-matter rather than by type of law.[103] There is, however, a clear intention underlying the devolution package that the Scottish Parliament should have general powers to amend and perhaps codify the private law and the criminal law of Scotland. The point is to provide (or restore) a law-making capacity to a legal system which has to its detriment lacked its own legislature in modern times. Arguably the law has failed to develop because of legislative congestion at

---

[102] For discussion of this subject in relation to the Government of Ireland Act 1920, see B. Hadfield, *"Scotland's Parliament:* A Northern Ireland Perspective on the White Paper" [1997] P.L. 660. See also T. Jones "Scottish Devolution and Demarcation Disputes" [1997] P.L. 283.

[103] Although it is true that the unofficial list of devolved matters contained in the White Paper and set out above does include "Civil law" and "Criminal law".

Westminster. But the general amendment or codification of the law could easily affect subject-matter on the "reserved" side of the devolution dichotomy as much as on the "devolved" side. Such changes in the law cut across the two categories as would be seen, for instance, if the general rules of the law of contract were reformed. This could easily affect "housing" or "passenger transport" and many other topics on the devolved side of the divide. It could easily also affect, however, reserved matters such as "financial services" or "insolvency". The same applies to the reform of the criminal law which may readily be seen as largely affecting devolved matters but many reserved matters also depend on rules relating to criminal offences, evidence and penalties in their enforcement aspect.

Returning to the qualification in *clause 28(6)*, what it does is to prevent the extension of the "incidentally affecting" rule to modifications of private law, criminal law or "any enactment". Initially they are *not* "saved" by the device of deeming them to be not reserved. *But,* one has then to look at *clause 28(4)* and *(5)* because those subclauses *do* operate to save such modifications in certain circumstances. They do so not by redefining "reserved matters" as such but instead by refining the meaning to be given to "legislative competence". *Clause 28(4)* states that a provision of a Scottish Act is not outside the legislative competence of the Parliament on grounds of relating to reserved matters "merely because it makes modifications of Scots private law, or Scots criminal law, as it applies to reserved matters if the provision does so in such a way that the law in question applies consistently to devolved and reserved matters". The effect here is to bring back into the fold of competence general modifying or reforming laws which do undoubtedly relate to reserved matters but do so "consistently" with their treatment of devolved matters. There is some ambiguity in the word "consistently"[104] but it presumably means that the new provisions must apply without distinction or discrimination to both devolved and reserved matters. Another possible cause of difficulty in the application of the subclause (and also of *clause 28(6)*) is some uncertainty about what "Scots private law" will embrace e.g. in relation to the law of actions. Could a Scottish Act to reform the grounds of judicial review (which could certainly relate to reserved matters) be saved by *clause 28(4)*?

Another twist in the tail of *clause 28(4)* is that three of the listed categories of reserved matters in *Schedule 5* to the Bill do themselves explicitly define as outside the legislative competence of the Parliament certain areas of potential legislative activity which affect Scots private law and which might otherwise be defined as within the competence by virtue of *clause 28(4)*.[105] Plainly these reflect an insistence that, even if private law reform were carried out "consistently" as between devolved and reserved matters, it would nevertheless represent an unacceptable intrusion into those particular aspects of the reserved matters.[106]

---

[104] As indeed there is also in the phrase "law in question" where it is unclear what "law" is referred to.
[105] *Sched. 5, Part II, Head 1, S. 1; Head 5, S. 3; Head 6, S. 3.*
[106] See also the observations on *clauses 31(1)(b), 54(4)(b)* below.

Clause 28(5) is related to *28(4)* and may also be seen as addressing the consequences of *clause 28(6)*. *Clause 28(5)* declares a provision to be not outside the Parliament's legislative competence "merely because it makes modifications of any enactment as it applies to reserved matters which are incidental to or consequential on provision made (whether by the Act in question or another enactment) for purposes relating to any devolved matters". This, in general, contributes further to saving the legislative competence of "incidental or consequential" intrusions into reserved matters.

However, both *clause 28(4)* and *(5)* have to be read in the light of *clauses 31(1)(b)* and *54(4)(b)*. As will be seen, one of the grounds on which the Secretary of State may intervene to prohibit the submission of a Bill for Royal Assent and one of the grounds on which he or she may revoke subordinate legislation made by a member of the Scottish Executive is that legislation whose competence is saved only by *clause 28(4)* (in relation to *private* law) or *clause 28(5)* "would have an adverse effect on the operation of an enactment as it applies to reserved matters".

Finally and perhaps most importantly of all in this group of provisions, *clause 28(9)* states that: "[a]ny provision of an Act of the Scottish Parliament is to be read, so far as possible, so as to be within the legislative competence of the Parliament and is to have effect accordingly". It is to be a rule of interpretation of Scottish Acts that there be a strong presumption in favour of their compliance with all the rules relating to the Parliament's legislative competence. It has been pointed out at various stages in the account of this part of the Bill that uncertainties will arise in its interpretation and it may well be that this subclause will overcome many of the difficulties. It will, however, be interesting to discover how the words "so far as possible" will themselves come to be interpreted. How far will the presumption they create displace other countervailing presumptions e.g. that statutes creating criminal offences or adversely affecting rights of property be restrictively interpreted? And, even if *clause 28(9)* makes a useful contribution in a dispute at the margins of the devolved and reserved matters, what will be its effect in relation to the other rules on legislative competence? If, for instance, a question of the compatibility of a Scottish Act with a Convention right arises, will the presumption in *clause 28(9)* be invoked in favour of a broader "margin of appreciation"? Could the presumption affect a decision on compatibility with Community law? Another thing that has to be remembered is that when the competence of a Scottish Act is challenged, it will by no means always be an interest of the Scottish Executive or Parliament which is at stake. Often it will be in a conflict between one citizen and another that the issue of an Act's validity will be raised.

CHALLENGING A BILL OR ACT OF THE SCOTTISH PARLIAMENT

It is a general principle of the law that bodies created by statute must act within the powers conferred on them. They must act *intra vires* and if, on the other hand, they act beyond their powers (*ultra vires*), anything done will be invalid and of no legal effect. This principle will apply to the Scottish Parliament as it does to other statutory bodies and, therefore, any provision in a Scottish Act which is held to be beyond the legislative competence of the Parliament - for example, because it relates to reserved matters or is incompatible with the ECHR - will be invalid.

The principle is reinforced by *clause 28(1)* of the Bill which, as we have seen, expressly states that an "Act of the Scottish Parliament is not law so far as any provision of the Act is outside the legislative competence of the Parliament". If nothing more were said, this would simply leave Scottish Acts open to challenge in ordinary proceedings in the courts, e.g. in judicial review in the Court of Session by a person with the necessary standing. The Scotland Bill does, however, make two sets of provisions to supplement this general position. The Bill contains special procedural provisions for the way in which "devolution issues" are to be handled by the courts and these are considered below.

In addition, however, the Scotland Bill contains rules designed to prevent some Bills in the Scottish Parliament from becoming Acts at all if they are thought to include provisions which are beyond the Parliament's legislative competence. These rules supplement those which will regulate the normal legislative proceedings of the Parliament and which will doubtless provide the opportunity for routine debate on the desirability and quality of the measures under discussion including their legal validity. In the first place, *clause 30* requires that a member of the Scottish Executive in charge of a Bill[107] shall, on or before introduction of the Bill in the Parliament, make a written statement to the effect that in his or her view "an Act of the Scottish Parliament containing the same provisions as those in the Bill would be within the legislative competence of the Parliament". Such a statement does not, of course, guarantee that a court would take the same view as the minister. It does, however, provide some assurance that the issue of the validity of the proposed measure has been seriously addressed. A form of screening, based on legal advice available to the minister, has taken place.[108]

But the rules do not leave this judgment to be made by the minister alone. *Clause 31* requires that the Parliament's standing orders must ensure that a Bill is not introduced in the Parliament if the Presiding Officer decides, subject to the possibility of overruling by the Parliament itself, that the Bill or any provision in it would not be within the legislative competence of the Parliament. There must also be a requirement in standing orders that it is the Presiding Officer who submits Bills for Royal Assent.[109] This is a requirement used to enable a Bill to be subjected to two forms of pre-Assent scrutiny. There is, on the one hand, the possibility of a reference to the Judicial Committee of the

---

[107] There is no equivalent requirement made where a Private Member's Bill, for which provision will presumably be made in standing orders, has no member of the Scottish Executive "in charge". A similar question may arise in relation to "private legislation", for which provision may also presumably be made. Future use of the Private Legislation Procedure (Scotland) Act 1936 will be confined to the making of provisional orders by the Secretary of State and to confirming them at Westminster; and excluding powers wholly within the competence of the Scottish Parliament. See *clause 88(3)* and *Sched. 7, para. 2.*

[108] A similar procedure is being introduced at Westminster in relation to Convention rights under the current Human Rights Bill.

[109] Royal Assent is itself required by *clause 27(2)*.

Privy Council on an issue of legislative competence.[110] Secondly, there is the possibility of an order from the Secretary of State forbidding a Bill to proceed to Royal Assent. The Parliament's standing orders must ensure that the Presiding Officer does not submit a Bill for Royal Assent during the period of four weeks following the passing of the Bill[111] to enable either or both forms of external scrutiny to be exercised.

As to legislative competence, it is open to either the Advocate General or the Lord Advocate or the Attorney General to "refer the question of whether a Bill or any provision of a Bill would be within the legislative competence of the Parliament to the Judicial Committee for decision" (*clause 32(1)*). Standing orders of the Parliament must ensure that, if the Judicial Committee does decide that a Bill (or provision of a Bill) would not be within the legislative competence of the Parliament, then the Presiding Officer does not submit the unamended Bill for Royal Assent (*clause 31(5)*). There must be an opportunity for the reconsideration of the Bill and for a final parliamentary stage at which the Bill can be approved (as amended) or rejected (*clause 34(3), (4)*). The Scotland Bill does not itself contain detailed rules about the manner in which reference proceedings before the Judicial Committee are to be conducted but it enables such rules to be made (*clause 94(3)*). The Bill does, however, make special provision as to the membership of the Judicial Committee when it handles Scotland Act matters (including the resolution of "devolution issues" discussed below). A judge must not only be a member of the Committee but also a holder (or previous holder) of the office of Lord of Appeal in Ordinary or of "high judicial office" (i.e. to the exclusion of Commonwealth judges) (*clause 94(2)*).[112] Also laid down by *clause 94(1)* of the Bill is that "[a]ny decision of the Judicial Committee in proceedings under this Act[113] shall be stated in open court and shall be binding in all legal proceedings (other than proceedings before the Committee)". Presumably a reference to the Judicial Committee in which an issue of Community law is raised may be the subject of a further reference to the European Court of Justice under Article 177 of the EC Treaty.

The type of pre-enactment review of legislative measures which is introduced by *clause 32* and which requires the court to rule in an abstract way (i.e. without the focus imposed by the concrete facts of a particular case between parties) is something of a constitutional novelty in the United Kingdom[114] and it will be interesting to see what use of it is made and with what effect. It will provide the occasions for the interpretative difficulties surrounding the definition of the legislative competence of the Parliament to be explored. There will

---

[110] For earlier discussion of the preference for the Privy Council rather than the House of Lords, see C. Boyd "Parliament and Courts" in *Devolution to Scotland: The Legal Aspects* (T. St.J. N. Bates, ed., 1997).

[111] Or the period of four weeks from the date of reconsideration of the Bill, following an earlier reference to the Judicial Committee or an order made by the Secretary of State.

[112] See White Paper, para. 4.17.

[113] Which means proceedings in relation to "devolution issues" discussed below as well as proceedings under *clause 32*.

[114] There was a little-used power of reference to the Judicial Committee under s.51 of the Government of Ireland Act 1920.

also be interesting questions about the relationship between pre-Assent review and the review of legislation in proceedings raised after enactment - to which the impact of *clause 94(1)* will be immediately relevant. It is unclear, for instance, how a pre-Assent decision by the Judicial Committee that a whole Bill of the Scottish Parliament is within the Parliament's legislative competence would be treated by another court subsequently invited to determine a "devolution issue" on a more specific point. The possible difficulties involved in integrating Convention rights and Community law issues into this process have already been considered.

The second form of intervention which may be made at the pre-Assent stage of a Scottish Bill is where, under certain circumstances, the Secretary of State may make an order, subject to annulment by either House at Westminster, prohibiting the Bill's submission for Royal Assent (*clause 33*). The Secretary of State may intervene in one or other of two situations. The first is where he or she has reasonable grounds to believe that a Bill contains provisions which would be incompatible with any "international obligations" - defined to mean any international obligations of the United Kingdom *other than* those under Community law or obligations not to do acts incompatible with any of the Convention rights (*clause 111(7)*). Breach of such obligations does not in itself take the Scottish Parliament beyond its legislative competence (and it should be noted that "observing and implementing international obligations" is specifically stated not to be reserved under *Schedule 5, paragraph 6(2)*) but the Secretary of State's right to intervene is presumably to be defended nevertheless in terms of the UK Government's continuing responsibilities for international relations. The other situation in which the Secretary of State may make an order under *clause 33* is where provisions in a Bill are, again, *within* the legislative competence of the Parliament but are so by virtue of[115] *clause 28(4)* (as it applies in relation to Scots private law) or *clause 28(5)*. These are the subclauses which save a provision, which would otherwise be outside the legislative competence of the Parliament because it relates to reserved matters, on the ground either (*28(4)*) that it is competent merely because it makes modifications of Scots private law[116] as it applies to reserved matters but does so in a way that "the law in question applies consistently to devolved and reserved matters"; or (*28(5)*) that it is competent because it makes modifications to an enactment in a "reserved" area "which are incidental to or consequential on provision made (whether by the Act in question or another enactment) for purposes relating to any devolved matters". The general difficulties involved in the interpretation of these subclauses have already been discussed. The further complication in their application to *clause 33* is that there will be no way at all, on the face of a Bill,[117] that it will be apparent that provisions do rely upon the subclauses for their competence. It may perhaps be necessary in some circumstances for the legislative competence of the provisions to be tested in Judicial

---

[115] With "by virtue of" to be read as including "by" and "under", *clause 111(8)*.

[116] Or Scots criminal law, but that aspect is not referred to in *clause 33*.

[117] Nor necessarily, in an authoritative way, by virtue of anything contributed by the ministerial statement under *clause 30*, nor in parliamentary debates.

Committee proceedings under *clause 32* before their challenge by the Secretary of State under *clause 33*.

At all events, *clause 33* authorises the Secretary of State to intervene in relation to provisions so saved but which he or she "has reasonable grounds to believe would have an adverse effect on the operation of an enactment as it applies to reserved matters". The Bill does not spell out further the sort of circumstances in which this power of intervention may be used by the Secretary of State but it is presumably to be seen as a means of adding ad hoc extensions to the list of three "Scots private law" exceptions from the operation of *clause 28(4)* already included in *Schedule 5*.[118]

The order which the Secretary of State may make in either of the two situations covered by *clause 33* and which prohibits the Presiding Officer from submitting a Bill for Royal Assent, must itself identify the Bill and the provisions in question and must state the reasons for making the order (*clause 33(2)*). It is to be made by statutory instrument subject to annulment by either House of the UK Parliament (*clause 101(6)*). An order would presumably be itself challengeable in proceedings for judicial review.

Finally in this section, a note on the timetabling of pre-Assent scrutiny, whether on grounds of legislative competence or by intervention of the Secretary of State, and its impact on the progress of a Bill. The basic rule is that a reference to the Judicial Committee or an order by the Secretary of State must be made within four weeks of the initial passing of the Bill in question (*clauses 32(2)(a), 33(3)(a)*). However, the relevant law officer and the Secretary of State are, subject to one qualification, barred from making a reference or order if he or she has notified the Presiding Officer of an intention not to do so (*clauses 32(3), 33(4)*). The rules also provide for an extended time-limit where a Bill has already been the subject of a reference or order followed by reconsideration and approval (in amended form) by the Parliament. In that event, a further period of four weeks is permitted within which another reference or order may be made (*clauses 32(2)(b), 33(3)(b)*). Approval of a Bill in amended form cancels the effect of notification of an intention not to intervene issued prior to that approval (*clauses 32(3), 33(4)*).

POST-ENACTMENT CHALLENGE AND "DEVOLUTION ISSUES"

Whether it was referred at its pre-Assent stage to the Judicial Committee of the Privy Council or not, a provision in an Act of the Scottish Parliament will remain open to the possibility of challenge to its legal validity. Such a challenge might come in the course of proceedings between a UK minister and a member of the Scottish Executive; or between an individual and a member of the Scottish Executive or between two individuals where the issue between them turns directly or indirectly upon the validity of a Scottish Act. The full range of possibilities is difficult to predict but a typical instance may turn out to be a challenge by judicial review of a decision made by a member of the Scottish Executive where, in part at least, the validity of the decision depends

---

[118]   See *Sched. 5, Pt II, Head 1, S. 1; Head 5, S. 3; Head 6, S. 3.*

upon the validity of the provision of the Scottish Act under which it purports to be made.

Schedule 6 to the Scotland Bill makes special provision for the manner in which such questions of validity are to be resolved (*clause 91*). It starts by defining a "devolution issue" as a question "whether an Act of the Scottish Parliament or any provision of an Act of the Scottish Parliament is within the legislative competence of the Parliament" (*para. 1*).[119] It is also provided, however, that a "devolution issue shall not be taken to arise in any proceedings merely because of any contention of a party to the proceedings which appears to the court or tribunal ..... to be frivolous or vexatious" (*para. 2*). The Schedule then provides special mechanisms which, in summary:-

(a) enable a devolution issue which arises in civil proceedings below the level of the Inner House of the Court of Session to be separated from other issues in the case and referred for decision by the Inner House, with an appeal available to the Judicial Committee of the Privy Council (*paras. 7, 12, 13*);

(b) enable a devolution issue arising in the Inner House to be referred to the Judicial Committee (*para. 10*);

(c) require the House of Lords to refer a devolution issue to the Judicial Committee unless the House considers it more appropriate to determine the issue itself (*para. 32*);

(d) require courts to order intimation of a devolution issue which arises before them to the Advocate General and the Lord Advocate and enable those law officers to take part in proceedings so far as they relate to a devolution issue (*paras. 5-6*);

(e) enable a law officer to institute proceedings for the determination of a devolution issue (*para. 4*); and

(f) enable a law officer to require any court to refer a devolution issue direct to the Judicial Committee and to refer to the Judicial Committee a devolution issue which is not the subject of proceedings (*paras. 33-34*).

Schedule 6 makes further provision for the award of expenses and for the regulation of procedure (*paras. 36-37*). It also extends the mechanism for dealing with devolution issues to criminal proceedings (where the taking of issues on reference or appeal to the Judicial Committee is a particular novelty)[120] and to tribunals. Parallel provision is also made for devolution issues which may arise in proceedings in England and Wales and in Northern Ireland.

The Bill makes provision for certain situations consequential upon legal proceedings taken to challenge the validity of legislation made by the Scottish Parliament or action taken by members of the Scottish Executive. On the one hand *clause 92* authorises the making of such subordinate legislation by a UK minister[121] as is necessary or expedient in consequence of incompetent acts by

---

[119] In addition, several forms of Executive decision-making may raise devolution issues defined in the same paragraph. These are discussed in Chap. 6.

[120] See also the amendment made to the Criminal Procedure (Scotland) Act 1995 in *Sched. 7* to the Bill.

either the Parliament or members of the Scottish Executive. Then *clause 93* permits a court or tribunal which has made a finding of invalidity to temper the impact of the decision by varying any retrospective effect or by suspending its effect. The Lord Advocate must be given intimation of the possibility of such an order and the opportunity to be a party to the proceedings.

Finally, lest this chapter end on a note implying that all issues surrounding the legislative competence of the Scottish Parliament will become hotly contested and require legal proceedings (especially between the Scottish and UK Governments) for their resolution, it should be remembered that this need not necessarily be the case and, if the optimism expressed in the White Paper is justified, will turn out not to be so. There it is made clear that it is very much the hope of the present Government that "given an open and constructive relationship between the UK Government and the Scottish Executive, problems will usually be resolved quickly and amicably."[122] The focus will be upon promoting good communication between the two parties.[123]

---

[121] See *clause 102.*
[122] para. 4.15.
[123] para. 4.12.

CHAPTER 6
THE SCOTTISH ADMINISTRATION

Although much of the campaigning for devolution has focused on the need to establish a Parliament and the benefits in terms of power and democracy that a Parliament would bring, there is no doubting the importance to the future governance of Scotland of the executive branch of government. The Scottish Parliament will represent the people of Scotland. It will make laws for Scotland. But the Parliament will not itself govern. It will not take over the decision-making functions of the Secretary of State for Scotland or other UK ministers. It is the intention of the devolution scheme proposed in the White Paper and now contained in the Scotland Bill that executive power should instead pass to a Scottish Executive consisting of ministers drawn from and accountable to the Parliament. Although there are some important differences built into the Bill and further differences can be expected to develop in practice, the general scheme adopted is that of the Westminster model of parliamentary government. The Scottish government will be made up of the Scottish Executive (the First Minister and other Scottish Ministers including, with separate powers, the Lord Advocate and the Solicitor General for Scotland), junior Scottish Ministers, and civil servants (drawn from the Home Civil Service of the United Kingdom). Most of the relevant provisions are to be found in *Part II* of the Bill "The Scottish Administration".[124]

FORMATION OF THE SCOTTISH ADMINISTRATION

In UK government practice, the first and most important step in the formation of a new administration is the appointment of the Prime Minister. In law, the appointment is made by the Queen in the exercise of a prerogative power but, by convention, any element of discretion in the selection of the Prime Minister is virtually ruled out in normal circumstances, because the person must be selected from the House of Commons and must be the person best able to command the support of a majority of MPs, usually the leader of the largest party.

For the formation of an administration under the Scotland Bill, the same basic rules are to apply with the exception that the terminology changes and, rather than relying upon the emergence of non-legal conventions, more is to be specifically laid down by statute. Thus the appointment of the person formally entitled First Minister - some suspect that the title Prime Minister will develop in popular parlance - is to be by the Queen and is to be made from among the

---

[124] Although the term "Scottish Administration" is not used elsewhere in *Part II* itself, it is used in *clause 62* (Payments out of the Scottish Consolidated Fund) and in amendments made to earlier legislation by *Schedule 7* (e.g. the Crown Proceedings Act 1947, where there are interesting references to proceedings against "the Scottish Administration" and to a "part of the Administration") to include the Registrar General of Births, Deaths and Marriages for Scotland, the Keeper of the Registers for Scotland and the Keeper of the Records for Scotland. See *clause 111(5)*.

members of the Parliament (*clause 42(1)*). The Queen is to act on the recommendation of the Presiding Officer of the Parliament who must, in turn, base the recommendation on a nomination made by the Parliament (*clause 43(4)*). That nomination must itself be made within a period of 28 days beginning on the day of one of four specified events -

(a) the holding of a poll at a general election;

(b) the previous First Minister tendering his or her resignation;

(c) the office of First Minister becoming vacant (other than by resignation); or

(d) the First Minister ceasing to be a member of the Parliament otherwise than by virtue of a dissolution (*clause 43(2), (3)*).[125]

Once appointed, the First Minister holds office "at Her Majesty's pleasure". The First Minister may, however, tender his or her resignation at any time and *must* do so "if the Parliament resolves that the Scottish Executive no longer enjoys the confidence of the Parliament" (*clause 42(2)*). There is provision, in the case of a vacancy or if the First Minister is unable to act, for the designation by the Presiding Officer of another member of the Parliament as a temporary substitute (*clause 42(4), (5)*).

In accordance with the principle of *parliamentary* government, the ministers whom the First Minister may appoint must be drawn from members of the Parliament (*clause 44(1)*). The Bill goes further, however, and adopts the spirit of a recommendation of the Scottish Constitutional Convention by requiring that the First Minister must, before seeking the Queen's formal approval for the appointment of a minister, obtain the Parliament's agreement to the appointment (*clause 44(2)*). Once appointed, a minister holds office on much the same formal terms as the First Minister, save that he or she may be removed from office by the First Minister (*clause 44(3)*).

Separate provision is made for the appointment of the Scottish Law Officers, the Lord Advocate and the Solicitor General for Scotland. As with other ministers, appointments are effectively to be made by the First Minister who must make recommendations to the Queen for appointment or dismissal, with the agreement in either case of the Parliament (*clause 45(1)*). Law Officers do not, however, have to be members of the Parliament but are assured of the opportunity to participate in its proceedings (*clause 26*).

The First Minister, ministers and Law Officers, once appointed, constitute "the Scottish Executive", whose members are referred to collectively in the Bill as "the Scottish Ministers" (*clause 41(2)*). In addition the First Minister is to appoint from the membership of the Parliament "junior Scottish Ministers" whose function is "to assist the Scottish Ministers in the exercise of their functions" (*clause 46(1), (2)*).[126] There is no requirement, in the case of junior Scottish Ministers, that their appointment has the individual agreement of the Parliament but the terms on which they hold office thereafter are the same as

---

[125] For the consequences of a failure by the Parliament to nominate a First Minister, see Chap. 4.

[126] The Bill does not include any express power to delegate to junior ministers but this power is presumably to be implied. Rather different questions may arise in relation to the delegation of functions by ministers to civil servants.

for the Scottish Ministers proper *(clause 46(3))*. They are not members of the Scottish Executive as it is defined. All ministers must, on appointment, take the oaths required by *clause 79*. Provision for their remuneration (salaries, allowances and pensions) is made by *clause 76*.

Nothing is laid down in the Bill about how the Scottish Executive should organise the government of Scotland but it will doubtless be structured on departmental (and perhaps agency) lines with individual Scottish ministers, assisted by junior ministers, heading departments with responsibilities distributed on a functional basis. What the Bill does determine is that those departments will draw their staff from the Home Civil Service *(clause 47)* initially, doubtless, on transfer from the Scottish Office in most cases. As the White Paper explained, this will place civil servants who are in the service of the Scottish Executive under terms and conditions common to other parts of the civil service. It is expected that arrangements for civil servants to move between the Scottish Executive and UK departments will continue along the same lines as the existing practice between the Scottish Office and other departments. It is hoped this will foster good working relationships between the two governments.[127]

THE FUNCTIONS OF SCOTTISH MINISTERS

The responsibilities of the new Scottish Ministers and their departments will be to carry out, formally on behalf of the Queen, the executive functions of government within the devolved areas. To enable this to happen, the Scotland Bill includes two main provisions, or sets of provisions. In the first place, *clause 48* makes general provision for the exercise of functions. Functions are to be conferred by statute (made by the Scottish Parliament) on "the Scottish Ministers" and, once so conferred, are to be exercisable by any of the ministers constituting the Scottish Executive *(clause 48(1), (3))*. The two exceptions to this general rule are the functions specifically conferred on the First Minister[128] and the "retained functions" of the Lord Advocate[129] which are exercisable by, or on behalf of, those ministers alone *(clause 48(5), (6))*.

In the course of time, most of the functions of the Scottish Ministers will come to be directly conferred on them by the Scottish Parliament, as it enacts new legislation or modifies existing Westminster legislation in the devolved areas. In the early days of devolved government, however, the Scottish Ministers will be required to carry out executive functions in relation to the devolved areas which are currently exercised by UK ministers, in particular the Secretary of State for Scotland. Thus, the second principal set of provisions in the Scotland Bill relating to executive power are those which give effect to a general transfer of powers from UK ministers to the Scottish Ministers - enabling

[127] White Paper, para. 10.12.
[128] Examples in the Scotland Bill itself include the power under *clause 89* to make recommendations for the appointment and removal of judges. Doubtless some others will be added in legislation enacted by the Scottish Parliament.
[129] See below.

us, in other words, to interpret statutes which include, for example, the formula "the Secretary of State may ....." as "the Scottish Ministers may .....". There is no attempt made in the Bill to comb the whole statute book and make the necessary adjustments by the separate amendment of individual provisions![130]

The principal general transfer provisions in the Bill are contained in *clause 49* which states that "(a) those of Her Majesty's prerogative and other executive functions which are exercisable on behalf of Her Majesty by a minister of the Crown, and (b) functions conferred on a minister of the Crown by any pre-commencement enactment[131]" are to be exercisable "so far as they are exercisable in or as regards Scotland", by the Scottish Ministers. There is again a specific exclusion from this transfer of the "retained functions of the Lord Advocate" and, in line with the same logic that applies to the devolution of legislative power, the functions transferred to the Scottish Ministers do not include "any functions so far as they relate to reserved matters" - the same "reserved matters" as are set out in *Schedule 5* to the Bill in relation to the Parliament's legislative competence. There is, however, a power contained in *clause 59* of the Bill which may be used to transfer, by subordinate legislation made by a UK minister, additional powers exercisable by a minister of the Crown "in or as regards Scotland" either to the Scottish Ministers outright or to the Scottish Ministers concurrently with the minister of the Crown or by the minister of the Crown acting with the agreement, or after consultation with, the Scottish Ministers. By this means, the powers of the Scottish Ministers may be extended into the areas included within the reserved matters. An indication of the extensions likely to be made was given in the White Paper which refers, amongst others, to powers and duties in relation to electricity supply, some transport responsibilities, civil nuclear emergency planning and some powers in relation to the National Lottery and gaming functions.[132]

What the power in *clause 59* anticipates are situations in which executive powers will be shared or be exercised concurrently by the Scottish Ministers and UK ministers. This is a circumstance for which specific provision has to be made. Although, in the legislative area, the UK Parliament will retain, through the doctrine of parliamentary sovereignty, the power to pass Acts of Parliament affecting devolved matters, there will be no general power in the hands

[130] But see *clause 104* which provides for references in pre-commencement enactments and other documents to a minister of the Crown to be construed as including the Scottish Ministers.
[131] Defined to mean (a) an Act passed before or in the same session as the Scotland Act and any other "enactment" made before the passing of the Act, and (b) an "enactment" made before the commencement of *clause/section 49* under such an Act or "enactment" (*clause 49(3)*). For "enactment" see *clause 111(1)* and s.21 of the Interpretation Act 1978 as amended by *Sched. 7* to the Scotland Bill. Exceptions to the general scope of *clause 49* include the Secretary of State's powers (in relation to provisional orders etc.) under the Private Legislation Procedure (Scotland) Act 1936 (*clause 88*) and under the Parliamentary Commissioner Act 1967 (*clause 86*).
[132] para. 2.7. No doubt the "statutory functions" referred to in *clause 23* (power of the Parliament to call for witnesses) include functions exercisable by the Scottish Ministers in relation to reserved matters. N.B. the separate use of "Scottish functions" in *clause 106* (Consolidated Fund etc.).

of UK ministers to make executive decisions in the areas transferred to the Scottish Ministers. *Clause 59* apart, however, some specific provision is already made in the Bill for UK ministers to continue to make decisions in the transferred areas. *Clause 52* contains a list of statutory powers which are stated to be exercisable, despite the general transfer in *clause 49*, in or as regards Scotland, by the relevant UK minister as well as by the Scottish Ministers.[133] For instance, powers under the Road Traffic Act 1988 in relation to road safety information and training which are specifically excepted from being reserved matters,[134] and therefore are devolved, are declared exercisable by ministers in both governments. There is no doubt the hope and expectation that the exercise of such shared powers will be done in a spirit of co-operation and agreement. If, however, a dispute arises as to whether the decision of one minister should prevail over that of the other, is it to be presumed that the later decision in time will prevail? There is also *clause 53* which makes special provision in relation to European Community law.[135]

A very important aspect of the powers of the Scottish Ministers will be the powers transferred to them to make subordinate legislation and *clause 50* of the Bill makes interesting provision for the making of subordinate legislation by members of the Scottish Executive which supplements the general powers in *clause 49,* i.e. where an existing power of a UK minister to make rules, regulations, etc., is to be transferred to the Scottish Ministers. It is stated, first, that provision "may be made in subordinate legislation if, and only if, the provision would be within the legislative competence of the Parliament if it were included in an Act of the Scottish Parliament" (*clause 50(2)*). Secondly, to add greater specificity to that requirement, it is provided that the restrictions in *clause 49* which apply to any functions of the Scottish Ministers and confine them to functions exercisable "in or as regards Scotland" and "otherwise than in relation to reserved matters" are to be read in accordance with the same obligation to legislate only within the scope of the legislative competence of the Parliament (*clause 50(3)*).[136]

Important to the interpretation of all the restrictions on the power of a member of the Scottish Executive to make subordinate legislation is *clause 50(5)* which states that "[a]ny provision of subordinate legislation made or purporting to be made by a member of the Scottish Executive is to be read, so far as possible, so as to be within the powers conferred by virtue of the Act and is to have effect accordingly". This is a provision parallel to that contained in *clause 28(9)* in relation to Acts of the Scottish Parliament and is clearly designed to create a strong presumption of compliance with the terms of the Scotland Act.

---

[133] There is also a power under *clause 87* of the Bill to make "agency arrangements" for the performance of "administrative, professional or technical services" between the two governments and public bodies.

[134] *Sched. 5, Part II, Head 5, S. 1.*

[135] See Chap.9.

[136] See also *clause 50(4).*

THE SCOTTISH LAW OFFICERS

It was acknowledged in the White Paper that, once the decision had been made to devolve the responsibilities of the Lord Advocate (currently the principal law officer for Scotland in the UK Government) for the prosecution and investigation of crimes, it was appropriate that the Lord Advocate and the junior minister, the Solicitor General for Scotland, should become the new Scottish Executive's Law Officers. They should cease to be the Law Officers of the UK Government where there would be created in their place the new post of Advocate General for Scotland.[137]

We have already seen that *clause 41* of the Bill constitutes the Lord Advocate and the Solicitor General as members of the Scottish Executive, after their appointment on the First Minister's recommendation under *clause 45*. This establishes the availability of legal advice to the Scottish Executive. But what the White Paper also emphasised was the need to maintain the "traditional independence of the Lord Advocate as public prosecutor"[138] and this is a principle which is carried forward into the Bill. It has clearly been seen as a matter of importance not only for the devolved government itself but also for the UK Government. The Lord Advocate will have responsibilities not only for the prosecution of offences in all those areas of the criminal law to be devolved but also for the prosecution of offences within the scope of the reserved matters - such as treason but also, more routinely, in relation to the misuse of drugs, firearms offences, consumer protection and many others. There is to be no separate UK level prosecution authority for all these offences but there is a clear UK level interest in the independent and efficient prosecution of them.

Thus in *clause 45(2)*, a clause which is not itself amendable by the Scottish Parliament, it is provided that "[a]ny decision of the Lord Advocate in his capacity as head of the systems of criminal prosecution and investigation of deaths in Scotland shall continue to be taken by him independently of any other person". One of the specific restrictions on the legislative competence of the Scottish Parliament is that no provision in a Scottish Act is law if "it would remove the Lord Advocate from his position as head of the systems of criminal prosecution and investigation of deaths in Scotland" (*clause 28(2)(e)*) and the Bill takes further steps to protect what are called the "retained functions" of the Lord Advocate. These are defined as "(a) any functions exercisable by him immediately before he ceases to be a minister of the Crown, and (b) other statutory functions conferred on him alone" (*clause 48(6)*). As we have seen, the effect of ring-fencing these "retained functions" is to prevent them from becoming exercisable (whether as original functions or as transferred at the time of devolution) by "the Scottish Ministers" in general and, therefore, by any member of the Scottish Executive. The Lord Advocate's retained functions, including any powers to make subordinate legislation, are exercisable

[137] paras. 4.8, 4.9. One necessary consequence of the creation of the new office is the series of amendments made to the Crown Suits (Scotland) Act 1857, the Crown Proceedings Act 1947 and the Criminal Procedure (Scotland) Act 1995 by *Sched. 7*. See also the repeals in *Sched. 8*.
[138] para. 4.8.

by the Lord Advocate or Solicitor General alone (*clauses 48-50* and *105*) - although, as with other members of the Scottish Executive, the Law Officers' staff will be civil servants (*clause 47*).[139]

The Lord Advocate's new responsibilities (in association with the Advocate General and the Attorney General) under the Scotland Bill in relation to the pre-Assent reference of Scottish Bills to the Judicial Committee of the Privy Council (*clauses 31, 32*) and in relation to the handling of "devolution issues" (*Schedule 6*) are dealt with below.

THE ACCOUNTABILITY OF THE SCOTTISH ADMINISTRATION

Parliamentary Controls

In so far as a principal objective of the process of devolution is establishing a higher level of democratic governmental accountability in Scotland, success will be measured largely by reference to the accountability of the Scottish Executive to the Parliament. This will, in turn, depend largely on procedures to be established by the Parliament and, therefore, on political configurations and the will of parliamentarians themselves once the institutions have been formed. The Scotland Bill makes very few direct contributions to establishing the mechanisms of parliamentary accountability although *clause 86* does impose the positive requirement that the Parliament should make provision for the investigation of complaints made to its members in respect of action taken by or on behalf of a member of the Scottish Executive.[140] The clause gives latitude to the Parliament as to the institutions and procedures it establishes but, by its reference to the investigation of complaints under the Parliamentary Commissioner Act 1967, plainly anticipates something along the same lines as the UK Parliamentary Ombudsman.

Also important to the general maintenance of accountability are the requirements imposed by *clause 66* for the Parliament to establish statutory procedures for the keeping of accounts, financial control and audit.[141]

"Control" by the UK Government

In the discussion, earlier in this chapter, of the powers of the Scottish Executive it was explained that the Scottish Ministers will, on the whole, acquire exclusive authority in the areas transferred to them from UK ministers. There will, however, be certain "shared powers" (*clause 52*); there is the power to make "agency arrangements" (*clause 87*); and there is the possibility of the further transfer of powers to Scottish Ministers, some of which may be established on a "shared" or concurrent basis (*clauses 59, 97*). Overarching the whole of the relationship between the Scottish Executive and the UK Government will be the financial arrangements and, in particular, the provisions for the

---

[139]   See also *clauses 57, 58* concerning the property and liabilities of the Lord Advocate.
[140]   Or of the Registrar General of Births, Deaths and Marriages, the Keeper of the Registers or the Keeper of the Records.
[141]   See Chap. 7.

payment of annual grants to the Scottish Executive[142] and, of course, there
will be, in the background, the opportunity for UK ministers to introduce legislation in the Westminster Parliament further to adjust the powers of the Scottish Executive by amendment of the Scotland Act. It may also be said that
some of the very broadly cast powers to make subordinate legislation by, for
instance, *clauses 95* and *96* represent very considerable powers retained by
UK ministers.

These possibilities apart, however, UK ministers have no general powers
to direct, restrain or otherwise guide Scottish Ministers in the exercise of their
powers. The one exception to this principle is the group of powers "to prevent
or require action" in *clause 54* of the Scotland Bill. It parallels the provision
made by *clause 33* in relation to Bills of the Scottish Parliament and enables
the Secretary of State, if he or she "has reasonable grounds to believe that any
action proposed to be taken by a member of the Scottish Executive would be
incompatible with any international obligations" (defined to exclude European
Community or ECHR obligations[143]), to direct that the proposed action be not
taken. A direction is to be made by order as a statutory instrument and "action"
for this purpose includes making, confirming or approving subordinate legislation (*clause 54(3)*). There is a similar power to *compel* action where the Secretary of State wishes to require compliance with international obligations
(*clause 54(2)*), in which event "action" includes introducing a Bill in the Parliament - although the Secretary of State can hardly compel the passing of such
a Bill and there may be a more general doubt about how the Secretary of State
may compel compliance with orders made. Presumably the answer would lie,
in the more routine cases, in a petition for judicial review.

Finally, there is a power under which the Secretary of State may by order
revoke subordinate legislation made, or which could be revoked, by a member
of the Scottish Executive. This power may be used (a) where, again, he or she
has reasonable grounds to believe provisions are[144] incompatible with international obligations; or (b) where the provisions would, if contained in an Act of
the Scottish Parliament, be within its legislative competence by virtue of *clause
28(4)* or *28(5)*[145] but which the Secretary of State has reasonable grounds to
believe are having or may have[146] an adverse effect on the operation of an
enactment as it applies to reserved matters. Reasons for revocation must be
given.[147]

Control by the Courts and "Devolution Issues"
As members of the Scottish Executive assume the mainly statutory functions
inherited from UK ministers they will become subject to the same forms of

---

[142] See Chap. 7.
[143] *Clause 111(7).*
[144] The Bill, as it stands, has "would be" at this point.
[145] For discussion, see Chap. 5.
[146] The Bill as it stands has "would have".
[147] *Clause 54(5)*, but there is presumably a drafting error in that subclause which makes it unclear
whether reasons must also be given for other types of order under the clause.

legal control as their predecessors. At some points these are imposed by statute and the decisions made by and on behalf of the Scottish Ministers will become appealable to courts and tribunals. More broadly, however, the Scottish Minis-ters will become subject to the non-statutory supervisory jurisdiction of the Court of Session and the general principles of judicial review. Some particular circumstances in which the discharge of the new obligations of the Scottish Ministers to be imposed by the Scotland Act itself will be reviewable have already been noted.

What judicial review in these and other circumstances may raise is the need to resolve "devolution issues" similar to those which may arise in rela-tion to legislation enacted by the Scottish Parliament.[148] *Clause 91* and *Sched-ule 6* make the necessary provision, and *Schedule 6* applies the same rules requiring reference of a "devolution issue" to a higher court (and on appeal to the Judicial Committee of the Privy Council) as are laid down for the "devolu-tion issues" raising questions about the legislative competence of the Parlia-ment.

In relation to "devolution issues" arising in connection with the acts (or failures to act) of members of the Scottish Executive (and also UK ministers), the categories of "issue" are laid down in *para. 1(b)-(f)* of *Schedule 6*. The same qualification as to the contentions of parties in proceedings held to be "frivolous or vexatious" applies as it does to legislative devolution issues (*para. 2*). The five categories of devolution issue are as follows:

1. The first relates solely to subordinate legislation, and is a question about whether subordinate legislation (or a provision of such legislation) pur-ported or proposed to be made by a member of the Scottish Executive would be within the Parliament's legislative competence if included in an Act of the Scottish Parliament (*para. 1(b)*). This reflects the requirement contained in *clause 50(2)* for the validity of subordinate legislation. As with issues raised in relation to an Act, it defines as "devolution issues" questions which do not relate to devolution as such (e.g. concerning human rights and Com-munity law).

2. The second devolution issue arises where subordinate legislation is not in-volved but there is a question of whether some other function relates to a reserved matter (*para. 1(c)*). This too reflects the rule in *clause 49(2)* which does generally prevent members of the Scottish Executive from straying into functions relating to reserved matters. It is clear, however, that the transfer of additional functions to the Scottish Ministers by *clause 59*[149] is intended to permit members of the Scottish Executive to exercise functions in relation to some reserved matters.

3. The third devolution issue in the list is where, again, subordinate legisla-tion is not involved and there is a question of whether the purported or proposed exercise of a function would be incompatible with any Conven-tion right or with Community law (*para. 1(d)*). This reflects the obligation

---

[148] See Chap. 5.
[149] Other powers might also be conferred directly by an Act of the UK Parliament.

imposed on members of the Scottish Executive by *clause 53(2)* but raises the same questions about the recasting of human rights and Community law issues as "devolution issues". Presumably, once again, the possibility of a fast-track reference to the Judicial Committee on an administrative decision by a member of the Scottish Executive where a human rights or Community law issue is raised should be seen as a precursor of other action by the UK Government.

4. The same question may be raised about the fourth category of devolution issue which is whether a *failure to act* by a member of the Scottish Executive is incompatible with a Convention right or with Community law (*para. 1(e)*).

5. The final category of devolution issue looks to the obligations not of members of the Scottish Executive but of UK ministers. It is a devolution issue if there is a question of whether a matter in relation to which a UK minister has purported (or proposed) to exercise a function is a devolved matter (*para. 1(f)*). The purpose here must be to achieve a measure of reciprocity and to enable a challenge to a UK minister if he or she trespasses beyond the limits of reserved matters in relation to Scotland. It should be noted, however, that, in some instances, it will be perfectly lawful for a UK minister to exercise functions in relation to devolved matters, for example where there are "shared powers" under *clause 52*.

CHAPTER 7

FINANCIAL ARRANGEMENTS FOR SCOTTISH GOVERNMENT

In any system of decentralised government, from fully-fledged federalism to democratic local self-government, financial arrangements are of the highest importance. It may be that the provisions devoted to finance in the Scotland Bill itself are themselves rather brief but this belies their significance for the scheme of devolution as a whole. As the Constitution Unit said: "The heart of the devolution settlement will be the arrangements for financing the Scottish Executive's actions".[150] Their report went on:

> "The design of the financing provisions for Scottish devolution is crucial. The danger is that central government control of the purse strings will lead to control, or at least undue influence, over the Scottish Parliament's policies. Ideally, therefore, the financial provisions might satisfy the following criteria:
>
> 1. They should be equitable as between the nations and regions of the UK.
> 2. They should respect the principle of equalisation according to need between the nations and regions of the UK.
> 3. They should be politically sustainable, providing reasonable financial certainty for the Parliament even when political relations between Edinburgh and London are not good.
> 4. Partly to redress point 3, they should leave the Scottish Executive as little dependent on detailed negotiation with HM Treasury as possible.
> 5. They should operate within the financial constraints imposed on and from the centre (national and international constraints of macroeconomic policy).
> 6. Within those constraints, they should provide for maximum policy and spending autonomy for the Scottish Executive.
> 7. They should ensure accountability to the Scottish electorate for spending decisions. This is closely related to point 6 about autonomy, and also requires the allocation mechanism and other data to be publicly accessible.
> 8. They should be practical, and not so complex or time-consuming that they introduce unmanageable delay into the budget process either in the UK or Scotland."[151]

Similar criteria appeared in the Government's White Paper as the objectives to underpin the financing of devolved government:

> "The financial arrangements for the Scottish Parliament will be designed to ensure that:
> - Scotland will continue to benefit from its appropriate share of UK public expenditure;
> - the Scottish Parliament's assigned budget is determined by a method which is objective, transparent and widely accepted;
> - the Scottish Parliament has the maximum freedom to determine its own expenditure priorities;

---

[150] *Scotland's Parliament: Fundamentals for a New Scotland Act* (1996), para. 202.
[151] Above at para. 203.

- the Scottish Parliament has a defined and limited power to vary central government taxation in Scotland and alter its overall spending accordingly;
- the UK Government can maintain proper control over public expenditure and public borrowing at the UK level;
- there are clear lines of accountability for local government spending and taxation; and
- UK taxpayers as a whole will be insulated from the effects of local decisions which add to Exchequer-funded expenditure in Scotland."[152]

Overall the arrangements to be made should "provide a structure for funding the Scottish Parliament that will establish that Parliament on a sound financial basis both on its own terms and in terms of its relationship with the UK. The system will provide an important element of continuity and the stability necessary for sensible long-term planning. It crucially will introduce direct accountability for spending priorities in Scotland. The proposals provide new opportunities. They will support the establishment of a powerful and effective Scottish Parliament capable of serving fully Scotland's interests and at the same time they recognise and acknowledge the continuing and legitimate interests of the UK as a whole."[153]

THE BLOCK AND FORMULA SYSTEM

The Government proposed that the way to meet these objectives would be by a continuation in relation to the Scottish Parliament of the arrangements currently in place for the funding of most Scottish Office expenditure. This is done by means of what is called the "block and formula" system according to which a "block" from overall UK resources is made available annually to the Secretary of State.[154] Each year the size of the block is calculated by reference to the previous year's figure adjusted by increases in line with a formula, "the Barnett formula" which ensures that, in relation to each spending programme within the block, any increase (or decrease) is in line with equivalent changes in expenditure south of the border. The formula, named after Joel (now Lord) Barnett, Chief Secretary to the Treasury at the time, was first deployed at the time of the last plans for devolution in 1978 and provided that, for each £85 of planned expenditure on equivalent services in England, Scotland would receive £10 - a position adjusted in 1992 to take account of different population distributions.

In broad terms, the Government's proposal is that the Scottish Parliament should have an overall assigned budget and that resources currently made available under this block and formula system to the Scottish Office would be made available on the authority of the UK Parliament by grant to the Scottish Parliament under new block arrangements. The Scottish Executive (subject to the consent of the Parliament) would then have the same sort of freedom enjoyed

---

[152] para. 7.2.
[153] para. 7.28.
[154] Chap. 5 and see the White Paper, Annex B.

by the Scottish Office to allocate funds within the assigned budget to Scottish spending programmes.

The above simplified account describes the principal source of funding for the Scottish Parliament and the mechanism for deciding its size each year. It should, however, be read subject to two main qualifications:

1. The position described is one which will be complicated by some, largely technical, adjustments to the block arrangements which will, for instance, bring into the block system some budgets (including some Agriculture, Fisheries and Food expenditure and the Crown Office) which have been excluded hitherto.[155]

2. Another complicating factor is that the whole block system and the assumptions about the fair distribution of funding between Scotland and the rest of the United Kingdom on which it is based have become a matter of intense scrutiny and debate. The question of whether the original "needs-based" funding calculations made prior to 1978 which gave an apparent advantage to Scottish spending has, in fact, given Scotland higher levels of public expenditure and, if so, whether this is justified, is hotly contested. Leading the assault have been politicians and business people from England. Their concerns were reflected in evidence given to the Treasury Select Committee of the House of Commons which held a brief inquiry into the formula in November/December 1997. The report of the Committee was brief and did not contain detailed recommendations for the future. The Committee did urge, however, that the needs assessment, on which the future use of the Barnett Formula (or a successor formula) would be based, should be brought up to date.[156] However, the Government, in particular the Chancellor Gordon Brown, has shown a continuing loyalty to the Barnett Formula in its present form. Gordon Brown is reported as saying: "The Treasury Select Committee is the Treasury Select Committee - it's not the Treasury".[157]

Turning to the Bill itself, one finds very little of the detail of these arrangements spelt out. The means of ensuring the revenue funding for Scottish government is by establishing a Scottish Consolidated Fund (*clause 61(1)*) and then providing that "[t]he Secretary of State shall from time to time make payments into the Fund out of money provided by Parliament of such amounts as he may determine" (*clause 61(2)*). Nothing further is specified as to the level at which the Secretary of State may fix the funding to be provided nor the procedures to be followed. Presumably these will, in practice, involve substantial consultation between the Secretary of State and the Scottish Executive. The White Paper made no commitment, however, to setting up an independent body - a commission politically independent of either government - to make recommendations in the light of an objective economic assessment. The need for such a body in order to reduce the number of disputes based merely upon

---

[155] White Paper, Annex B.
[156] The Barnett Formula (1997-98) H.C. 341, para. 12.
[157] *The Scotsman*, November 1, 1997.

subjective and politically-generated assessments of the relative deserts of Scotland and the rest of the United Kingdom has been stressed by some commentators.[158]

Thereafter, the remainder of *Part III* of the Bill on "Financial Provisions" contains similarly cryptic clauses including those dealing with the payments which may be made from the Scottish Consolidated Fund (*clause 62*),[159] the limited borrowing powers of the Scottish Ministers (*clause 63*), and the corresponding lending power of the Secretary of State (*clause 64*). There is separate provision in *clause 90* enabling the Treasury to require the Scottish Ministers to supply such information as they may reasonably specify.

THE TAX-VARYING POWER
One of the most distinctive and best known proposals of the Scottish Constitutional Convention was that the Scottish Parliament should have an independent power to vary levels of income tax in Scotland. They said:
"In the Western democracies all principal levels of national and local government have powers over taxation. While the Parliament's income will be principally based on totals of expenditure set at UK level, the power to vary the rate of tax is vital if the Parliament is to be properly accountable. Critics of the proposal to establish a Parliament in Scotland repeatedly state that such a power is essential for an effective Parliament.

Scotland's Parliament will have the power to increase or cut the basic rate of income tax for Scottish taxpayers by a maximum of 3p in the pound. This will give it a greater degree of independence."[160]
Such a power to vary income tax in Scotland was not included in the 1978 Act and the total dependence of the proposed Assembly on funding decisions made by the UK Government had, as the Convention said, been criticised. Their tax-varying proposal was taken forward in the White Paper which announced that, subject to the outcome of the referendum, the Scottish Parliament should have such a power.[161] It was not, however, made clear whether the necessary statutory scheme would be included in the Scotland Bill or whether separate provision would be made. In the event, the Bill has itself made provision for the tax-varying power and *Part IV* of the Bill is considered briefly below.

In the White Paper, the Government did outline the main provisions of the scheme. They remained committed, in the first instance, to providing a tax-varying power by way of a power to vary income tax rather than any other tax. Income tax, they claimed, was broadly based and easy to administer, relatively

[158] See especially the Constitution Unit's *Scotland's Parliament: Fundamentals for a New Scotland Act* (1996), Chap. 5.
[159] See also *clause 106* which includes *inter alia* important provision for the carrying forward from the rules of the UK Consolidated Fund to the Scottish Consolidated Fund the exemption of certain payments from the need for further (annual) approval/appropriation by the relevant Parliament - including judicial salaries.
[160] *Scotland's Parliament: Scotland's Right* (1995), p.27.
[161] para. 7.11. See also the Constitution Unit, *Scotland's Parliament: Fundamentals for a New Scotland Act* (1996), paras. 287-303. For the referendum and its outcome, see Chap. 2.

simple and easy to understand, and free of the difficulties associated with the other major tax bases such as VAT, corporation tax, or National Insurance. They also ruled out the use of the council tax or non-domestic rates for this purpose as liable to "over-burden the local government finance system and undermine the accountability of local government to its electorate".[162]

Thus the Scottish Parliament would have the power to increase or decrease the basic rate of income tax set by the UK Parliament by a maximum of 3p which would currently be the equivalent of a power to raise or forgo £450m in a year. The White Paper recognised, however, that attaching the tax-varying power to the basic rate of income tax made it vulnerable to changes to the UK income tax structure, and so an undertaking was given to preserve the Scottish Parliament's ability to vary its income through the tax structure by up to £450m, index-linked to maintain its value. Changes in the mechanism for protecting that tax take would be the subject of joint discussion between the Scottish Executive and the UK Government.[163]

Beyond the commitment to the principle of the tax-varying power, the White Paper did not go into much more detail. It was, however, made clear that the savings and dividend income of individuals would not be subject to the tax-varying power.[164] One consequence of this would be to simplify somewhat the identification of those people subject to any variation ordered by the Scottish Parliament. The test of liability would be "residence" - a concept described by the White Paper as well established in tax law: "A Scottish resident will be an individual who is resident in the UK for income tax purposes and who in any tax year either spends at least half of his time in Scotland (when in the UK) or whose principal home is in Scotland. These concepts will be set out in legislation."[165]

Tax collection would be done by the Inland Revenue, with employees paying as usual by PAYE.[166] The White Paper estimated the costs to the Government of establishing the mechanisms for tax variation at £10m, with running costs at about £8m per annum. The Scottish Parliament would be required to meet the administration costs incurred by the Inland Revenue but there would also be additional costs in setting up PAYE collection which would be borne by employers.[167]

In the Scotland Bill itself, the key provisions are those which, on the one hand, ensure that "taxes and excise duties" are in general "reserved matters" for the UK Parliament[168] and, on the other hand, *clause 69* under which "a tax-varying resolution"[169] of the Scottish Parliament may be made. Such a resolution must be made for a particular year of assessment (for income tax

[162] para. 7.12. But see also "Local Taxation and Local Expenditure" below.
[163] paras. 7.13 - 7.14.
[164] para. 7.15
[165] para. 7.16
[166] para. 7.17.
[167] paras. 7.18 - 7.19.
[168] See *Sched. 5, Part II, Head 1, S. 1.*
[169] Defined in *clause 70* to include a resolution to cancel a previous such resolution.

purposes) and provide for an increase or reduction in the percentage determined by the UK Parliament[170] to be the basic rate of income tax for that year. The variation in the percentage must not exceed 3 and must be expressed as either a whole or half number (*i.e.* 0.5, 1.5, 2, 2.5, 3). The variation contained in the resolution then applies to "Scottish taxpayers" (*clause 69(1)*).[171]

A person is defined as a "Scottish taxpayer" if, in relation to any year of assessment, he or she is (a) an individual who, for income tax purposes, is treated as resident in the United Kingdom in that year and (b) Scotland is the part of the United Kingdom with which he or she has the closest connection during that year (*clause 71(1)*). The concept of "residence" for income tax purposes is one which, as the White Paper said, is reasonably well settled in its meaning and is unlikely to be unduly problematic in its application to the tax-varying power but the idea of a person's having a "closest connection" with Scotland rather than some other part of the United Kingdom is new and may cause more difficulties. *Clause 71* does, however, provide further assistance. There it is stated that a person has his or her closest connection with Scotland in a particular year of assessment only if one or more of three specified conditions applies:

1. He or she is a person who
    (a) spends at least a part of that year in Scotland;
    (b) for at least a part of that time, his or her principal UK home is located in Scotland and he or she makes use of it as a place of residence; and
    (c) the times in the year when Scotland is where his or her principal UK home is located comprise (in aggregate) at least as much of that year as the times (if any) in that year when the location of his or her principal UK home is not in Scotland (*clause 71(2), (3)*).

This is the "principal home" test of closest connection and will doubtless be the test which will come to define the vast majority of "Scottish taxpayers" as such. It requires that a part of the year be spent in Scotland and then that for *a part of that part* the person's principal UK home is in Scotland and is made use of as a place of residence. But, in addition, the person's principal UK home must be located for at least as long in Scotland as elsewhere.

Some further assistance is provided by the Bill on both the "spending" of time and on the location of a principal home. As to the spending of time, it is provided that (a) an individual spends a day in Scotland if, but only if, he is in Scotland at the beginning or end of that day, and similarly that (b) an individual spends a day elsewhere in the United Kingdom, if, but only if, he or she is elsewhere in the United Kingdom at the beginning or end of that day *and* it is not a day that he or she spends in Scotland (*clause 71(4)*).

Secondly, it is provided that an individual's principal UK home at any time is located in Scotland if at that time (a) he or she is an individual with a place[172]

---

[170] Such determination to include a declaration under the Provisional Collection of Taxes Act 1968.

[171] It should be noted that, by virtue of *clause 98*, the individuals to be treated as "Scottish taxpayers" and the consequences for those individuals for social security purposes fall to be determined by the Secretary of State.

of residence in Scotland, and (b) in the case of an individual with two or more places of residence in the United Kingdom, Scotland is the location of such one of those places as at that time is his or her main place of residence in the United Kingdom (*clause 71(5)*).

2. The number of days which he or she spends in Scotland in the year of assessment is equal to or exceeds the number of days in that year which he or she spends elsewhere in the United Kingdom.

This is perhaps the "days spent" test and, as with the rules of the "principal home" test, must be read together with the further rules on the spending of time in *clause 71(4)* mentioned above. It ensures that some of those who do not qualify as "Scottish taxpayers" by virtue of the location of (and residence in) their principal home will nevertheless qualify on grounds of days spent in Scotland. Perhaps the most obvious people qualifying on this ground will be UK taxpayers whose work brings them to Scotland but who return to their principal home for weekends or, for example, for a week in each month.

3. The person is an individual who, for the whole or part of the year of assessment, is an MP, MEP or MSP.

Just in case they do not establish a "closest connection" with Scotland on either of the other two grounds, this "MP test" brings into the fold of "Scottish taxpayers" all types of Scotland-based parliamentarian. No doubt this is felt to be constitutionally appropriate. It also avoids the politically embarrassing possibility that the people's own representatives might otherwise escape liability to pay any higher level of taxation imposed on Scottish taxpayers. Thus if Robin Cook, the Secretary of State for Foreign Affairs and MP for Livingston, were to maintain his principal home in England and to spend more days in London in the course of a year than in the Lothians, he would nevertheless be treated as a Scottish taxpayer.

Supplementing these core provisions on liability are three other important clauses relating to the tax-varying power. *Clause 72* takes account of the possibility anticipated in the White Paper that changes to the general UK income tax structure may have a "significant effect on the practical extent" of the Scottish Parliament's tax-varying powers. Provision is made for an assessment of the situation by the Treasury and, if appropriate, proposals for the amendment of the existing powers. Any such proposals must satisfy certain conditions laid down, the main one being that the "practical extent of the Parliament's tax-varying powers would remain broadly the same from year to year" (*clause 72(4)*). The actual amendment of the existing powers would require an Act of the UK Parliament.

Clauses 73 and *74* make the accounting provision necessary for the transfers into or out of the Scottish Consolidated Fund consequential upon a decision either to increase or to reduce the rate of tax for Scottish taxpayers. There is further provision in *clause 75* for the Treasury to make statutory amendments consequential upon the introduction of the tax-varying power.

---

[172] This may include a place on board a vessel or other means of transport (*clause 71(6)*).

LOCAL TAXATION AND LOCAL EXPENDITURE

As noted above, it has been the Government's view that the Scottish Parliament and Executive should be funded almost entirely by means of the assigned revenues as a successor to the block and formula system. The single "independent" source of revenue will be the tax-varying power operated by reference to the basic rate of income tax. The Government rejected the option of the use of, amongst others, the council tax as a source of tax flexibility.

It is also the case, however, that, because Scottish local government including local finance will be devolved to the Parliament and Executive, they will, in effect, have the power to regulate the balance of local authority revenue drawn, on the one hand, from the Scottish Executive grant to local authorities and, on the other, from the council tax or a successor to that tax. It would be permissible for the Scottish Parliament and Executive (a) to provide reduced "central" funding for local authorities and (b) to relax "capping" controls on council tax levels and thus (c) to finance an overall increase in public expenditure in Scotland.

In acknowledging these freedoms which would be conferred on the Scottish Parliament and Executive, however, the White Paper also indicated two important limitations. In the first place, it was noted that:

"The Scottish Parliament will have the powers to control local authority current expenditure, through capping or other means, and it will be for the Scottish Parliament to decide whether and how to exercise these powers. Should self-financed expenditure start to rise steeply, the Scottish Parliament would clearly come under pressure from council tax payers in Scotland to exercise its powers. If growth relative to England were excessive and were such as to threaten targets set for public expenditure as part of the management of the UK economy, and the Scottish Parliament nevertheless chose not to exercise its powers, it would be open to the UK Government to take the excess into account in considering the level of their support for expenditure in Scotland."[173]

This is not a sanction reflected directly in the Bill itself, but the necessary flexibility to adjust levels of grant is inherent in *clause 61(2)*.

The other limitation on the financial freedom of the Scottish Parliament noted in the White Paper was in response to the possibility that some of its decisions on the funding of devolved matters might have a direct impact upon the costs of non-devolved services:

"Decisions by local authorities on their council tax levels and their housing rent levels could lead to expenditure on council tax benefits and rent rebates growing more rapidly in Scotland than in England. This could put an unfair burden on UK taxpayers. Arrangements will therefore be made to include the resources for these benefits in the Block, so that any resultant extra costs would have to be found by the Scottish Parliament."[174]

Once again, this will be something within the power of the UK Government to control under *clause 61(2)*.

[173] para. 7.24.

FINANCIAL PROPRIETY AND VALUE FOR MONEY

A final concern mentioned in the White Paper was that of the scrutiny and control of the spending of the Scottish Executive. This would be a matter for the Scottish Parliament and the Scotland Bill would itself lay down only a general obligation to establish the necessary arrangements. The detailed machinery would need to be agreed before the Scottish Parliament became fully operational in order to ensure that the accountability of the Scottish Executive could be established as soon as it assumed its responsibilities.[175]

The general obligation to be imposed on the Scottish Parliament is represented in the Bill by *clause 66* which requires the Parliament to make statutory provision for rules on the preparation of accounts by the Scottish Ministers; for the publication of the accounts; and the laying of accounts and financial reports before the Parliament (*clause 66(1)*). There is in addition the requirement to establish an office equivalent to that of the Comptroller and Auditor General. This will be an "independent person" - defined as someone "not subject to the direction or control of any member of the Scottish Executive or of the Parliament" - whose tasks will include the auditing of accounts both in relation to the legality of payments made and the "economy, efficiency and effectiveness" with which the Scottish Ministers and the Lord Advocate have used their resources (*clause 66(1)-(4)*).[176]

---

[174] para. 7.25.
[175] para. 7.27.
[176] The Secretary of State's own responsibilities under the Act will be scrutinised by the Comptroller and Auditor General (*clause 68*).

CHAPTER 8
RELATIONS WITH LOCAL GOVERNMENT AND OTHER BODIES

Local government in Scotland was reorganised by the Local Government etc. (Scotland) Act 1994 with effect from April 1, 1996, when the present structure of 32 unitary authorities was established. Nothing proposed in the White Paper or now contained in the Scotland Bill will in itself change that structure. However, from the point of view of local government in Scotland, the effect of devolution is going to be to insert a new tier of government between the local authorities themselves and the United Kingdom Government and Parliament and this will have important consequences.

The same applies to other public bodies established and operating in Scotland. The Bill contains no provisions for the reform or reorganisation of the National Health Service or of the large number of other non-departmental public bodies (NDPBs) which are presently within the responsibility of the Secretary of State for Scotland. Like the local authorities, however, their position within the overall framework of government will be affected by the creation of the Scottish Parliament and Executive.

This chapter considers the consequences of the White Paper proposals and of the Bill's provisions for Scottish local government and public bodies.

LOCAL GOVERNMENT
The Bill itself makes little direct provision for local government. This is partly because no immediate reorganisation is proposed. The other reason is the method of allocation of powers to the Scottish Parliament and Executive. The intention is to devolve responsibility for local government. As the White Paper said: "The Scottish Parliament will have general responsibility for legislation and policy relating to local government. The Scottish Parliament will have the power to set the framework within which local government operates and to legislate to make changes to the powers, boundaries and functions of local authorities. The Scottish Executive will be responsible for supporting local authority current expenditure and for controlling and allocating capital allocations to Scottish councils. It will also be responsible for the system of local taxation."[177]

To achieve this measure of devolution, however, it is, as explained in Chapter 5, not necessary for specific powers concerning the structure and functions of local authorities to be spelled out. All powers in relation to the structure (including the system of elections but not eligibility to vote),[178] organisation and financing of local government itself and then in relation to functions currently undertaken by local councils such as school education, social work, housing, or town and country planning are devolved - except to the extent that any aspects are expressly reserved to the Westminster Parliament and the UK Government.

The White Paper set out a long list of powers intended to be devolved

---

[177] para. 6.5.
[178] *Sched. 5, Part II, Head 2, S. 3.*

which included those mentioned above as well as many other local authority functions. These are all within the legislative competence of this Scottish Parliament as defined in *clause 28* of the Bill. Because local authorities are not much concerned with the "General Reservations" set out in *Part I* of *Schedule 5* to the Bill, (the constitution, foreign affairs, defence, etc.), the devolution to the Scottish Parliament of powers to legislate for local government is not greatly affected by them.[179] However, some of the "Specific Reservations" in *Part II* of *Schedule 5* do affect certain functions which are carried out by local authorities and will serve to keep legislative power at Westminster in respect of these. They include powers in relation to entertainment licensing, consumer protection, and road traffic regulation.[180] These exceptional cases apart, however, the scheme of the Bill is to place the general law-making responsibility for local government and its functions in the hands of the Scottish Parliament.

The same principle applies to administrative powers and the Bill provides for a general transfer of the responsibilities of the Secretary of State to the Scottish Ministers (*clause 49*). At present, the Secretary of State has many administrative responsibilities in relation to local authorities and the way in which he exercises his powers is very important to the operation of local government. At many points local authorities do, in effect, exercise their powers under the supervision and control of the Secretary of State. Sometimes his consent is required for specific actions; sometimes local authority decisions are subject to appeal to the Secretary of State; and in many areas local authorities must exercise their powers subject to rules laid down in subordinate legislation or codes of guidance made by the Secretary of State.[181] All these powers pass under the Bill to the Scottish Ministers unless they relate to reserved matters (*clause 49(3)*) and, as we have seen, reserved matters relevant to local government are few in number. The power to transfer additional functions (in relation to reserved matters) to the Scottish Ministers under *clause 59* has already been noted. This could be used to transfer local government-related functions from UK ministers to the Scottish Ministers.

Perhaps most importantly, control over the financing of local authorities will pass to the Scottish Parliament and Scottish Executive. Within the existing legislative framework, the substantial powers presently vested in the Secretary of State[182] to control levels of capital spending by local authorities will go to the Scottish Ministers. The same applies to the existing controls by the Secretary of State over levels of revenue expenditure. At present local authorities make individual decisions to determine the level of the council tax in their

---

[179] Although it is made clear by *para. 6(2)* of *Sched. 5* that the regulation of "observing and implementing international obligations, obligations under the Human Rights Convention and obligations under Community law" *is* a devolved matter.

[180] *N.B.* also, however, the exception from reservation of some local authority responsibilities in relation to "social security schemes".

[181] For a fuller discussion see C.M.G. Himsworth, *Local Government Law in Scotland* (1995), Chap. 10.

[182] S.94 of the Local Government (Scotland) Act 1973.

areas for each year.[183] But, on average, authorities raise only about one-sixth of their income from the council tax. Most of the rest comes in the form of an annual grant from the Secretary of State made in accordance with a formula devised in consultation with the Convention of Scottish Local Authorities (COSLA). A part of the total grant to councils derives from the business rate levied on commercial and industrial premises at levels prescribed by the Secretary of State. The remainder is made available from the total Scottish Office budget and, overall, distributions to individual authorities are made at levels which take account of the population of the authority's area weighted in accordance with a formula based on assumed levels of service provision.

In the calculation and distribution of grants to local authorities, the Secretary of State exercises very considerable powers of control, and the control extends a stage further in that the Secretary of State also retains the power to "cap" the total level of an authority's annual expenditure and thus impose a limit on the amount an authority may raise by way of the council tax levied on its own residents.[184]

These important financial controls conferred by existing legislation will all pass (subject to any modifications made between 1998 and 2000) to the Scottish Executive. It will be for the Scottish Ministers rather than the Secretary of State to make decisions about the level at which Scottish local government as a whole will be funded; the division of the burden of that funding between local sources (mainly the council tax but also including charges for services provided) and central grants from the Scottish Executive; and the rules which, by formula, determine which local authorities benefit most and which least from those central grants. All these decisions are of prime importance to local authorities and for the provision of local services. They are also, however, decisions which may have a wider impact upon the overall funding of Scottish government.[185]

It has also to be remembered that not only will the Scottish Ministers inherit the existing powers of the Secretary of State in relation to local government, but the Scottish Parliament will have broad and theoretically unrestrained powers to legislate in the same area. The Parliament would be able to reorganise local government; to modify, expand or reduce the functions of local authorities; amend the financial basis of local government; or, indeed, to abolish local government as we know it altogether.

This proposed substantial power of the Scottish Parliament to determine the future of local government has attracted much attention. There has been a fear that the new Parliament and Executive, anxious to expand their own governmental space between the upper millstone of Westminster and Whitehall and the lower millstone of local government, might seek to make unwarranted inroads into the area presently occupied by local government. As the Scottish Constitutional Convention put it:

[183]   S.93 of the Local Government Finance Act 1992.
[184]   Local Government Finance Act 1992, s.94, Sched. 7.
[185]   See Chap. 7.

"The Convention regards it as vital that the relationship between the Parliament and local authorities be positive, co-operative and stable. It expects the Parliament to investigate new ways of co-operative working between levels of government. Relations between local and central government have too often fallen victim to confrontational Government policies aimed at systematically removing powers from elected local representatives. The creation of Scotland's Parliament will mark a distinct change of approach, by placing a culture of co-operation and stability at the heart of the relationship between the Parliament and local authorities.

The value of local government stems from three essential attributes: first, it provides for the dispersal of power both to bring the reality of government nearer to the people and also to prevent the concentration of power at the centre; second, participation, local government is government by local communities ....; and thirdly, responsiveness through which it contributes to meeting local needs by delivering services."[186]

What these views of the Convention reflect is not only a specific concern about local government in Scotland following devolution but also a more general concern about the condition of local government in Great Britain as a whole and the relationship between central government and local authorities. The later years of the Conservative administrations up to 1997 were characterised by fraught relations between the two tiers of government. The poll tax experiment was probably the most prominent single cause of complaint from the local authority side but the Conservative commitment to a philosophy of local government which saw authorities as enablers rather than as providers of services; the introduction and expansion of compulsory competitive tendering; the removal of water and sewerage functions from local government; and, for many, the abolition of the regions and creation of the unitary authorities - some of them small and under-resourced - in April 1996 were all seen as developments hostile to local government as a whole.[187]

It was against this background that the Government expressed in the White Paper its determination that local government should flourish under the Scottish Parliament:

"In establishing a Scottish Parliament to extend democratic accountability, the Government do not expect the Scottish Parliament and its Executive to accumulate a range of new functions at the centre which would be more appropriately and efficiently delivered by other bodies within Scotland. The Government believe that the principle that decisions should be made as close as possible to the citizen holds good within Scotland as it does within the United Kingdom ..... The Government recognise that the relationship between the Scottish Parliament and Scottish Executive and local authorities is particularly crucial to the good governance of Scotland and

---

[186] *Scotland's Parliament: Scotland's Right,* p.16.
[187] For a full treatment, covering Great Britain as a whole, see the report of the House of Lords Select Committee on Relations between Central and Local Government "Rebuilding Trust" (1995-96) H.L. Paper 97.

the effective provision of services to its people ..... The Government believe the Scottish people will be served best by a Scottish Parliament and
Scottish Executive working closely with strong democratically elected local government."[188]

In this connection the White Paper also referred to the new Government's signing
in June 1997 of the European Charter of Local Self-Government. This is a
treaty drawn up under the auspices of the Council of Europe in 1985 and which
has been ratified by most of the 40 members of the council. The terms of the
Charter are designed to require states to protect the status of local government.
They must, for example, ensure that local authorities have "adequate financial
resources" which are "commensurate with the responsibilities" they are given.[189]
There are restrictions on the "administrative supervision" which may be imposed on local authorities.[190]

It was the view of the Conservative Governments between 1985 and 1997
that there would be no advantage to the United Kingdom in signing the Charter[191] but the incoming Labour Government moved quickly to sign the Charter
on coming into office to demonstrate a commitment to the value of local government. It would, they said, "be for the Scottish Parliament and its Executive
to determine the details of their relationships with local authorities and funding and taxation arrangements for local government in the light of developments"[192] between the publication of the White Paper and the eventual establishment of the Scottish Parliament.

One suggestion made by the Scottish Constitutional Convention was that
the Scotland Act should itself include a provision "committing Scotland's Parliament to secure and maintain a strong and effective system of local government, and embodying the principle of subsidiarity so as to guarantee the important role of local government in service delivery."[193] The inclusion of a
commitment to the principle of subsidiarity and also the possibility of conferring on local authorities a "general competence" to undertake in their areas any
functions they thought appropriate (and not expressly forbidden by statute)
were later discussed in the Constitution Unit's report[194] but none of these proposals was adopted by the Government for inclusion in the Bill itself. As we
have seen, the Bill is silent on these matters.

What the Government did promise in the White Paper, however, was the
early appointment of an independent committee (subsequently referred to as a
"commission") whose function would be "to study how to build the most effective relations between the Scottish Parliament and Scottish Executive and a
strong and effective local government".[195] The commission's report would be

---

[188] paras. 6.2, 6.4, 6.6.
[189] Charter, Art. 9.
[190] Charter, Art. 8.
[191] Evidence to "Rebuilding Trust" above.
[192] White Paper, para. 6.6.
[193] *Scotland's Parliament: Scotland's Right*, p.17.
[194] *Scotland's Parliament: Fundamentals for a New Scotland Act*, pp.123-127.
[195] para. 6.4.

laid before the Scottish Parliament. In a further consultation paper, the Government set out some thoughts as to its remit. These included the need for the commission to investigate the possibility of a "concordat" between local government and the Scottish Parliament.[196]

One other matter of specific concern to Scottish local government has been another question raised by the Constitutional Convention and discussed further by the Constitution Unit, the possibility of a prohibition on simultaneous dual membership of the Scottish Parliament and a local authority. The Convention expressed the view that membership of the Scottish Parliament should be considered a full-time appointment and that members should not, therefore, be permitted to have a "dual mandate", combining membership of the Parliament with membership of a local authority.[197] Such a restriction on "dual mandates" was, however, opposed by the Constitution Unit[198] and rejected by the White Paper. As noticed in Chapter 4, the Bill contains no prohibition on a "dual mandate", so it is a matter for individual political parties to make up their minds about.

OTHER PUBLIC BODIES

It is a well-recognised feature of British public administration that much of it is conducted not by the central departments (and their executive agencies) headed by ministers, nor by local authorities, but by other public bodies at an "intermediate" level of government. Often termed Non-Departmental Public Bodies (NDPBs) or, more popularly "quangos", they take many different forms and are not easily classified. Some are responsible for the administration of the remaining nationalised industries (such as the Post Office); some regulate privatised industries (e.g. the electricity and gas regulators); some have other regulatory functions (such as the Scottish Environmental Protection Agency); some have a more executive role (such as the three water authorities in Scotland); some have an advisory or consultative role; and often tribunals with a judicial function are seen as public bodies at this intermediate level. Whilst it would be unfair to assume that criticisms which apply to some of these bodies apply to all, it is true that in recent years NDPBs have not had a good press. There have been problems with their financial accountability and their efficiency. Complaints about appointments based on political patronage attracted the attention of the (then) Nolan Committee on Standards in Public Life.[199] Above all, it has been the lack of direct accountability either to Parliament or to other elected bodies that has been criticised. In the White Paper the Government itself recognised that, while it was acceptable for some functions of government to be carried out by public bodies established for particular purposes,

[196] See also the Constitution Unit, *Scotland's Parliament: Fundamentals for a New Scotland Act* (1996) paras. 476-478.
[197] *Scotland's Parliament: Scotland's Right*, p.25. A transitional exemption would have permitted new members of the first Scottish Parliament to serve out their terms in another parliament or authority.
[198] *Scotland's Parliament: Fundamentals for a New Scotland Act* (1996) paras. 479-482.
[199] First Report of the Committee on Standards in Public Life, Cm. 2850 (1995), Chap.4.

it was "concerned at the extent to which Scotland's vital public services are now run by unelected bodies."[200]

This is not, however, an issue addressed in the devolution proposals themselves. In contrast with the Government of Wales Bill, the Scotland Bill does not contain provisions directly designed to lead either to the abolition of quangos or to their reform, although there may be an underlying assumption in the proposals that the creation of a Scottish Parliament will produce the conditions in which reform may take place. It is instead the concern of the White Paper and Bill to address the specific problems that the general devolution of legislative and administrative powers creates for NDPBs. Simply put, there are two issues. The first is to draw the line between those bodies which are to be devolved and those which are not. The second is to establish ground rules for how the Scottish Parliament and Executive will relate to those bodies which fall on the non-devolved side of the line but in whose work there is a significant Scottish interest.

The response to these issues is principally to be found in what emerges in the White Paper and Bill as a tripartite scheme of division of NDPBs. The three types of public body are:

1. Those which will fall wholly within the responsibility of the Scottish Parliament and Executive.
2. Those which, because of the "reserved" nature of their functions, will remain within the remit of the UK Parliament and Government but in respect of which there will be a limited consultative role for the Scottish institutions.
3. Those which fall into an intermediate category of "cross-border public bodies" which will have responsibilities in the devolved areas and for which special provision for the involvement of the Scottish Parliament and Executive will be made.

Devolved Bodies

Some Scottish public bodies will fall within the remit of the Scottish Parliament simply by virtue of the standard rules governing the Parliament's legislative competence.[201] Their functions are confined to Scotland and do not concern the reserved matters and the Parliament will have the power to make new legislation in respect of them. The Parliament could alter the structure of existing bodies or could wind them up and create new ones.[202] The Parliament will be entitled to receive reports from these bodies and to subject their members and officials to questioning by parliamentary committees.

The scheme of devolution adopted in the Bill means that the names of these bodies are not to be listed in the legislation but a list was set out in Annex A to the White Paper. The list contained many executive bodies (including Highlands and Islands Enterprise, the National Library of Scotland, the Scottish

---

[200] para. 6.7.
[201] *Clauses 28, 29* and *Sched. 5.*
[202] White Paper, para. 2.9.

Arts Council, the Scottish Environmental Protection Agency, Scottish Homes, the Scottish Legal Aid Board and many others); advisory bodies (including the General Teaching Council for Scotland, the Royal Fine Art Commission for Scotland and the Scottish Law Commission); three nationalised industries (the Scottish Transport Group, Highlands and Islands Airports Ltd. and Caledonian MacBrayne Ltd.); a number of tribunals (including the children's panels and the Lands Tribunal for Scotland); the three water authorities; and health bodies (including the Common Services Agency, the health boards and the health service trusts).

In addition to being within the legislative remit of the Parliament, all these bodies will also come under the administrative responsibility of members of the Scottish Executive (*clause 49*) who will inherit the existing powers of UK ministers to make appointments to the bodies, to fund them and to direct their activities.[203] The White Paper also stipulated that the "Scottish Executive will be required to put arrangements in place to ensure that appointments to public bodies are subject to independent scrutiny and conform to the Commissioner of Public Appointments' Code of Practice".[204]

UK or GB Public Bodies with "Reserved" Responsibilities

At the other end of the scale are those bodies which are at present established on a UK or GB basis and which, in terms of the scheme of allocation of powers in the Bill, exercise functions in relation to the reserved matters. Although these too are not, in the main, expressly identified in the Bill,[205] the White Paper picked out the energy regulators (OFFER and OFGAS); the Office of Passenger Rail Franchising and the Office of the Rail Regulator; the Health and Safety Commission, the Commission for Racial Equality and the Equal Opportunities Commission; the Employment Service and the Benefits Agency; the BBC and the Independent Television Commission; and the Post Office.

These bodies will remain the responsibility of the UK authorities. However, the White Paper did recognise that some of their activities "will continue to be significant in the economic or social life of Scotland, and therefore likely to be of interest to the Scottish Parliament".[206] The Government proposed that the Scottish Parliament should be able to invite the submission of reports and the presentation of oral evidence on the work of these bodies as it affects Scotland.[207]

---

[203] White Paper, para. 2.9.
[204] para. 6.8 (although it is not clear from the terms of the Bill how those requirements are to be imposed).
[205] Exceptions are the Post Office and the BBC.
[206] para. 2.11.
[207] The White Paper also promised that the Scottish Executive would be "consulted on the appointment of the National Governor of the BBC who represents Scottish interests, and on corresponding appointments to other broadcasting bodies" (p.9).

Cross-Border Public Bodies

The third category of public bodies includes those which currently operate on a UK or GB basis but in relation to the devolved areas. Because they do deal with devolved matters it will be competent for the Scottish Parliament to replace them with separate Scottish bodies. The White Paper envisaged, however, that "the Scottish Parliament will want to continue most such UK or GB arrangements in the light of the advantages of sharing knowledge and expertise on a UK or GB basis and of the greater efficiency in the use of resources".[208] Examples of such bodies provided in the White Paper were the UK Sports Council, the Central Council for Education and Training in Social Work, the Criminal Injuries Compensation Authority and the Meat Hygiene Service.

For as long as such bodies continue to operate, the intention is that the Scottish Parliament will have the right to receive copies of the reports which they are already obliged to lay before the Westminster Parliament (*clause 83(3)*) and the Scottish Executive will be entitled to be consulted on the appointment of members and officers and on "any specific function ..... whose exercise might otherwise affect devolved matters concerning Scotland" (*clause 83(2)*).

The mechanism used in the Bill to achieve these purposes is the creation of the relevant UK or GB body as a "cross-border public body" which is to be done in subordinate legislation by a UK minister. To qualify, a potential cross-border public body must be a body or tribunal established by an enactment and "which, in addition to other functions, has functions exercisable in or as regards Scotland which do not relate to reserved matters".[209] The Bill also contains a provision enabling specific powers in relation to a cross-border public body to be transferred to the Scottish Ministers from the relevant UK minister.[210]

---

[208] para. 2.10.
[209] *Clause 83(5)*. It is not completely clear what rules apply to a body which appears to satisfy the basic criteria to qualify for recognition by the relevant UK minister but in respect of which no order has been made.
[210] *Clause 84* and see also *clause 85* which deals with the property and other consequences of an eventual splitting up of the UK or GB body.

CHAPTER 9
RELATIONS WITH THE EUROPEAN UNION

One of the biggest constitutional and political changes to affect the United Kingdom since the time of the Scotland Act 1978 has been the growing impact of the European Community and Union. European policy and legislation binding on member states cover much broader areas and penetrate more deeply into the social and economic fabric. Established European policies affecting economic development, agriculture and fisheries have been joined by an expanding influence on environmental policy and in many other areas. The devolution of power to Scotland by 2000 is, therefore, taking place in a very different European context from that of the late 1970s.

In one sense, however, UK relations with the European Union will remain unaffected by the devolution proposals. Whatever re-arrangements of governmental authority are made within the United Kingdom, it is the United Kingdom itself which will continue to be the member of the European Union and, as the White Paper made clear, relations with Europe will be the formal responsibility of the UK Parliament and Government.[211] That position is established in the Bill where, in *Schedule 5* the European Union (along with other aspects of foreign policy) is declared to be a "reserved matter" (*Schedule 5, Part I, para. 6*).

On the other hand, the White Paper also stated the Government's view that the Scottish Parliament and Executive should have an important role in those aspects of European Union business which affect devolved areas. This would be in the context of what the Government called its "more active and constructive approach to the European Union."[212]

Some of the involvement of the Scottish Parliament and Executive will arise because the obligation to implement in Scotland that EC legislation which is binding on the United Kingdom and which is in the devolved fields will, in the main, fall to them. Other aspects of Scottish Parliament and Executive involvement in the EU will be extra-statutory in character and these do not attract a direct reference in the Bill. It is, however, helpful to have the full picture of the proposed Scottish governmental involvement in the EU in mind and so it is appropriate to discuss different aspects of it.[213]

EU POLICY FORMULATION AND NEGOTIATION

An important aspect of relations with the EU, which was given prominence in the White Paper, was the Government's wish to involve members of the Scottish Executive in policy formulation and negotiation conducted in European institutions. These processes would continue to reflect existing practice which includes the participation of Scottish Office Ministers in EU Councils where

---

[211] para. 5.1.
[212] paras. 5.1-5.2.
[213] A good pre-White Paper discussion of these issues is T.StJ.N. Bates, "Devolution and the European Union" in *Devolution to Scotland: The Legal Aspects* (Bates, ed., 1997).

Scottish interests are on the agenda, and the involvement of Scottish Office officials in discussions of relevant EU matters with their colleagues in other departments.[214]

Although there would indeed be some continuity of practice here, the White Paper implicitly recognises that devolution will bring important changes and especially that it will produce governments at the Scottish and UK levels which may well have rather different strategies in relation to EU policy formulation. Instead of the co-ordination of ministers and departments all of whom have a loyalty to the same policy decided under the umbrella of the Cabinet, devolution is quite liable to produce a situation in which Scottish Ministers and officials may have different ideas about the best EU policy on, for example, agriculture or fisheries.

The Government's concern about the changed conditions that devolution will produce is reflected in their insistence in the White Paper that, when UK policy is being formulated in discussion involving representatives of both the UK Government and the Scottish Executive, it will "require, of course, mutual respect for the confidentiality of those discussions and adherence to the resultant UK line, without which it would be impossible to maintain such close working relationships".[215] The White Paper continued:

"Our proposals are designed to give the Scottish Parliament and Scottish Executive the opportunity to work constructively for the common interests of Scotland and the UK. The success of such a close working relationship, and the ability to sustain it, will depend upon the way in which the Scottish Parliament and Executive respond to that opportunity.

"The Government also propose that Ministers and officials of the Scottish Executive should have a role to play in relevant council meetings and other negotiations with our EU partners. Policy does not remain static in negotiations; and continuing involvement is a necessary extension of involvement in formulating the UK's initial policy positions. The role of Scottish Ministers and officials will be to support and advance the single UK negotiating line which they have played a part in developing. The emphasis in negotiations has to be on working as a UK team; and the UK lead minister will retain overall responsibility for the negotiations and determine how best each member of the team can contribute to securing the agreed policy position, so that, in appropriate cases, Scottish Executive Ministers could speak for the UK in councils. They would do so with the full weight of the UK's status as a large member state behind them, because the policy positions advanced will have been agreed among the UK interests".[216]

SCRUTINY AND IMPLEMENTATION OF EU LEGISLATION

The Government has given the further assurance that, when EU negotiations

---

[214] White Paper, paras. 5.2 and 5.4.
[215] para. 5.4.
[216] paras. 5.5-5.6.

lead to the formulation of legislative proposals, the Scottish Parliament will be given the opportunity to scrutinise them "to ensure that Scotland's interests are properly reflected".[217] The problem of timetabling these procedures is acknowledged but the Government has affirmed that it will take into account the views of the Scottish Parliament and that the UK Parliament may also wish to do so in its own scrutiny processes.[218]

Perhaps most importantly of all, the Government made it clear in the White Paper that, in relation to devolved matters, it would be the Scottish Executive which would be responsible for ensuring the implementation in Scotland of EU obligations.[219] Thus where an EC Directive required implementation in Scotland, it would be for the Executive to ensure that the necessary legislation be made. Typically this would not necessitate the passing of an Act of the Scottish Parliament but would be done under the general powers conferred on Scottish Ministers to make subordinate legislation (*clause 50*).

These arrangements for the implementation of EU obligations by the Scottish Executive would not preclude the possibility that this could "include the option of agreeing to GB or UK legislation, if it judges it appropriate. It is implicit in the sovereignty of the UK Parliament that it will continue to have the ability to legislate to give effect to EU obligations in Scotland".[220] In other words, rather than devising its own rules, the Scottish Executive could conveniently enter into arrangements for implementation common to the whole of Great Britain or the United Kingdom. As the White Paper suggested, if the implementation were done by the UK Parliament, this might be by an Act extending both to Scotland and to the rest of Great Britain or the United Kingdom. If it were to be done by regulations made by ministers, this could be done by UK ministers and Scottish Executive Ministers adopting the same form of words in their separate instruments.

As the White Paper also made clear, however, the promulgation of the same rules of implementation in the different UK jurisdictions may not be merely a matter of convenience: "Where EU obligations are to be implemented separately for Scotland, there will be arrangements with the UK Government to ensure that differences of approach are compatible with the need for consistency of effect; and to avoid the risk of financial penalties falling on the UK for any failure of implementation or enforcement."[221] The mention of "financial penalties" is a reference to the impact of the rule in the *Francovich* case[222] which makes member states of the EU liable to pay compensation to those injured by the failure of a state to implement its EU obligations. The White Paper continued: "If any such financial penalties were imposed on the UK, or penalties arose from infraction proceedings, responsibility for meeting them would have to be borne by the Scottish Executive if it were responsible for the

---

[217] White Paper, para. 5.7.
[218] *ibid.*
[219] para. 5.8.
[220] White Paper, para. 5.8.
[221] para. 5.8.
[222] *Francovich and Bonifaci v. Italy,* Cases C-6 and 9/90 [1991] E.C.R. I-5357.

failure; and the same principle would apply to the other parts of the UK."[223] This is evidence of an understandable wish on the part of the UK Government to ensure that breaches of EU Treaty obligations with possible accompanying financial penalties are avoided or, failing that, to ensure that the Scottish Executive is ultimately made responsible for any penalties imposed. What is perhaps less clear is why, breach of EU obligations apart, the UK Government should be entitled or indeed should wish to insist on "consistency of effect" in devolved matters. At all events, these concerns and the approach expressed more generally in the White Paper are now reflected in the Scotland Bill itself.

In the first place, as already noted, the terms of *Schedule 5* to the Bill define relations with the European Union and its institutions as "reserved matters" and, therefore, beyond the legislative scope of the Scottish Parliament and also beyond the powers of the Scottish Executive. Secondly, however, the Bill recognises that, although "relations" with the European Union like other aspects of international relations should be reserved to the UK Parliament and Government, there will be ways in which the Scottish Parliament and Executive can and must be involved in EU issues and, above all, they must, within their devolved areas of competence, observe and implement obligations under Community law. There is, therefore, an express exclusion of these obligations from the category of reserved matters.[224] If there are EC policies to be implemented in Scotland and they fall within the devolved matters, it will be the obligation of the Scottish Executive, initiating legislation in the Parliament if necessary, to ensure that the implementation is effected. Where such new legislation is not required, then, as explained in Chapter 6, the Scottish Ministers will have available to them the administrative powers and the powers to make subordinate legislation which are currently exercisable by UK ministers but which will, if exercisable in or as regards Scotland, be transferred to members of the Scottish Executive by *clauses 49-50* of the Bill. These powers will include that contained in section 2 of the European Communities Act 1972[225] to make legislation for the implementation of Community law.

Then, thirdly, there is an important modification of the transfer arrangements in so far as they concern "functions in relation to observing and implementing obligations under Community law" in that *clause 53(1)* of the Bill provides that, despite the general transfer to the Scottish Ministers, "any function of a minister of the Crown in relation to any matter shall continue to be exercisable by him as regards Scotland for the purposes specified in section 2(2) of the European Communities Act 1972". The language of this clause is not entirely unambiguous and it is not, for instance, completely clear whether action by a UK minister would always prevail over action taken by a member of the Scottish Executive, but it is presumably the means by which the UK Government would expect to try to achieve "consistency of effect" in the implementation of Community law.

---

[223] para. 5.8.
[224] *Sched. 5, para. 6(2)*.
[225] As amended by *Sched. 7* to the Bill.

Finally, it should be recalled that neither the Scottish Parliament nor a member of the Scottish Executive, when making subordinate legislation, will be permitted to enact anything incompatible with Community law.[226] This limitation is built into the restrictions on legislative competence and will, of course, apply to all legislative measures, whether or not intended to implement Community law as such. Challenges on the ground of incompatibility may go, in the case of Bills, on a pre-Assent reference to the Judicial Committee of the Privy Council and, in the case of either primary or subordinate legislation, may raise "devolution issues" for special treatment by the courts.[227] The requirement of compatibility with Community law is extended by *clause 53(2)* to "other acts" of members of the Scottish Executive, and challenges on grounds of incompatibility in respect of these may also be taken as "devolution issues".[228]

LINKS WITH EUROPEAN INSTITUTIONS

There are other features of relations with the European Union which were anticipated in the White Paper but are not directly reflected in the Bill itself. These concern, in the main, the ways in which Scotland will maintain less formal links with EU institutions. The White Paper anticipated that: "Scotland will be able to play its part in the less formal discussions with the institutions of the EU and interests within other member states."[229] As the White Paper went on to explain, Scotland already has representatives (8 MEPs) in the European Parliament and it will be the responsibility of the Scottish Executive to make proposals to the Scottish Parliament on nominations to Scotland's share of representation on the Committee of the Regions and the Economic and Social Committee, both of which have an advisory role in relation to EU decision-making. The White Paper promised that the UK Government would consult the Scottish Executive on appointments to other European institutions, where appropriate.

The White Paper also anticipated that the Scottish Executive may well consider that, in line with the practice of some regional governments of other European countries, it should maintain a separate office in Brussels. This would assist Scotland's relationship with such regional governments and also with the Brussels institutions themselves. The Government's view was that the Scottish Executive office in Brussels should complement rather than cut across the work of UKREP which would continue to represent the United Kingdom to the EU institutions and would continue to include staff from Scotland - with the secondment arrangements from the Scottish Executive replacing those from the Scottish Office. The Government concluded:

"The guiding principle which the UK Government sets out to establish in the relationship with the Scottish Executive on EU matters is that there

---

[226] *Clauses 28(2)(d), 50(2).*
[227] See Chap. 5.
[228] Including incompatibility by virtue of a failure to act. See *Sched. 6, para. 1(e).*
[229] para. 5.9.

should be the closest possible working relationships and involvement. Provided the Scottish Executive is willing to work in that spirit of collaboration and trust, there will be an integrated process which builds upon the benefits of the current role of the Scottish Office within government. Taken together these arrangements will allow Scotland, within the UK, to develop its role in the European Union."[230]

---

[230]   para. 5.12.

The Scotland Bill

Presented by Mr Secretary Dewar
supported by
the Prime Minister, Mr Secretary Prescott,
Mr Chancellor of the Exchequer,
Mr Secretary Cook, Mr Secretary Straw,
Secretary Margaret Beckett,
Dr John Cunningham,
Mr Secretary Robertson,
Secretary Harriet Harman,
Mr Secretary Davies and Mr Henry McLeish.

Ordered to be Printed by The House of Commons, *17th December 1997.*

EXPLANATORY AND FINANCIAL MEMORANDUM

The Bill provides for the establishment of a Scottish Parliament and the Scottish Administration.

Part I establishes the Parliament and makes provision about elections. Part II establishes the Administration and makes provision for the transfer of functions. Part III makes provision for financing the Administration, including provision for audit and accounting. Part IV makes provision for the Parliament's tax-varying power. Parts V and VI provide for various miscellaneous, general and supplementary matters.

PART I
THE SCOTTISH PARLIAMENT

Clause 1 establishes a Scottish Parliament. Members of the Scottish Parliament ("MSPs") are to be constituency members elected by the simple majority system or regional members elected by proportional representation. Schedule 1 makes provision for the constituencies, regions and the number of regional members (including provision for changes to the regions and the number of regional members).

Clauses 2 and 3 make provision for dissolution of the Parliament, the timing of ordinary general elections and the circumstances in which extraordinary general elections are to be held. In general, ordinary general elections are to be held on the first Thursday in May every fourth calendar year. Extraordinary general elections are held where the Parliament resolves by a majority of not less than two-thirds of its membership that it should be dissolved, or if the Parliament does not nominate a First Minister during the period specified in Clause 43

Clause 4 deals with candidates for general elections. It provides for registered political parties to submit a regional list of their candidates to be regional members and identifies those who may not be candidates to be regional or constituency members.

Clauses 5 to 7 set out the proportional representation system by which regional members are returned at a general election. Voters may give a vote for a registered political party which has submitted a regional list or for an individual candidate. That vote is in addition to any right to vote for the return of a constituency member. The process for determining the return of regional members is based on the number of votes given for each party and for each individual, and on the number of candidates of the party returned as constituency members for the constituencies in the region.

Clause 8 provides for constituency by-elections where the seat of a constituency member is vacant.

Clause 9 provides that a vacancy in a regional member seat which had been allocated to a registered political party will be filled by the nomination of another person from the same party list. If the vacancy is not filled in accordance with that procedure or the seat has been held by an individual candidate, the seat will remain vacant until the next general election.

Clause 10 provides that those who are properly registered and are entitled to vote in a local government election in an area falling wholly or partly within a constituency are entitled to vote in that constituency in an election to the Parliament.

Clause 11 enables the Secretary of State to make provision by order for the conduct of elections and related matters.

Clauses 12 and 13 provide for the term of office of an MSP and the procedure for his resignation.

Clauses 14 to 17 provide the grounds of disqualification from being an MSP and the exceptions from, consequences of, and legal proceedings as to, disqualification.

Clause 18 provides for the election of a Presiding Officer and two deputies from among the MSPs.

Clause 19 provides for the appointment of a Clerk of the Parliament by the Scottish Parliamentary Corporate Body ("SPCB").

Clause 20 provides for the establishment, membership and functions of the SPCB. Schedule 2 makes further provision about the SPCB including provision about its powers and staff.

Clause 21 requires the proceedings of the Parliament to be regulated by standing orders. Schedule 3 makes further provision as respects the content of the standing orders.

Clause 22 requires the standing orders to provide for the registration and declaration of interests of MSPs and for the prohibition of MSPs from promoting any matter in return for payment. It provides that any MSP who contravenes provisions of the standing orders under the clause commits an offence.

Clauses 23 to 25 enable the Parliament to require certain persons to attend to give evidence, or to produce documents, relating to specified matters. Failure to comply is an offence. Persons giving evidence in proceedings of the Parliament may be required to take an oath. A refusal to do so when so required is an offence.

Clause 26 makes provision for the Lord Advocate and the Solicitor General for Scotland to participate in the proceedings of the Parliament (but not vote) when they are not MSPs. It also provides for them to be able to refuse to answer any question or produce any document if they consider that it might prejudice particular criminal proceedings or might otherwise be contrary to the public interest.

Clause 27 provides that the Scottish Parliament may make laws, to be known as Acts of the Scottish Parliament, and that Bills shall becomes Acts of the Scottish Parliament when they have been passed by the Parliament and have received Royal Assent. The clause states that it does not affect the power of the Parliament of the United Kingdom to make laws for Scotland.

Clause 28 makes provision as to the legislative competence of the Scottish Parliament. In particular, the Parliament cannot legislate in relation to reserved matters (which are defined in Schedule 5) and can only legislate as a matter of the law of Scotland. European Community law, rights under the European Convention on Human Rights which are given effect to in UK law and provisions of the Bill (other than those set out in Schedule 4) are also protected as is the position of the Lord Advocate as head of the criminal prosecution system and system of investigation of deaths in Scotland

Clause 29 introduces Schedule 5 and also provides for modifications of that Schedule to be made by subordinate legislation.

Clause 30 provides that a member of the Scottish Executive in charge of a Bill shall, on or before its introduction, make a statement to the effect that in his view an Act of the Scottish Parliament containing the same provisions as those in the Bill would be within the legislative competence of the Parliament.

Clause 31 requires the standing orders to ensure that no Bill can be introduced if the Presiding Officer decides that it would be outside the legislative competence of the Parliament. Standing orders may provide for the Parliament to overrule such a decision by the Presiding Officer. The standing orders are required to ensure that it is the Presiding Officer who submits Bills for Royal Assent and to impose certain limitations on his power to do so.

Clause 32 provides that questions as to whether a Bill would be within the legislative competence of the Parliament may be referred to the Judicial Committee of the Privy Council by the Advocate General, the Lord Advocate or the Attorney General.

Clause 33 enables the Secretary of State by order to prohibit the submission of a Bill for Royal Assent within 4 weeks of its passing by the Parliament if he believes (and states his reasons) that it contains provisions which would be incompatible with international obligations; or that, in certain cases, the provisions would have an adverse effect on the operation of an enactment as it applies to reserved matters.

Clause 34 requires the standing orders to make provision as to the procedural stages of a Bill, including reconsideration of a Bill following a decision of the Judicial Committee that the Bill is not within the legislative competence of the Parliament or following an order by the Secretary of State under Clause 33.

Clause 35 provides that the Acts of Union have effect subject to the Bill.

Clause 36 provides for the use of Letters Patent under the Scottish Seal for the signification of Royal Assent to a Bill, and for proclamations under the Scottish Seal in connection with general elections.

Clause 37 makes provision about defamation. Statements made in proceedings of the Parliament and statements published under the Parliament's authority are to be absolutely privileged.

Clause 38 disapplies the rule of strict liability for contempt of court in relation to publications made in, or reports of, certain proceedings of the Parliament.

Clause 39 provides for the Parliament to be a public body for the purposes of the Prevention of Corruption Acts 1889 to 1916.

Clause 40 provides for the exclusion of certain days in calculating when Parliament should meet after a general election.

PART II
THE SCOTTISH ADMINISTRATION

Clause 41 establishes a Scottish Executive, comprising the First Minister, the Ministers appointed by the First Minister under Clause 44, the Lord Advocate and the Solicitor General for Scotland. They are to be known collectively as the Scottish Ministers.

Clauses 42 to 44 provide for the appointment and term of office of the First Minister and the Ministers. The Parliament nominates one of its members to be First Minister and the Ministers are only appointed with the agreement of the Parliament.

Clause 45 makes provision in relation to the appointment and removal of the Lord Advocate and the Solicitor General for Scotland. It provides for the continuation of the independence of the Lord Advocate in relation to his prosecution functions and functions relating to the investigation of deaths in Scotland, and for the Lord Advocate and the Solicitor General for Scotland to cease to be Ministers of the Crown.

Clause 46 provides for the appointment and term of office of Junior Scottish Ministers.

Clause 47 provides for the appointment of staff by the Scottish Ministers. Service in their staff and in certain other positions is to be service in the Home Civil Service. It also makes provision in relation to the salary, allowances and pension payable in respect of such persons.

Clause 48 makes provision concerning the conferral of statutory functions on the Scottish Ministers and the exercise of functions of the Scottish Ministers, the First Minister or the Lord Advocate; and for the treatment of acts and omissions of, and property acquired or liabilities incurred by, a member of the Scottish Executive.

Clause 49 provides for the transfer to the Scottish Ministers of functions exercisable by a Minister of the Crown in or as regards Scotland which are not functions so far as they relate to reserved matters or retained functions of the Lord Advocate or.

Clause 50 defines the scope of the powers to make subordinate legislation transferred under Clause 49. Provision may be made in the subordinate legislation if, and only if, the provision would be within the legislative competence of the Parliament if it were included in an Act of the Scottish Parliament.

Clause 51 provides that, subject to one exception, any statutory requirement for a function to be exercised only with the agreement of, or after consultation with, another Minister of the Crown does not apply to the exercise of the function by a member of the Scottish Executive by virtue of Clause 49.

Clause 52 provides for the concurrent exercise of certain powers by Ministers of the Crown despite the transfer of functions under Clause 49.

Clause 53 prohibits a member of the Scottish Executive from doing anything which is incompatible with European Community law or with the rights in the European Convention on Human Rights which are given effect to in law in the United Kingdom. Despite the transfer to the Scottish Ministers of functions in relation to observing and implementing obligations under Community law made by virtue of Clause 49, Ministers of the Crown continue to exercise functions as regards Scotland for the purposes specified in section 2(2) of the European Communities Act 1972

Clause 54 enables the Secretary of State by order to direct that any proposed action by a member of the Scottish Executive shall not be taken if it would be incompatible with international obligations of the United Kingdom. It also enables the Secretary of State by order to direct the Scottish Executive to take specified action where to do so is required for the purpose of giving effect to such obligations. The Secretary of State is also given power by order, in certain circumstances, to revoke subordinate legislation made by a member of the Scottish Executive

Clauses 55 and 57 make provision for the holding of property and the incurring of liabilities by the Scottish Ministers and the Lord Advocate; and for the acquiring of rights and the incurring of liabilities by the First Minister.

Clauses 56 and 58 enables subordinate legislation to provide for the transfer of certain property and liabilities to the Scottish Ministers in connection with the exercise of devolved functions and to the Lord Advocate in connection with the exercise of his retained functions.

Clause 59 enables subordinate legislation to provide for the transfer to the Scottish Ministers of statutory functions and for the adaptation of such functions.

Clause 60 provides for the transfer of certain property and liabilities to the Scottish Ministers in connection with the exercise of any functions transferred under Clause 59.

PART III
FINANCIAL PROVISIONS

Clause 61 establishes a Scottish Consolidated Fund and provides for the Secretary of State to make payments into the Fund out of money provided by Parliament. It also makes provision as to receipts of the Scottish Executive and other receipts which are payable into the Fund and provision as to banking services in respect of the Fund.

Clause 62 makes provision as to the circumstances in which sums may be paid out of the Scottish Consolidated Fund and as to the purposes for which such sums may be applied.

Clause 63 provides for the Scottish Ministers to have power to borrow from the Secretary of State in certain circumstances and subject to certain conditions.

Clause 64 provides a power for the Treasury to issue to the Secretary of State out of the National Loans Fund the sums required by him to lend to the Scottish Ministers under Clause 63, and sets a limit of £500m on the sum outstanding on loan at any time. This limit may be increased by the Secretary of State by order.

Clause 65 makes provision as to the interest rate to be charged on loans made by the Scottish Executive to bodies established by enactment. It also provides that such bodies may not, under a power conferred by an Act of the

Scottish Parliament, borrow in a currency other than sterling except with the consent of the Scottish Ministers and the approval of the Treasury.

Clause 66 requires rules made by or under an Act of the Scottish Parliament to provide for a number of matters relating to financial control, accounts and audit. It also requires provision to be made for independent persons to exercise certain functions relating to these matters.

Clause 67 provides for certain outstanding sums which were lent by the Secretary of State out of the National Loans Fund to be repaid to the Scottish Ministers and paid into the Scottish Consolidated Fund, and for the Scottish Ministers to repay the sums received to the Secretary of State.

Clause 68 requires the Secretary of State to prepare for each financial year an account of the sums paid and received by him under Clauses 63, 64 and 67. This account is to be sent to the Comptroller and Auditor General, who will then examine it and report on it to Parliament.

PART IV
THE TAX-VARYING POWER

Clause 69 provides that the Scottish Parliament may pass a resolution providing for the basic rate of income tax for Scottish taxpayers to be increased or reduced so as to differ, by not more than 3%, from that determined by the UK Parliament.

Clause 70 requires a tax-varying resolution of the Scottish Parliament to relate to only a single year of assessment beginning after, but no more than 12 months after, the resolution. The clause prevents the tax-varying power from applying in relation to any year before the year 2000-01. Standing orders shall ensure that only a member of the Scottish Executive may move a motion for a tax-varying resolution.

Clause 71 defines the expression "Scottish taxpayer". A person is a Scottish taxpayer for a particular year if he is resident in the UK for tax purposes, and Scotland is the part of the UK with which he has the closest connection. Generally speaking, the latter criterion is satisfied by a person who has his principal UK home in Scotland or spends more of the year in Scotland than elsewhere in the UK. Special provision is made for members of the UK, European and Scottish Parliaments

Clause 72 makes provision to take account of changes in the UK income tax structure which would have a significant effect on the extent of the Scottish Parliament's tax-varying powers. It imposes a duty on the Treasury to indicate to the House of Commons whether an amendment of the tax-varying power is required as a consequence of such changes and, if they think an amendment is required, to make appropriate proposals.

Clause 73 applies where the basic rate of income tax has been increased for Scottish taxpayers. It requires the Inland Revenue to pay into the Scottish Consolidated Fund an amount equal to the estimated yield of the increased rate of tax to be paid by Scottish taxpayers in consequence of the Scottish Parliament's resolution.

Clause 74 applies where the basic rate of income tax has been reduced for

Scottish taxpayers. It requires a payment to be made out of the Scottish Consolidated Fund to the Inland Revenue to allow for the shortfall in the yield of income tax resulting from the reduced rate of tax to be paid by Scottish taxpayers.

Clause 75 permits the Treasury by order to modify enactments as they consider necessary or expedient to take account of the fact that the Scottish Parliament has, is to have or has exercised tax-varying powers. It also provides power by order to exclude the effect of any tax-varying resolution in relation to certain enactments and to postpone the effect of such a resolution in relation to the operation of the PAYE system.

PART V
MISCELLANEOUS AND GENERAL

Clauses 76 to 78 provide for the payment by the Parliament of salaries, pensions, gratuities and allowances in respect of MSPs and members of the Scottish Executive (including junior Scottish Ministers). The Parliament is to abate the salary of any MSP where he receives a salary as a Member of Parliament or a Member of the European Parliament.

Clause 79 requires all MSPs, members of the Scottish Executive and junior Scottish Ministers to take an oath of allegiance. Members of the Scottish Executive are also required to take an official oath.

Clause 80 provides for MSPs, members of the Scottish Executive and junior Scottish Ministers to be excused from jury service.

Clause 81 concerns Scottish representation at Westminster. It repeals the rule in the Parliamentary Constituencies Act 1986 which provides that Scotland is to have not less than 71 parliamentary constituencies. It also provides for the Boundary Commission for Scotland in its next full review of Scottish parliamentary constituencies to regard the electoral quota for Scotland as the electoral quota then current for England. No constituency including the Orkney or Shetland Islands is to include any area other than those islands

Clause 82 provides for a new Ministerial office of the Advocate General for Scotland in the Government of the United Kingdom.

Clauses 83 to 85 make provision in relation to certain statutory public bodies which are specified in subordinate legislation as cross-border public bodies. Clause 83 requires Ministers of the Crown to consult the Scottish Ministers in relation to such bodies and Clause 84 confers a power to adapt such bodies by subordinate legislation. Clause 85 enables the transfer by subordinate legislation of certain property and liabilities of such bodies where an Act of the Scottish Parliament has provided for any of its functions to be no longer exercisable in or as regards Scotland

Clause 86 requires the Parliament to make provision for the investigation of certain complaints made to its members in respect of members of the Scottish Executive, the Registrar General of Births, Deaths and Marriages for Scotland, the Keeper of the Registers of Scotland and the Keeper of the Records of Scotland.

Clause 87 provides for arrangements to be made between the Scottish Ministers or the Lord Advocate and any Minister of the Crown, government department, holder of a public office, or public body for administrative, professional or technical services to be provided by one of them for the other.

Clause 88 modifies the effect of enactments dealing with private legislation where the power to make, confirm or approve orders has been transferred to the Scottish Ministers and provides for the Parliament to provide for its own special procedure.

Clause 89 sets out the role of the First Minister in the appointment and removal of Scottish judges. A recommendation of the First Minister for their removal from office requires the approval of two thirds of the members of the Parliament.

Clause 90 provides that the Treasury may in certain circumstances require the Scottish Ministers to provide information.

Clause 91 gives effect to Schedule 6 which establishes a procedure to ensure that certain questions about the legislative competence of the Parliament, the powers of the Scottish Executive and the powers of a Minister of the Crown in relation to Scotland can be dealt with by a special procedure of the courts. Generally speaking, the Judicial Committee of the Privy Council will be the final court for deciding such questions.

Clause 92 enables provision to be made by subordinate legislation to remedy any purported provision made by or under an Act of the Scottish Parliament, or any purported exercise of functions by a member of the Scottish Executive.

Clause 93 provides for a court or tribunal to remove, limit or suspend any retrospective effect of its decision that a provision of an Act of the Scottish Parliament or subordinate legislation is not within the powers of the Parliament or person making it.

Clause 94 provides for the membership of the Judicial Committee of the Privy Council for the purpose of proceedings under the Bill and enables certain powers to be conferred on the Judicial Committee in relation to such proceedings.

Clause 95 enables subordinate legislation to make such provision as is considered necessary or expedient in consequence of any provision made by or under an Act of the Scottish Parliament.

Clause 96 enables subordinate legislation to make such modifications in any pre-commencement enactment as appear necessary or expedient in consequence of the Bill.

Clause 97 enables subordinate legislation to make such provision as is considered appropriate for enabling or otherwise facilitating the transfer to the Scottish Ministers by virtue of clause 49 and 59 of functions exercisable by a Minister of the Crown. It also provides power to enable functions of government departments to be exercised separately in or as regards Scotland.

Clause 98 enables the Secretary of State by order to provide for individuals to be treated for the purposes of any of the matters that are reserved by virtue of Head 6 (Social Security) of Schedule 5 as if they were, or were not, Scottish taxpayers; and to provide in relation to any year of assessment that, for those purposes, the basic rate in relation to the income of Scottish taxpayers shall be treated as being such rate as is specified in the order instead of the rate increased or reduced for that year by virtue of a tax-varying resolution of the Parliament passed after the beginning of the year

Clause 99 provides that Her Majesty may by Order in Council make provision for regulating fishing for salmon, trout, eels and freshwater fish in the River Tweed and the River Esk.

PART VI
SUPPLEMENTARY

Clauses 100 to 103 make general provision about the exercise of powers to make subordinate legislation under the Bill.

Clause 104 provides for certain statutory and documentary references to a Minister of the Crown to be read as, or to include, a reference to the Scottish Ministers where appropriate.

Clause 105 modifies the effect of enactments in relation to the exercise, by a member of the Scottish Executive or other persons, of certain functions to make, confirm or approve subordinate legislation.

Clause 106 provides that references in enactments to money paid into or out of the Consolidated Fund or out of money provided by Parliament cease to have effect in relation to functions, other than functions relating to reserved matters, which are exercisable in or as regards Scotland by any person other than a Minister of the Crown by virtue of Clause 52 or 53. References to sums charged on the Consolidated Fund are to be read instead as references to the Scottish Consolidated Fund

Clause 107 provides for reports which are required to be laid before Parliament to be laid instead, or in addition, before the Scottish Parliament.

Clause 108 extends the application of enactments to Crown land so that references to Ministers of the Crown and government departments include Scottish Ministers, the Lord Advocate and a member of the Scottish Executive as appropriate.

Clause 109 extends the Crown exemption from stamp duty to cover the Scottish Ministers, the Lord Advocate and the SPCB.

Clause 110 gives effect to Schedules 7 and 8 which contain modifications to enactments and repeals.

Clauses 111 to 116 deal with interpretation, expenses, commencement, extent and the short title of the Bill.

Financial effects of the Bill

This Bill will not lead to any increase in overall public expenditure funded by UK taxpayers as a whole. All expenditure under, or as a consequence of, this Bill will be contained within an overall budget for the Parliament or, in the case of costs incurred by UK Government Departments as employers as a result of the exercise of the Parliament's tax-varying power, will be contained within those Departments' programmes. The Parliament's budget will be the same as if the budget for the services under the control of the Parliament had continued to be provided under present arrangementsThe Bill makes provision for payments into the Scottish Consolidated Fund by the Secretary of State. This will merely replace the funding for that part of the services under the control of the Parliament which is currently voted by Parliament. Self-financed public expenditure in Scotland -i.e. spending not financed by UK taxpayers as a whole - may increase or decrease depending on how the Scottish Parliament elects to use its tax-varying powers and how it decides to treat self-financed spending by Scottish local authorities

The site, design and procurement method will determine the eventual cost of the Scottish Parliament building.

The additional annual running costs of the Scottish Parliament and Administration can only be estimated at this stage since the legislation allows the Parliament itself to make most decisions about its own procedures and the Scottish Executive to decide on its shape, the allocation of functions and its administrative requirements, including staff and accommodation. All running costs will be met from the Parliament's assigned budget. The costs will also depend on the decisions about the pay of MSPs which will in turn depend on advice to be submitted in due course by the Senior Salaries Review Body (SSRB)The best current estimate is that the total additional annual running costs, including salaries, pensions and allowances for MSPs, staff costs and accommodation costs will amount to between £20m and £30m.

The direct costs to the Government of establishing the mechanisms for administering the Parliament's tax varying power are estimated at around £10m. These costs will be incurred largely by the Inland Revenue. Running costs for the Government of the tax-varying power, again to be incurred by the Inland Revenue, are expected to be around £8m per annum, but may vary depending upon whether or not the Scottish Parliament chooses to vary the rate of tax. The Department of Social Security will also incur set-up costs of around £6m in changing its systems to accommodate the tax-varying power. Their annual running costs are expected to be around £1m, but that estimate may vary depending on whether the Parliament chooses to vary the rate of tax. The administration costs incurred by the Inland Revenue and Department of Social Security will be met from the Scottish Consolidated Fund once it is established, and from the Scottish Block before then. Further work is being done to refine the provisional estimates quoted above.

If the Scottish Parliament should decide to use the tax-varying power, there would be consequential effects on eligibility to income-related benefits and on liabilities for child maintenance. These would involve extra public expenditure, estimated at up to £5 million a year, which would be met from the Scottish Consolidated Fund. If the full flexibility to vary tax is used there could be costs on appropriate personal pensions of the order of £4m, including set up costs.

Elections to the Parliament, which will normally be held every 4 years, will cost around £6m. The costs of the first elections will be met from the Consolidated Fund and offsetting savings will be found from other Scottish provision. The costs of subsequent elections will be met from the Scottish Consolidated

Fund within the overall budget allocated to the Parliament.

Effect of the Bill on public service manpower
The provisional estimate is that some 200 staff will be needed to serve the Scottish Parliament. These staff will not be civil servants. The Parliament will decide on the most appropriate staffing structure.

The Scottish Executive will inherit responsibility for the staff of The Scottish Office and other Departments for which the Secretary of State for Scotland is currently responsible and the Lord Advocate's departments. The Scottish Executive is likely to need some increase in staff over and above current staff numbers to deal with new responsibilities currently falling to the Cabinet Office and HM Treasury; new responsibilities for policy development presently undertaken by Whitehall Departments; and to respond to the Scottish Parliament

The Secretary of State for Scotland will need the support of a small staff, as will the Advocate General for Scotland.

The Inland Revenue and Department for Social Security will need some additional manpower to establish and maintain the mechanisms for administering the Parliament's tax-varying power.

Business compliance cost assessment
Other than the tax-varying power, the Bill will have no significant direct impact on businesses, charities or voluntary organisations.

Collection of income tax from employees at the Scottish variable rate through the PAYE system will generate additional costs for employers in both the private and public sectors. Their setting up costs are estimated to be around £50m (which could be phased) and running costs at around £6-£15m. Costs will vary from employer to employer.

ARRANGEMENT OF CLAUSES

PART I
THE SCOTTISH PARLIAMENT
The Scottish Parliament

A
BILL
TO

Provide for the establishment of a Scottish Parliament and Administration and other changes in the government of Scotland; to provide for changes in the constitution and functions of certain public bodies; to provide for the variation of the basic rate of income tax in relation to income of Scottish taxpayers in accordance with a resolution of the Scottish Parliament; to amend the law about parliamentary constituencies in Scotland; and for connected purposes.

BE IT ENACTED by the Queen's most Excellent Majesty, by and with the advice and consent of the Lords Spiritual and Temporal, and Commons, in this present Parliament assembled, and by the authority of the same, as follows:-

PART I
THE SCOTTISH PARLIAMENT
The Scottish Parliament

The Scottish Parliament.

1.-(1) There shall be a Scottish Parliament.

(2) One member of the Parliament shall be returned for each constituency (under the simple majority system) at an election held in the constituency.

(3) Members of the Parliament for each region shall be returned at a general election under the additional member system of proportional representation provided for in this Part and vacancies among such members shall be filled in accordance with this Part.

(4) The validity of any proceedings of the Parliament is not affected by any vacancy in its membership.

(5) Schedule 1 (which makes provision for the constituencies and regions for the purposes of this Act and the number of regional members) shall have effect.

General elections

Ordinary general elections.

2.-(1) The poll at the first ordinary general election for membership of the Parliament shall be held on a day appointed by order made by the Secretary of State.

(2) The poll at subsequent ordinary general elections shall be held on the first Thursday in May in the fourth calendar year following that in which the previous ordinary general election was held, unless the day of the poll is determined by a proclamation under subsection (5).

(3) If the poll is to be held on the first Thursday in May, the Parliament-

(a) is dissolved by virtue of this section at the beginning of the minimum period which ends with that day, and

(b) shall meet within the period of seven days beginning immediately after the day of the poll.

(4) In subsection (3), "the minimum period" means the period determined

in accordance with an order under section 11(1).

(5) If the Presiding Officer proposes a day for the holding of the poll which is not more than one month earlier, nor more than one month later, than the first Thursday in May, Her Majesty may by proclamation under the Scottish Seal-

(a) dissolve the Parliament,

(b) require the poll at the election to be held on the day proposed, and

(c) specify a day, within the period of seven days beginning immediately after the day of the poll, on which the Parliament is to meet.

(6) In this Act "the Scottish Seal" means Her Majesty's Seal appointed by the Treaty of Union to be kept and used in Scotland in place of the Great Seal of Scotland.

Extraordinary general elections.

3.-(1) The Presiding Officer shall propose a day for the holding of a poll if-

(a) the Parliament resolves that it should be dissolved and, if the resolution is passed on a division, the number of members voting in favour of it is not less than two-thirds of the total number of seats for members of the Parliament, or

(b) any period during which the Parliament is required under section 43 to nominate one of its members for appointment as First Minister ends without such a nomination being made.

(2) If the Presiding Officer makes such a proposal, Her Majesty may by proclamation under the Scottish Seal-

(a) dissolve the Parliament and require an extraordinary general election to be held,

(b) require the poll at the election to be held on the day proposed, and

(c) specify a day, within the period of seven days beginning immediately after the day of the poll, on which the Parliament is to meet.

(3) If a poll is held under this section within the period of six months ending with the day on which the poll at the next ordinary general election would be held (disregarding section 2(5)), that ordinary general election shall not be held.

(4) Subsection (3) does not affect the year in which the subsequent ordinary general election is to be held.

Candidates.

4.-(1) At a general election, the candidates may stand for return as constituency members or regional members.

(2) A person may not be a candidate to be a constituency member for more than one constituency.

(3) The candidates to be regional members shall be those included in a list submitted under subsection (4) or individual candidates.

(4) Any registered political party may submit to the regional returning officer a list of candidates to be regional members for a particular region (referred to in this Act, in relation to the region, as the party's "regional list").

(5) Not more than twelve persons may be included in the list.

(6) A registered political party's regional list must not include a person-

(a) who is included in any other list submitted under subsection (4) for the region or any list submitted under that subsection for another region,

(b) who is an individual candidate to be a regional member for the region or another region,

(c) who is a candidate to be a constituency member for a constituency not included in the region, or

(d) who is a candidate to be a constituency member for a constituency included in the region but is not a candidate of that party.

(7) A person may not be an individual candidate to be a regional member for a particular region if he is-

(a) included in a list submitted under subsection (4) for the region or another region,

(b) an individual candidate to be a regional member for another region,

(c) a candidate to be a constituency member for a constituency not included in the region, or

(d) a candidate of any registered political party to be a constituency member for a constituency included in the region.

(8) In this Act, "registered political party" means a political party registered under any enactment providing for the registration of political parties.

Poll for regional members.

5.-(1) This section and sections 6 and 7 are about the return of regional members at a general election.

(2) In each of the constituencies for the Parliament, a poll shall be held at which each person entitled to vote as elector may give a vote (referred to in this Act as a "regional vote") for-

(a) a registered political party which has submitted a regional list, or

(b) an individual candidate to be a regional member for the region.

(3) The right conferred on a person by subsection (2) is in addition to any right the person may have to vote in any poll for the return of a constituency member.

Calculation of regional figures.

6.-(1) The persons who are to be returned as constituency members for constituencies included in the region must be determined before the persons who are to be returned as the regional members for the region.

(2) For each registered political party which has submitted a regional list, the regional figure for the purposes of section 7 is-

(a) the total number of regional votes given for the party in all the constituencies included in the region, divided by

(b) the aggregate of one plus the number of candidates of the party returned as constituency members for any of those constituencies.

(3) Each time a seat is allocated to the party under section 7, that figure shall be recalculated by increasing (or further increasing) the aggregate in sub-

section (2)(b) by one.

(4) For each individual candidate to be a regional member for the region, the regional figure for the purposes of section 7 is the total number of regional votes given for him in all the constituencies included in the region.

Allocation of seats to regional members.

7.-(1) The first regional member seat shall be allocated to the registered political party or individual candidate with the highest regional figure.

(2) The second and subsequent regional member seats shall be allocated to the registered political party or individual candidate with the highest regional figure, after any recalculation required by section 6(3) has been carried out.

(3) An individual candidate already returned as a constituency or regional member shall be disregarded.

(4) Seats for the region which are allocated to a registered political party shall be filled by the persons in the party's regional list in the order in which they appear in the list, except that any candidate already returned as a constituency member shall be disregarded.

(5) Once a party's regional list has been exhausted (by the return of persons included in it as constituency members or by the previous application of subsection (1) or (2)) the party shall be disregarded.

(6) If (on the application of subsection (1) or any application of subsection (2)) the highest regional figure is the regional figure of two or more parties or individual candidates, the subsection shall apply to each of them.

Vacancies

Constituency vacancies.

8.-(1) Where the seat of a constituency member is vacant, an election shall be held to fill the vacancy (subject to subsection (4)).

(2) The date of the poll shall be fixed by the Presiding Officer.

(3) The date shall fall within the period of three months-

(a) beginning with the occurrence of the vacancy, or

(b) if the vacancy does not come to the notice of the Presiding Officer within the period of one month beginning with its occurrence, beginning when it does come to his notice.

(4) The election shall not be held if the latest date for holding the poll would fall within the period of three months ending with the day on which the poll at the next ordinary general election would be held (disregarding section 2(5)).

(5) For the purposes of this section, the date on which a vacancy is to be treated as occurring shall be determined under standing orders.

(6) A person may not be a candidate at such an election if he is a member of the Parliament or a candidate in another election to fill a vacancy.

Regional vacancies.

9.-(1) This section applies where the seat of a regional member is vacant.

(2) If the regional member was returned as an individual candidate, or the

vacancy is not filled in accordance with the following provisions, the seat shall remain vacant until the next general election.

(3) If the regional member was returned (under section 7 or this section) from a registered political party's regional list, the regional returning officer shall notify the Presiding Officer of the name of the person who is to fill the vacancy.

(4) He must be a person who-

(a) was included in that list,

(b) is not already a member of the Parliament, and

(c) is willing to serve as a regional member for the region.

(5) Where more than one person satisfies the conditions in subsection (4), the regional returning officer shall notify the name of whichever of them was higher, or highest, in the list.

(6) Where a person's name has been notified under subsection (3), this Act shall apply as if he had been declared to be returned as a regional member for the region on the day on which notification of his name was received by the Presiding Officer.

(7) For the purposes of this section, the date on which a vacancy is to be treated as occurring shall be determined under standing orders.

Franchise and conduct of elections

Electors.

10.-(1) The persons entitled to vote as electors at an election for membership of the Parliament held in any constituency are those who on the day of the poll-

(a) would be entitled to vote as electors at a local government election in an electoral area falling wholly or partly within the constituency, and

(b) are registered in the register of local government electors at an address within the constituency.

(2) A person is not entitled to vote as elector in any constituency-

(a) more than once at a poll for the return of a constituency member, or

(b) more than once at a poll for the return of regional members,

or to vote as elector in more than one constituency at a general election.

Power to make provision about elections.

11.-(1) The Secretary of State may by order make provision as to-

(a) the conduct of elections for membership of the Parliament,

(b) the questioning of such an election and the consequences of irregularities, and

(c) the return of members of the Parliament otherwise than at an election.

(2) The provision that may be made under subsection (1)(a) includes, in particular, provision-

(a) about the registration of electors,

(b) for disregarding alterations in a register of electors,

(c) about the limitation of the election expenses of candidates and registered political parties,

(d) for the combination of polls at elections for membership of the Parliament with polls at other elections, and

    (e) for modifying the application of section 6(1) where an election for the return of a constituency member is countermanded or abandoned.

(3) An order under subsection (1) may-

    (a) apply, with or without modifications or exceptions, any provision made by or under the Representation of the People Acts or the European Parliamentary Elections Act 1978 or by any other enactment relating to parliamentary elections, European Parliamentary elections or local government elections,

    (b) modify any form contained in, or in regulations or rules made under, the Representation of the People Acts so far as may be necessary to enable it to be used both for the original purpose and in relation to elections for membership of the Parliament, and

    (c) so far as may be necessary in consequence of any provision made by this Act or an order under subsection (1), modify any provision made by any enactment relating to the registration of parliamentary electors or local government electors.

(4) The return of a member of the Parliament at an election may be questioned only under Part III of the Representation of the People Act 1983 as applied by an order under subsection (1).

(5) For the purposes of this Act, the regional returning officer for any region is the person designated as such in accordance with an order made by the Secretary of State under this subsection.

Duration of membership

Term of office of members.

12. The term of office of a member of the Parliament begins on the day on which the member is declared to be returned and ends with the dissolution of the Parliament.

Resignation of members.

13. A member of the Parliament may at any time resign his seat by giving notice in writing to the Presiding Officer.

Disqualification

Disqualification from membership of the Parliament.

14.-(1) A person is disqualified from being a member of the Parliament (subject to section 15) if-

    (a) he is disqualified from being a member of the House of Commons under paragraphs (a) to (e) of section 1(1) of the House of Commons Disqualification Act 1975 (judges, civil servants, members of the armed forces, members of police forces and members of foreign legislatures),

    (b) he is disqualified otherwise than under that Act (either generally or in relation to a particular parliamentary constituency) from being a member of the House of Commons or from sitting and voting in it,

    (c) he is a Lord of Appeal in Ordinary, or

(d) he holds an office of a description specified in an Order in Council made under this subsection.

(2) A person who holds an office of a description specified in an Order in Council made under this subsection is disqualified from being a member of the Parliament for any constituency or region of a description specified in the Order in relation to that office.

Exceptions and relief from disqualification.

15.-(1) A person is not disqualified from being a member of the Parliament merely because-

(a) he is a peer (whether of the United Kingdom, Great Britain, England or Scotland), or

(b) he has been ordained or is a minister of any religious denomination.

(2) A citizen of the European Union who is resident in the United Kingdom is not disqualified from being a member of the Parliament merely because of section 3 of the Act of Settlement (disqualification of persons born outside the United Kingdom other than Commonwealth citizens and citizens of the Republic of Ireland).

(3) Subsection (4) applies where a person was, or is alleged to have been, disqualified from being a member of the Parliament (either generally or in relation to a particular constituency or region) on any ground other than one falling within section 14(1)(b).

(4) The Parliament may resolve to disregard any disqualification incurred by that person on the ground in question if it considers that-

(a) the ground has been removed, and

(b) it is proper to disregard any disqualification so incurred.

(5) A resolution under this section shall not-

(a) affect any proceedings under Part III of the Representation of the People Act 1983 as applied by an order under section 11, or

(b) enable the Parliament to disregard any disqualification which has been established in such proceedings or in proceedings under section 17.

Effect of disqualification.

16.-(1) If a person who is disqualified from being a member of the Parliament or from being a member for a particular constituency or region is returned as a member of the Parliament or (as the case may be) as a member for the constituency or region, his return shall be void and his seat vacant.

(2) If a member of the Parliament becomes disqualified from being a member of the Parliament or from being a member for the particular constituency or region for which he is sitting, he shall cease to be a member of the Parliament (so that his seat is vacant).

(3) Subsections (1) and (2) have effect subject to any resolution of the Parliament under section 15.

(4) The validity of any proceedings of the Parliament is not affected by the disqualification of any person from being a member of the Parliament or from being a member for the constituency or region for which he purports to sit.

Judicial proceedings as to disqualification.

17.-(1) Any person who claims that a person purporting to be a member of the Parliament is disqualified or has been disqualified at any time since being returned may apply to the Court of Session for a declarator to that effect.

(2) An application in respect of any person may be made whether the grounds on which it is made are alleged to have subsisted when the person was returned or to have arisen subsequently.

(3) No declarator shall be made-

(a) on grounds which subsisted when the person was returned, if an election petition is pending or has been tried in which the disqualification on those grounds of the person concerned is or was in issue, or

(b) on any ground, if a resolution under section 15 requires that any disqualification incurred on that ground by the person concerned is to be disregarded.

(4) The person in respect of whom an application is made shall be the defender.

(5) The applicant shall give such caution for the expenses of the proceedings as the Court of Session may direct; but any such caution shall not exceed £5,000 or such other sum as the Scottish Ministers may by order specify.

(6) The decision of the court on an application under this section shall be final.

(7) In this section "disqualified" means disqualified from being a member of the Parliament or from being a member for the constituency or region for which the person concerned purports to sit.

Presiding Officer and administration

Presiding Officer.

18.-(1) The Parliament shall, at its first meeting following a general election, elect from among its members a Presiding Officer and two deputies.

(2) A person elected Presiding Officer or deputy shall hold office until the conclusion of the next election for Presiding Officer under subsection (1), unless he previously resigns, ceases to be a member of the Parliament otherwise than by virtue of a dissolution or is removed from office by resolution of the Parliament.

(3) If the Presiding Officer or a deputy ceases to hold office before the Parliament is dissolved, the Parliament shall elect another from among its members to fill his place.

(4) Standing orders shall include provision for the exercise of the Presiding Officer's functions by a member of the Parliament if the office of Presiding Officer is vacant or the Presiding Officer is for any reason unable to act.

(5) The Presiding Officer may (subject to standing orders) authorise any deputy to exercise functions on his behalf.

(6) Standing orders may include provision as to the participation (including voting) of the Presiding Officer and deputies in the proceedings of the Parliament.

Clerk of the Parliament.

19.-(1) There shall be a Clerk of the Parliament.

(2) The Clerk shall be appointed by the Scottish Parliamentary Corporate Body (established under section 20).

(3) The Clerk's functions may be exercised by any Assistant Clerk if the office of Clerk is vacant or the Clerk is for any reason unable to act.

(4) The Clerk may authorise any Assistant Clerk or other member of the staff of the Parliament to exercise functions on his behalf.

Scottish Parliamentary Corporate Body.

20.-(1) There shall be a body corporate to be known as "The Scottish Parliamentary Corporate Body" (referred to in this Act as the Parliamentary corporation) to perform the statutory functions conferred on the corporation and any functions conferred on the corporation by resolution of the Parliament.

(2) The members of the corporation shall be-

(a) the Presiding Officer, and

(b) four members of the Parliament appointed in accordance with standing orders.

(3) The corporation shall provide the Parliament, or ensure that the Parliament is provided, with the property, staff and services required for the Parliament's purposes.

(4) The Parliament may give special or general directions to the corporation for the purpose of or in connection with the exercise of the corporation's functions.

(5) Proceedings by or against the Parliament shall be instituted by or (as the case may be) against the corporation on behalf of the Parliament.

(6) Any property or liabilities acquired or incurred in relation to matters within the general responsibility of the corporation to which (apart from this subsection) the Parliament would be entitled or subject shall be treated for all purposes as property or (as the case may be) liabilities of the corporation.

(7) Any expenses of the corporation shall be payable out of the Scottish Consolidated Fund.

(8) Any sums received by the corporation shall be paid into that Fund, subject to any provision made by virtue of an Act of the Scottish Parliament for the disposal of or accounting for such sums.

(9) Schedule 2 (which makes further provision about the corporation) shall have effect.

Proceedings etc.

Standing orders.

21.-(1) The proceedings of the Parliament shall be regulated by standing orders.

(2) Schedule 3 (which makes provision as to how certain matters are to be dealt with by standing orders) shall have effect.

Members' interests.

22.-(1) Standing orders shall include provision for a register of interests of members of the Parliament, and for-

(a) registrable interests (as defined in the standing orders) to be registered in it, and

(b) the register to be published and made available for public inspection.

(2) Standing orders shall include provision requiring that any member of the Parliament who has-

(a) a financial interest (as defined in the standing orders) in any matter, or

(b) any other interest, or an interest of any other kind, specified in the standing orders in any matter,

declares that interest before taking part in any proceedings of the Parliament relating to that matter.

(3) Standing orders made in pursuance of subsection (1) or (2) may include provision for preventing or restricting the participation in proceedings of the Parliament of a member with a registrable interest, or an interest mentioned in subsection (2), in a matter to which the proceedings relate.

(4) Standing orders shall include provision prohibiting a member of the Parliament from-

(a) advocating or initiating any cause or matter on behalf of any person, by any means specified in the standing orders, in consideration of any payment or benefit in kind of a description so specified, or

(b) urging, in consideration of any such payment or benefit in kind, any other member of the Parliament to advocate or initiate any cause or matter on behalf of any person by any such means.

(5) Standing orders may include provision for excluding from proceedings of the Parliament any member who fails to comply with, or contravenes, any provision made in pursuance of subsections (1) to (4).

(6) Any member of the Parliament who-

(a) takes part in any proceedings of the Parliament without having complied with, or in contravention of, any provision made in pursuance of subsections (1) to (3), or

(b) contravenes any provision made in pursuance of subsection (4),

is guilty of an offence.

(7) A person guilty of an offence under subsection (6) is liable on summary conviction to a fine not exceeding level 5 on the standard scale.

(8) In this section, references to members of the Parliament include references to the Lord Advocate and the Solicitor General for Scotland, whether or not they are such members.

Power to call for witnesses and documents.

23.-(1) The Parliament may require any person-

(a) to attend its proceedings for the purpose of giving evidence, or

(b) to produce documents in his custody or under his control,

relating to any of the matters mentioned in subsection (2).

(2) Those matters are-

(a) devolved matters concerning Scotland,

(b) matters in relation to which statutory functions are exercisable by the Scottish Ministers.

(3) The power in subsection (1) is not exercisable in relation to-

(a) a person outside Scotland,

(b) a Minister of the Crown, or

(c) a person in Crown employment, within the meaning of section 191(3) of the Employment Rights Act 1996,

unless he discharges functions relating to matters within subsection (2).

(4) That power is not exercisable in relation to-

(a) a person discharging functions of any body whose functions relate only to reserved matters, or

(b) a judge of any court or a member of any tribunal which exercises the judicial power of the State.

(5) That power may be exercised by a committee or sub-committee of the Parliament only if the committee or sub-committee is expressly authorised to do so (whether by standing orders or otherwise).

(6) The Clerk shall give the person in question notice in writing specifying-

(a) the time and place at which the person is to attend and the particular matters relating to which he is required to give evidence, or

(b) the documents, or types of documents, which he is to produce, the date by which he is to produce them and the particular matters to which they are to relate.

(7) Such notice shall be given-

(a) in the case of an individual, by sending it, by registered post or the recorded delivery service, addressed to him at his usual or last known address or, where he has given an address for service, at that address,

(b) in any other case, by sending it, by registered post or the recorded delivery service, addressed to the person at the person's registered or principal office.

(8) A person is not obliged under this section to answer any question or produce any document which he would be entitled to refuse to answer or produce in proceedings in a court in Scotland.

Witnesses and documents: offences.

24.-(1) Any person to whom a notice under section 23(6) has been given who-

(a) refuses, or fails without reasonable excuse, to attend proceedings as required by the notice,

(b) refuses, when attending proceedings as required by the notice, to answer any question relating to the matters specified in the notice,

(c) deliberately alters, suppresses, conceals or destroys any document which he is required to produce by the notice, or

(d) refuses, or fails without reasonable excuse, to produce any such document,

is guilty of an offence.

(2) Subsection (1) is subject to sections 23(8) and 26(3).

(3) A person guilty of an offence under this section is liable on summary conviction to a fine not exceeding level 5 on the standard scale or to imprisonment for a period not exceeding three months.

(4) Where an offence under this section which has been committed by a body corporate is proved to have been committed with the consent or connivance of, or to be attributable to any neglect on the part of-

    (a) a director, manager, secretary or other similar officer of the body corporate, or

    (b) any person who was purporting to act in any such capacity,

he, as well as the body corporate, is guilty of that offence and liable to be proceeded against accordingly.

Witnesses and documents: general.

25.-(1) The Presiding Officer or such other person as may be authorised by standing orders may-

    (a) administer an oath to any person giving evidence in proceedings of the Parliament, and

    (b) require him to take the oath.

(2) Any person who refuses to take an oath when required to do so under subsection (1)(b) is guilty of an offence.

(3) Subsection (3) of section 24 applies to an offence under subsection (2) as it applies to an offence under that section.

(4) Standing orders may provide for the payment of allowances and expenses to persons-

    (a) attending proceedings of the Parliament to give evidence, or

    (b) producing documents which they have been required or requested to produce,

whether or not in pursuance of a notice under section 23(6).

(5) For the purposes of sections 23 and 24 and this section, a person shall be taken to comply with a requirement to produce a document if he produces a copy of, or an extract of the relevant part of, the document.

Participation of the Scottish Law Officers.

26.-(1) If the Lord Advocate or the Solicitor General for Scotland is not a member of the Parliament-

    (a) he may participate in the proceedings of the Parliament to the extent permitted by standing orders, but may not vote, and

    (b) standing orders may in other respects provide that they are to apply to him as if he were such a member.

(2) Subsection (1) is without prejudice to section 22.

(3) The Lord Advocate or the Solicitor General for Scotland may, in any proceedings of the Parliament, decline to answer any question or produce any document relating to the operation of the system of criminal prosecution in any particular case if he considers that answering the question or producing the document-

    (a) might prejudice criminal proceedings in that case, or

(b) would otherwise be contrary to the public interest.

Legislation

Acts of the Scottish Parliament.

27.-(1) Subject to section 28, the Parliament may make laws, to be known as Acts of the Scottish Parliament.

(2) Proposed Acts of the Scottish Parliament shall be known as Bills; and a Bill shall become an Act of the Scottish Parliament when it has been passed by the Parliament and has received Royal Assent.

(3) A Bill receives Royal Assent at the beginning of the day on which Letters Patent under the Scottish Seal signed with Her Majesty's own hand signifying Her Assent are recorded in the Register of the Great Seal.

(4) The date of Royal Assent shall be written on the Act of the Scottish Parliament by the Clerk, and shall form part of the Act.

(5) The validity of any proceedings leading to the enactment of an Act of the Scottish Parliament shall not be called into question in any legal proceedings.

(6) Every Act of the Scottish Parliament shall be judicially noticed.

(7) This section does not affect the power of the Parliament of the United Kingdom to make laws for Scotland.

Legislative competence.

28.-(1) An Act of the Scottish Parliament is not law so far as any provision of the Act is outside the legislative competence of the Parliament.

(2) A provision is outside that competence so far as any of the following paragraphs apply-

   (a) it would form part of the law of a country or territory other than Scotland,

   (b) its effect would be to modify any provision of this Act,

   (c) it relates to reserved matters,

   (d) it is incompatible with any of the Convention rights or with Community law, or

   (e) it would remove the Lord Advocate from his position as head of the systems of criminal prosecution and investigation of deaths in Scotland.

(3) Subsection (2)(b) is subject to the provisions of Schedule 4.

(4) A provision is not outside that competence by reason of subsection (2)(c) merely because it makes modifications of Scots private law, or Scots criminal law, as it applies to reserved matters if the provision does so in such a way that the law in question applies consistently to devolved and reserved matters.

(5) A provision is not outside that competence by reason of subsection (2)(c) merely because it makes modifications of any enactment as it applies to reserved matters which are incidental to or consequential on provision made (whether by the Act in question or another enactment) for purposes relating to any devolved matters.

(6) A provision does not relate to reserved matters merely because it makes

provision for purposes relating to devolved matters which incidentally affects reserved matters unless it makes modifications of Scots private law or Scots criminal law, or of any enactment, as it applies to reserved matters.

(7) A provision is not outside that competence merely because it provides for rights or liabilities to which the Parliament is entitled or subject to be treated for any purposes as rights or (as the case may be) liabilities of the Parliamentary corporation or the Scottish Ministers.

(8) An Act of the Scottish Parliament may modify a provision made by or under an Act of Parliament, whenever passed or made, if the modification is otherwise within its legislative competence.

(9) Any provision of an Act of the Scottish Parliament is to be read, so far as possible, so as to be within the legislative competence of the Parliament and is to have effect accordingly.

(10) References in this section to modification of the law include re-enactment and codification.

Reserved matters.

29.-(1) Schedule 5 (which-

(a) defines reserved matters, and

(b) otherwise supplements section 28),

shall have effect.

(2) Subordinate legislation may make any modifications of that Schedule which the person making the legislation considers necessary or expedient.

(3) The subordinate legislation may modify any enactment (including any other provision of this Act), instrument or other document.

(4) In this Act "devolved matters" means matters other than reserved matters.

Scrutiny of Bills by the Scottish Executive.

30.-(1) A member of the Scottish Executive in charge of a Bill shall, on or before introduction of the Bill in the Parliament, make a statement to the effect that in his view an Act of the Scottish Parliament containing the same provisions as those in the Bill would be within the legislative competence of the Parliament.

(2) The statement shall be in writing and shall be published in such manner as the member of the Scottish Executive making the statement considers appropriate.

Scrutiny of Bills by the Presiding Officer.

31.-(1) Standing orders shall, subject to subsection (2), ensure that a Bill is not introduced in the Parliament if the Presiding Officer decides that the Bill or any provision of the Bill would not be within the legislative competence of the Parliament.

(2) Standing orders may provide for the Parliament to overrule any decision of the Presiding Officer of the kind mentioned in subsection (1) and for the Bill to be proceeded with accordingly.

(3) Standing orders shall ensure that it is the Presiding Officer who submits Bills for Royal Assent.

(4) Standing orders shall ensure that the Presiding Officer does not submit a Bill for Royal Assent at any time when-

    (a) the Advocate General, the Lord Advocate or the Attorney General is entitled to make a reference in relation to the Bill under section 32,

    (b) any such reference has been made but has not been decided or otherwise disposed of by the Judicial Committee, or

    (c) an order may be made in relation to the Bill under section 33.

(5) Standing orders shall ensure that, if the Judicial Committee have decided that a Bill or any provision of a Bill would not be within the legislative competence of the Parliament, the Presiding Officer does not submit the Bill in its unamended form for Royal Assent.

(6) In this Act-

"Advocate General" means the Advocate General for Scotland, and

"Judicial Committee" means the Judicial Committee of the Privy Council.

Scrutiny of Bills by the Judicial Committee.

32.-(1) The Advocate General, the Lord Advocate or the Attorney General may refer the question of whether a Bill or any provision of a Bill would be within the legislative competence of the Parliament to the Judicial Committee for decision.

(2) Subject to subsection (3), he may make a reference in relation to a Bill at any time during-

    (a) the period of four weeks beginning with the passing of the Bill, and

    (b) any period of four weeks beginning with any subsequent approval of the Bill in accordance with standing orders made by virtue of section 34(4).

(3) He shall not make a reference in relation to a Bill if he has notified the Presiding Officer that he does not intend to make a reference in relation to the Bill, unless the Bill has been approved as mentioned in subsection (2)(b) since the notification.

Power to intervene in certain cases.

33.-(1) If a Bill contains provisions-

    (a) which the Secretary of State has reasonable grounds to believe would be incompatible with any international obligations, or

    (b) which are within the legislative competence of the Parliament by virtue of subsection (4) (as it applies in relation to Scots private law) or subsection (5) of section 28 but which the Secretary of State has reasonable grounds to believe would have an adverse effect on the operation of an enactment as it applies to reserved matters,

he may make an order prohibiting the Presiding Officer from submitting the Bill for Royal Assent.

(2) The order must identify the Bill and the provisions in question and state the reasons for making the order.

(3) The order may be made at any time during-

(a) the period of four weeks beginning with the passing of the Bill, and

(b) any period of four weeks beginning with any subsequent approval of the Bill in accordance with standing orders made by virtue of section 34(4).

(4) The Secretary of State shall not make an order in relation to a Bill if he has notified the Presiding Officer that he does not intend to do so, unless the Bill has been approved as mentioned in subsection (3)(b) since the notification.

(5) An order in force under this section at a time when such approval is given shall cease to have effect.

Stages of Bills.

34.-(1) Standing orders shall include provision-

(a) for general debate on a Bill with an opportunity for members to vote on its general principles,

(b) for the consideration of, and an opportunity for members to vote on, the details of a Bill, and

(c) for a final stage at which a Bill can be passed or rejected.

(2) Standing orders may, in relation to different types of Bill, modify provisions made in pursuance of subsection (1).

(3) Standing orders shall provide for an opportunity for the reconsideration of a Bill after its passing if (and only if)-

(a) the Judicial Committee decide that the Bill or any provision of it would not be within the legislative competence of the Parliament, or

(b) an order is made in relation to the Bill under section 33.

(4) Standing orders shall, in particular, ensure that any Bill amended on reconsideration is subject to a final stage at which it can be approved or rejected.

(5) References in subsection (3), section 27(2) and 36(1)(a) to the passing of a Bill shall, in the case of a Bill which has been amended on reconsideration, be read as references to the approval of the Bill.

Miscellaneous

Acts of Union.

35. The Union with Scotland Act 1706 and the Union with England Act 1707 have effect subject to this Act.

Letters Patent and proclamations.

36.-(1) The Keeper of the Registers of Scotland shall record in the Register of the Great Seal-

(a) all Letters Patent signed with Her Majesty's own hand signifying Her Assent to a Bill passed by the Parliament, and

(b) all royal proclamations under sections 2(5) and 3(2),

which have passed under the Scottish Seal.

(2) On recording such Letters Patent he shall intimate the date of recording

to the Clerk.

(3) Her Majesty may by Order in Council make provision as to-

(a) the form and manner of preparation, and

(b) the publication,

of such Letters Patent and proclamations.

(4) If the First Minister so directs, impressions with the same device as the Scottish Seal shall be taken in such manner, of such size and on such material as is specified in the direction.

(5) Each such impression-

(a) shall be known as a Wafer Scottish Seal, and

(b) shall be kept in accordance with directions of the First Minister.

(6) If a Wafer Scottish Seal has been applied to Letters Patent or a proclamation mentioned in subsection (1), the document has the same validity as if it had passed under the Scottish Seal.

Defamatory statements.

37.-(1) For the purposes of the law of defamation-

(a) any statement made in proceedings of the Parliament, and

(b) the publication under the authority of the Parliament of any statement,

shall be absolutely privileged.

(2) In subsection (1), "statement" has the same meaning as in the Defamation Act 1996.

Contempt of court.

38.-(1) The strict liability rule shall not apply in relation to any publication-

(a) made in proceedings of the Parliament in relation to a Bill or subordinate legislation, or

(b) to the extent that it consists of a report of such proceedings.

(2) In subsection (1), "the strict liability rule" and "publication" have the same meanings as in the Contempt of Court Act 1981.

Corrupt practices.

39. The Parliament shall be a public body for the purposes of the Prevention of Corruption Acts 1889 to 1916.

Calculating time for meeting of the Parliament.

40. In calculating any period of days for the purposes of section 2(3)(b) or (5)(c) or section 3(2)(c), Saturday, Sunday, Christmas Eve, Christmas Day, Good Friday, a bank holiday in Scotland or a day appointed for public thanksgiving or mourning shall be disregarded.

PART II
THE SCOTTISH ADMINISTRATION
The Scottish Administration

The Scottish Executive.

41.-(1) There shall be a Scottish Executive, whose members shall be-

(a) the First Minister,

(b) such Ministers as the First Minister may appoint under section 44, and

(c) the Lord Advocate and the Solicitor General for Scotland.

(2) The members of the Scottish Executive are referred to collectively as the Scottish Ministers.

The First Minister.

42.-(1) The First Minister shall be appointed by Her Majesty from among the members of the Parliament and shall hold office at Her Majesty's pleasure.

(2) The First Minister may at any time tender his resignation to Her Majesty, and shall do so if the Parliament resolves that the Scottish Executive no longer enjoys the confidence of the Parliament.

(3) The First Minister shall cease to hold office if a person is appointed in his place.

(4) If the office of First Minister is vacant or he is for any reason unable to act, the functions exercisable by him shall be exercisable by a person designated by the Presiding Officer.

(5) A person shall be so designated only if-

(a) he is a member of the Parliament, or

(b) if the Parliament has been dissolved, he is a person who ceased to be a member by virtue of the dissolution.

(6) Functions exercisable by a person by virtue of subsection (5)(a) shall continue to be exercisable by him even if the Parliament is dissolved.

(7) The First Minister shall be the Keeper of the Scottish Seal.

Choice of the First Minister.

43.-(1) If one of the following events occurs, the Parliament shall within the period allowed nominate one of its members for appointment as First Minister.

(2) The events are-

(a) the holding of a poll at a general election,

(b) the First Minister tendering his resignation to Her Majesty,

(c) the office of First Minister becoming vacant (otherwise than in consequence of his so tendering his resignation), or

(d) the First Minister ceasing to be a member of the Parliament otherwise than by virtue of a dissolution.

(3) The period allowed is the period of 28 days which begins with the day on which the event in question occurs; but-

(a) if another of those events occurs within the period allowed, that period shall be extended (subject to paragraph (b)) so that it ends with the period of 28 days beginning with the day on which that other event occurred, and

(b) the period shall end if the Parliament passes a resolution under section

3(1)(a) or when Her Majesty appoints a person as First Minister.

(4) The Presiding Officer shall recommend to Her Majesty the appointment of any member of the Parliament who is nominated by the Parliament under this section.

Ministers.

44.-(1) The First Minister may, with the approval of Her Majesty, appoint Ministers from among the members of the Parliament.

(2) The First Minister shall not seek Her Majesty's approval for any appointment under this section without the agreement of the Parliament.

(3) A Minister appointed under this section-

(a) shall hold office at Her Majesty's pleasure,

(b) may be removed from office by the First Minister,

(c) may at any time resign and shall do so if the Parliament resolves that the Scottish Executive no longer enjoys the confidence of the Parliament,

(d) if he resigns, shall cease to hold office immediately, and

(e) shall cease to hold office if he ceases to be a member of the Parliament otherwise than by virtue of a dissolution.

The Scottish Law Officers.

45.-(1) It is for the First Minister to recommend to Her Majesty the appointment or removal of a person as Lord Advocate or Solicitor General for Scotland; but he shall not do so without the agreement of the Parliament.

(2) Any decision of the Lord Advocate in his capacity as head of the systems of criminal prosecution and investigation of deaths in Scotland shall continue to be taken by him independently of any other person.

(3) In Schedule 2 to the House of Commons Disqualification Act 1975 (Ministerial offices) and Part III of Schedule 1 to the Ministerial and other Salaries Act 1975 (salaries of the Law Officers), the entries for the Lord Advocate and the Solicitor General for Scotland are omitted.

Junior Scottish Ministers.

46.-(1) The First Minister may, with the approval of Her Majesty, appoint persons from among the members of the Parliament to assist the Scottish Ministers in the exercise of their functions.

(2) They shall be known as junior Scottish Ministers.

(3) A junior Scottish Minister-

(a) shall hold office at Her Majesty's pleasure,

(b) may be removed from office by the First Minister,

(c) may at any time resign and shall do so if the Parliament resolves that the Scottish Executive no longer enjoys the confidence of the Parliament,

(d) if he resigns, shall cease to hold office immediately, and

(e) shall cease to hold office if he ceases to be a member of the Parliament otherwise than by virtue of a dissolution.

The Civil Service.

47.-(1) The Scottish Ministers may appoint such staff as they consider appropriate.

(2) Service as-

(a) the Registrar General of Births, Deaths and Marriages for Scotland, the Keeper of the Registers of Scotland or the Keeper of the Records of Scotland, or

(b) a member of the staff of the Scottish Ministers, the Lord Advocate, or any person mentioned in paragraph (a),

shall be service in the Home Civil Service.

(3) Subsection (1) and the other enactments conferring power to appoint such persons shall have effect subject to any provision made in relation to the Home Civil Service by or under any Order in Council.

(4) Any Civil Service management function shall be exercisable by the Minister for the Civil Service in relation to the persons mentioned in subsection (2) as it is exercisable in relation to other members of the Home Civil Service; and, accordingly, section 1 of the Civil Service (Management Functions) Act 1992 (delegation of functions by Ministers) shall apply to any such function as extended by this section.

(5) Any salary or allowances payable to or in respect of the persons mentioned in subsection (2) (including contributions to any pension scheme) shall be payable out of the Scottish Consolidated Fund.

(6) The Scottish Ministers shall make payments to the Minister for the Civil Service, at such times as he may determine, of such amounts as he may determine in respect of-

(a) the provision of pensions, allowances or gratuities by virtue of section 1 of the Superannuation Act 1972 to or in respect of persons who are or have been in such service as is mentioned in subsection (2), and

(b) any expenses to be incurred in administering those pensions, allowances or gratuities.

(7) Amounts required for payments under subsection (6) shall be charged on the Fund.

(8) In this section-

"Civil Service management function" means any function to which section 1 of that Act applies and which is vested in the Minister for the Civil Service, and

"the Home Civil Service" means Her Majesty's Home Civil Service.

Ministerial functions

Exercise of functions.

48.-(1) Statutory functions may be conferred on the Scottish Ministers by that name.

(2) Statutory functions of the Scottish Ministers, the First Minister or the Lord Advocate shall be exercisable on behalf of Her Majesty.

(3) Statutory functions of the Scottish Ministers shall be exercisable by any member of the Scottish Executive.

(4) Any act or omission of, or in relation to, any member of the Scottish Executive shall be treated as an act or omission of, or in relation to, each of them; and any property acquired, or liability incurred, by any member of the Scottish Executive shall be treated accordingly.

(5) Subsections (3) and (4) do not apply in relation to the exercise of-

(a) functions conferred on the First Minister alone, or

(b) retained functions of the Lord Advocate.

(6) In this Act, "retained functions" in relation to the Lord Advocate means-

(a) any functions exercisable by him immediately before he ceases to be a Minister of the Crown, and

(b) other statutory functions conferred on him alone.

General transfer of functions.

49.-(1) The functions mentioned in subsection (2) shall, so far as they are exercisable in or as regards Scotland, be exercisable by the Scottish Ministers instead of by a Minister of the Crown.

(2) Those functions are-

(a) those of Her Majesty's prerogative and other executive functions which are exercisable on behalf of Her Majesty by a Minister of the Crown, and

(b) functions conferred on a Minister of the Crown by any pre-commencement enactment;

but do not include any retained functions of the Lord Advocate or any functions so far as they relate to reserved matters.

(3) In this Act, "pre-commencement enactment" means-

(a) an Act passed before or in the same session as this Act and any other enactment made before the passing of this Act, and

(b) an enactment made, before the commencement of this section, under such an Act or such other enactment.

Scope of powers to make subordinate legislation, etc.

50.-(1) Subsection (2) applies to the exercise by a member of the Scottish Executive of any function of making subordinate legislation which is exercisable by him by virtue of section 49.

(2) Provision may be made in the subordinate legislation if, and only if, the provision would be within the legislative competence of the Parliament if it were included in an Act of the Scottish Parliament.

(3) The restrictions in section 49 to the exercise of the function-

(a) in or as regards Scotland, and

(b) otherwise than in relation to reserved matters,

are to be read in accordance with subsection (2).

(4) Apart from subsection (3), subsection (2) does not affect any other restriction on the exercise of the function.

(5) Any provision of subordinate legislation made or purporting to be made by a member of the Scottish Executive is to be read, so far as possible, so as to be within the powers conferred by virtue of this Act and is to have effect ac-

cordingly.

Functions exercisable with agreement.

51.-(1) A statutory provision which provides for a Minister of the Crown to exercise a function with the agreement of, or after consultation with, any other Minister of the Crown shall not apply to the exercise of the function by a member of the Scottish Executive by virtue of section 49.

(2) In subsection (1) "statutory provision" means any provision in a pre-commencement enactment other than paragraph 5 or 15 of Schedule 32 to the Local Government (Planning and Land) Act 1980 (designation of enterprise zones).

Shared powers.

52. The powers of a Minister of the Crown under-
 (a) section 17(1) of the Ministry of Transport Act 1919 (power to make advances for certain purposes),
 (b) section 9 of the Industrial Organisation and Development Act 1947 (levies for scientific research, promotion of exports etc.),
 (c) section 5 of the Science and Technology Act 1965 (funding of scientific research),
 (d) section 1 of the Mineral Exploration and Investment Grants Act 1972 (contributions in respect of mineral exploration),
 (e) sections 10 to 12 of the Industry Act 1972 (credits and grants for construction of ships and offshore installations),
 (f) sections 7 to 14 of the Industrial Development Act 1982 (financial and other assistance for industry), and
 (g) sections 39 and 40 of the Road Traffic Act 1988 (road safety information and training),
shall, despite section 49, be exercisable in or as regards Scotland by him as well as by the Scottish Ministers.

Community law and Convention rights.

53.-(1) Despite the transfer to the Scottish Ministers by virtue of section 49 of functions in relation to observing and implementing obligations under Community law, any function of a Minister of the Crown in relation to any matter shall continue to be exercisable by him as regards Scotland for the purposes specified in section 2(2) of the European Communities Act 1972.

(2) A member of the Scottish Executive has no power to make any subordinate legislation, or to do any other act, so far as the legislation or act is incompatible with any of the Convention rights or with Community law.

Power to prevent or require action.

54.-(1) If the Secretary of State has reasonable grounds to believe that any action proposed to be taken by a member of the Scottish Executive would be incompatible with any international obligations, he may by order direct that the proposed action shall not be taken.

(2) If the Secretary of State has reasonable grounds to believe that any action capable of being taken by a member of the Scottish Executive is required for the purpose of giving effect to any such obligations, he may by order direct that the action shall be taken.

(3) In subsections (1) and (2), "action" includes making, confirming or approving subordinate legislation and, in subsection (2), includes introducing a Bill in the Parliament.

(4) If any subordinate legislation made or which could be revoked by a member of the Scottish Executive contains provisions-

    (a) which the Secretary of State has reasonable grounds to believe would be incompatible with any international obligations, or

    (b) which would be within the legislative competence of the Parliament by virtue of subsection (4) (as it applies in relation to Scots private law) or subsection (5) of section 28 if it were included in an Act of the Scottish Parliament, but which the Secretary of State has reasonable grounds to believe would have an adverse effect on the operation of an enactment as it applies to reserved matters,

the Secretary of State may by order revoke the legislation.

(5) An order under this section must state the reasons for revoking the legislation.

Property and liabilities
Property and liabilities of the Scottish Ministers.

55.-(1) Property may be held by the Scottish Ministers by that name.

(2) Property acquired by or transferred to the Scottish Ministers shall belong to, and liabilities incurred by the Scottish Ministers shall be liabilities of, the Scottish Ministers for the time being.

(3) In relation to property to be acquired by or transferred to, or belonging to, the Scottish Ministers or liabilities incurred by the Scottish Ministers, references to the Scottish Ministers-

    (a) in any title recorded in the Register of Sasines or registered in the Land Register of Scotland, or

    (b) in any other document,

shall be read in accordance with subsection (2).

(4) A document shall be validly executed by the Scottish Ministers if it is executed by any member of the Scottish Executive.

Transfers to the Scottish Ministers.

56.-(1) Subordinate legislation may provide-

    (a) for the transfer to the Scottish Ministers of any property to which this section applies, or

    (b) for the Scottish Ministers to have such rights or interests in relation to any property to which this section applies as the person making the legislation considers appropriate (whether in connection with a transfer or otherwise).

(2) This section applies to property belonging to a Minister of the Crown

which appears to the person making the legislation-

    (a) to be held or used wholly or partly for or in connection with the exercise of devolved functions, or

    (b) not to be within paragraph (a) but, when last held or used for or in connection with the exercise of any function, to have been within that paragraph.

(3) Subordinate legislation may provide for the transfer to the Scottish Ministers of any liabilities-

    (a) to which a Minister of the Crown is subject, and

    (b) which appear to the person making the legislation to have been incurred wholly or partly for or in connection with the exercise of devolved functions.

(4) In this section, "devolved functions" means any functions exercisable in or as regards Scotland other than-

    (a) functions relating to reserved matters, or

    (b) retained functions of the Lord Advocate.

Property and liabilities of the Lord Advocate and the First Minister.

57.-(1) Property may be held by the Lord Advocate by that name.

(2) Property acquired by or transferred to the Lord Advocate shall belong to, and liabilities incurred by the Lord Advocate shall be liabilities of, the Lord Advocate for the time being.

(3) In relation to property to be acquired by or transferred to, or belonging to, the Lord Advocate or liabilities incurred by the Lord Advocate, references to the Lord Advocate-

    (a) in any title recorded in the Register of Sasines or registered in the Land Register of Scotland, or

    (b) in any other document,

shall be read in accordance with subsection (2).

(4) Any rights and liabilities acquired or incurred by the First Minister shall be rights or (as the case may be) liabilities of the First Minister for the time being.

Transfers to the Lord Advocate.

58.-(1) Subordinate legislation may provide-

    (a) for the transfer to the Lord Advocate of any property to which this section applies, or

    (b) for the Lord Advocate to have such rights or interests in relation to any property to which this section applies as the person making the legislation considers appropriate (whether in connection with a transfer or otherwise).

(2) This section applies to property belonging to a Minister of the Crown which appears to the person making the legislation-

    (a) to be held or used wholly or partly for or in connection with the exercise of retained functions of the Lord Advocate, or

    (b) not to be within paragraph (a) but, when last held or used for or in connection with the exercise of any function, to have been within that paragraph.

(3) Subordinate legislation may provide for the transfer to the Lord Advocate of any liabilities-

(a) to which a Minister of the Crown is subject, and

(b) which appear to the person making the legislation to have been incurred wholly or partly for or in connection with the exercise of retained functions of the Lord Advocate.

Transfer of additional functions

Power to transfer functions.

59.-(1) Subordinate legislation may provide for any statutory functions, so far as they are exercisable by a Minister of the Crown in or as regards Scotland, to be exercisable-

(a) by the Scottish Ministers instead of by the Minister of the Crown,

(b) by the Scottish Ministers concurrently with the Minister of the Crown, or

(c) by the Minister of the Crown only with the agreement of, or after consultation with, the Scottish Ministers.

(2) Where subordinate legislation is made under subsection (1)(a) or (b) in relation to a function of a Minister of the Crown which is exercisable only with the agreement of, or after consultation with, another Minister of the Crown or other person, the function shall, unless the legislation provides otherwise, be exercisable by the Scottish Ministers free from any such requirement.

(3) Subordinate legislation under this section may, in particular, provide for any function exercisable by the Scottish Ministers by virtue of subordinate legislation under subsection (1)(a) or (b) to be exercisable subject to a requirement for the function to be exercised with the agreement of, or after consultation with, a Minister of the Crown or other person.

Transfers of property and liabilities in connection with functions.

60.-(1) Subordinate legislation may provide-

(a) for the transfer to the Scottish Ministers of any property to which this section applies, or

(b) for the Scottish Ministers to have such rights or interests in relation to any property to which this section applies as the person making the legislation considers appropriate (whether in connection with a transfer or otherwise).

(2) This section applies to property belonging to a Minister of the Crown which appears to the person making the legislation-

(a) to be held or used wholly or partly for or in connection with the exercise of any functions which are subject to subordinate legislation under section 59(1)(a) or (b), or

(b) not to be within paragraph (a) but, when last held or used for or in connection with the exercise of any function, to have been so held or used for or in connection with the exercise of such functions.

(3) Subordinate legislation may provide for the transfer to the Scottish Ministers of any liabilities-

(a) to which a Minister of the Crown is subject, and

(b) which appear to the person making the legislation to have been incurred wholly or partly for or in connection with the exercise of any functions which are subject to subordinate legislation under section 59(1)(a) or (b).

PART III
FINANCIAL PROVISIONS

Scottish Consolidated Fund.

61.-(1) There shall be a Scottish Consolidated Fund.

(2) The Secretary of State shall from time to time make payments into the Fund out of money provided by Parliament of such amounts as he may determine.

(3) Sums received by a member of the Scottish Executive shall be paid into the Fund.

(4) Subsection (3) is subject to any provision made by or under an Act of the Scottish Parliament for the disposal of or accounting for such sums.

(5) The Treasury may, after consulting with the Scottish Ministers, by order designate receipts of any description specified in the order which are payable into the Fund (or would be but for any provision made by or under an Act of the Scottish Parliament).

(6) The Scottish Ministers shall make payments to the Secretary of State, at such times and by such methods as the Treasury may from time to time determine, of sums equal to the total amount outstanding in respect of designated receipts.

(7) Amounts required for the payment of sums under subsection (6) shall be charged on the Fund.

(8) Banking services for the Fund shall be provided by the Office of Her Majesty's Paymaster General.

Payments out of the Fund.

62.-(1) A sum may only be paid out of the Scottish Consolidated Fund if-

    (a) it has been charged on the Fund by any enactment,

    (b) it is payable out of the Fund without further approval by virtue of this Act,

    (c) it is paid out for or in connection with any of the purposes mentioned in subsection (2) in accordance with rules made by or under an Act of the Scottish Parliament.

(2) Those purposes are-

    (a) meeting expenditure of the Scottish Administration,

    (b) meeting expenditure payable out of the Fund under any enactment (including this Act).

(3) A sum paid out of the Fund shall not be applied for any purpose other than that for which it was charged or (as the case may be) paid out.

Borrowing by the Scottish Ministers, etc.

63.-(1) The Scottish Ministers may borrow from the Secretary of State any sums required by them for the purpose of-

    (a) meeting a temporary excess of sums paid out of the Scottish Consolidated Fund over sums paid into that Fund, or

    (b) providing a working balance in the Fund.

(2) Amounts required for the repayment of, or the payment of interest on,

sums borrowed under this section shall be charged on the Fund.

(3) Sums borrowed under this section shall be repaid to the Secretary of State at such times and by such methods, and interest on them shall be paid to him at such rates and at such times, as the Treasury may from time to time determine.

(4) A member of the Scottish Executive may borrow money only under this section or under any power conferred by an Act of Parliament.

Lending by the Secretary of State.

64.-(1) The Treasury may issue to the Secretary of State out of the National Loans Fund such sums as are required by him for making loans under section 63.

(2) The aggregate at any time outstanding in respect of the principal of sums borrowed under that section shall not exceed £500 million.

(3) The Secretary of State may by order made with the consent of the Treasury substitute for the amount (or substituted amount) specified in subsection (2) such increased amount as may be specified in the order.

(4) Sums received by the Secretary of State under section 63(3) shall be paid into the National Loans Fund.

Borrowing by public bodies.

65.-(1) If a member of the Scottish Executive lends money to a body established under any enactment, the rate of interest on the loan shall not be less than the lowest rate determined by the Treasury under section 5 of the National Loans Act 1968 in respect of similar loans made out of the National Loans Fund on the day the loan is made.

(2) A body established under any enactment shall not, in pursuance of a power conferred by virtue of an Act of the Scottish Parliament, borrow money in a currency other than sterling except with the consent of the Scottish Ministers given with the approval of the Treasury.

Financial control, accounts and audit.

66.-(1) Rules made by or under an Act of the Scottish Parliament shall provide-

    (a) for proper accounts to be prepared by the Scottish Ministers, by the Lord Advocate and by other persons to whom sums are paid out of the Scottish Consolidated Fund, of the sums received by them from, or paid by them into, the Fund,

    (b) for the Scottish Ministers to prepare an account of payments into and out of the Fund,

    (c) for the appointment of an independent person to exercise, or ensure the exercise by other independent persons, of the functions mentioned in subsection (2),

    (d) for access to such documents as may reasonably be required for the purposes of rules made in pursuance of paragraph (c), and

    (e) for the publication of accounts and reports made in pursuance of any of the rules and for the laying of such accounts and reports before the Parliament.

(2) The functions referred to in subsection (1)(c) are-

(a) issuing credits for the payment of sums out of the Fund,

(b) examining the accounts referred to in subsection (1)(a) and (b) (which includes determining whether sums paid out of the Fund have been paid out and applied in accordance with section 62), and certifying and reporting on them,

(c) carrying out examinations into the economy, efficiency and effectiveness with which the Scottish Ministers and the Lord Advocate have used their resources in discharging their functions, and

(d) carrying out examinations into the economy, efficiency and effectiveness with which other persons determined under the rules to whom sums are paid out of the Fund or by the Scottish Ministers have used those sums in discharging their functions.

(3) Standing orders shall provide for the consideration by the Parliament of accounts and reports laid before it in pursuance of subsection (1)(e).

(4) For the purposes of this section, a person is independent in relation to a function if he is not subject to the direction or control of any member of the Scottish Executive or of the Parliament in exercising that function.

Existing debt.

67.-(1) This section applies where-

(a) power to lend money under a provision of a pre-commencement enactment was exercised by the Secretary of State,

(b) the sums required by him for the exercise of the power were issued by the Treasury out of the National Loans Fund, and

(c) the power is exercisable by the Scottish Ministers by virtue of section 49, or would have been so exercisable but for the repeal of the pre-commencement enactment.

(2) Any amount payable by way of repayment of or interest on the loan shall be paid to the Scottish Ministers and into the Scottish Consolidated Fund (instead of to the Secretary of State and into the National Loans Fund).

(3) Amounts equal to those which are to be received by the Scottish Ministers in repayment of principal shall be treated as being amounts of advances made on the commencement of this section to the Scottish Ministers by the Secretary of State.

(4) Such advances shall be repaid to the Secretary of State at such times and by such methods, and interest on them shall be paid to him at such rates and at such times, as the Treasury may from time to time determine.

(5) Sums required to be paid under subsection (4) shall be charged on the Scottish Consolidated Fund.

(6) Sums received under subsection (4) shall be paid into the National Loans Fund.

Accounts of loans to the Scottish Ministers.

68. The Secretary of State shall, for each financial year-

    (a) prepare, in such form and manner as the Treasury may direct, an account of sums paid and received by him under sections 63, 64 and 67, and

    (b) send the account to the Comptroller and Auditor General not later than the end of November in the following financial year,

and the Comptroller and Auditor General shall examine, certify and report on the account and shall lay copies of it and of his report before each House of Parliament.

PART IV
THE TAX-VARYING POWER

Power to fix basic rate for Scottish taxpayers.

69.-(1) Subject to section 70, this section applies for any year of assessment for which income tax is charged if-

(a) the Parliament has passed a resolution providing for the percentage determined to be the basic rate for that year to be increased or reduced for Scottish taxpayers in accordance with the resolution,

(b) the increase or reduction provided for is confined to an increase or reduction by a number not exceeding three which is specified in the resolution and is either a whole number or half of a whole number, and

(c) the resolution has not been cancelled by a subsequent resolution of the Parliament.

(2) Where this section applies for any year of assessment the Income Tax Acts (excluding this Part) shall have effect in relation to the income of Scottish taxpayers as if any rate determined by the Parliament of the United Kingdom to be the basic rate for that year were increased or reduced in accordance with the resolution of the Scottish Parliament.

(3) In subsection (2) the reference to the income of Scottish taxpayers does not include a reference to any income of Scottish taxpayers which, had it been income for the year 1997-98, would have been income to which section 1A of the Income and Corporation Taxes Act 1988 (income from savings and distributions) applied for that year.

(4) In this section-

(a) a reference, in relation to any year of assessment, to income tax being charged for that year includes a reference to the passing of a PCTA resolution that provides for the charging of that tax for that year, and

(b) a reference, in relation to a year of assessment, to the determination by the Parliament of the United Kingdom of a rate to be the basic rate for that year includes a reference to the passing of a PCTA resolution specifying a percentage to be the basic rate for that year.

(5) In this section "a PCTA resolution" means a resolution of the House of Commons containing such a declaration as is mentioned in section 1(2)(b) of the Provisional Collection of Taxes Act 1968.

Supplemental provision with respect to resolutions.

70.-(1) This section applies to any resolution of the Parliament ("a tax-varying resolution") which-

(a) provides, in accordance with section 69, for an increase or reduction for Scottish taxpayers of the basic rate for any year of assessment, or

(b) cancels a previous resolution of the Parliament providing for such an increase or reduction.

(2) Subject to subsection (3), a tax-varying resolution-

(a) must be expressed so as to relate to no more than a single year of assessment beginning after, but no more than twelve months after, the passing of the resolution, but

(b) shall have effect in relation to a determination by the Parliament of the United Kingdom of the rate to be the basic rate for that year irrespective of whether that determination had been made at the time of the passing of the resolution.

(3) Subsection (2) shall not prevent a tax-varying resolution relating to any year of assessment from being passed and having effect where-

(a) a determination by the Parliament of the United Kingdom of the rate to be the basic rate for that year is made after, or less than a month before, the beginning of that year,

(b) that determination is not confined to the passing of the enactment by which a determination of the same rate by a PCTA resolution is ratified, and

(c) the tax-varying resolution is passed within the period of one month beginning with the day of the making by the Parliament of the United Kingdom of its determination.

(4) Where, in a case to which subsection (3) applies, a tax-varying resolution is passed after the beginning of the year of assessment to which it relates-

(a) the resolution shall have effect as from the beginning of that year, and

(b) all such payments, repayments, deductions and other adjustments shall be made as are required to restore the position to what it would have been if the resolution had been passed before the beginning of that year.

(5) Standing orders shall ensure that only a member of the Scottish Executive may move a motion for a tax-varying resolution.

(6) A tax-varying resolution shall not be passed so as to have effect in relation to any year of assessment before the year 2000-01.

(7) Subsections (4) and (5) of section 69 apply for the purposes of this section as they apply for the purposes of that section.

Scottish taxpayers.

71.-(1) For the purposes of this Part a person is a Scottish taxpayer in relation to any year of assessment if-

(a) he is an individual who, for income tax purposes, is treated as resident in the United Kingdom in that year, and

(b) Scotland is the part of the United Kingdom with which he has the closest connection during that year.

(2) For the purposes of this section an individual who is treated for income tax purposes as resident in the United Kingdom in any year of assessment has his closest connection with Scotland during that year if, but only if, one or more of the following paragraphs applies in his case-

(a) he is an individual to whom subsection (3) applies for that year,

(b) the number of days which he spends in Scotland in that year is equal to or exceeds the number of days in that year which he spends elsewhere in the United Kingdom,

(c) he is an individual who, for the whole or any part of that year, is a member of Parliament for a constituency in Scotland, a member of the European Parliament for Scotland or a member of the Scottish Parliament.

(3) This subsection applies to an individual for a year of assessment if-

(a) he spends at least a part of that year in Scotland,

(b) for at least a part of the time that he spends in Scotland in that year, his principal UK home is located in Scotland and he makes use of it as a place of residence, and

(c) the times in that year when Scotland is where his principal UK home is located comprise (in aggregate) at least as much of that year as the times (if any) in that year when the location of his principal UK home is not in Scotland.

(4) For the purposes of this section-

(a) an individual spends a day in Scotland if, but only if, he is in Scotland at the beginning or end of that day, and

(b) an individual spends a day elsewhere in the United Kingdom if, but only if, he is elsewhere in the United Kingdom at the beginning or end of that day and it is not a day that he spends in Scotland.

(5) For the purposes of this section an individual's principal UK home at any time is located in Scotland if at that time-

(a) he is an individual with a place of residence in Scotland, and

(b) in the case of an individual with two or more places of residence in the United Kingdom, Scotland is the location of such one of those places as at that time is his main place of residence in the United Kingdom.

(6) In this section "place" includes a place on board a vessel or other means of transport.

Changes to income tax structure.

72.-(1) This section applies where-

(a) there has been a proposal for the modification of any provision made by or under the Income Tax Acts,

(b) that proposal is one made and published by the Treasury or the Board, or (without having been so made and published) appears to the Treasury to be a proposal to which effect is likely to be given by Act of Parliament, and

(c) it appears to the Treasury that the proposed modification would have a significant effect on the practical extent for any year of assessment of the Parliament's tax-varying powers.

(2) It shall be the duty of the Treasury, as soon as reasonably practicable after the publication of the proposal, or (as the case may be) as soon as reasonably practicable after it first appears to the Treasury that the proposal is likely to be enacted, to lay before the House of Commons-

(a) a statement of whether, in the Treasury's opinion, an amendment of the Parliament's tax-varying powers is required as a consequence of the proposal, and

(b) if in their opinion an amendment of those powers is required, the Treasury's proposals for amending those powers.

(3) Any proposals for amending the Parliament's tax-varying powers that

are laid before the House of Commons by the Treasury under this section-

    (a) must be confined to income tax,

    (b) must appear to the Treasury to satisfy the conditions set out in subsections (4) and (5), and

    (c) must not contain any proposal for the Parliament's tax-varying powers to be exercisable in relation to the taxation of income from savings or distributions.

    (4) The first condition mentioned in subsection (3)(b) is that the proposals would secure-

    (a) so far as possible, and

    (b) after making due allowance for annual changes in the retail prices index,

that the practical extent of the Parliament's tax-varying powers would remain broadly the same from year to year as it would be if (apart from any resolution of the Parliament) the law relating to income tax were the same from year to year as it was in relation to the year 1997-98.

    (5) The second condition so mentioned is that the proposals would not enable the Parliament's tax-varying powers to be exercised for any year of assessment so as to have an effect on the levels of the after-tax income of Scottish taxpayers generally that would be significantly different from the effect their exercise could have had in any previous year of assessment.

    (6) References in this section to the practical extent of the Parliament's tax-varying powers are references to the amounts of income tax for any year of assessment which appear to be or (as the case may be) to have been the maximum amounts capable of being raised and foregone in that year in pursuance of a resolution of the Parliament.

    (7) In this section "income from savings or distributions" means income which, had it been income for the year 1997-98, would have been income to which section 1A of the Income and Corporation Taxes Act 1988 applied for that year.

Accounting for additional Scottish tax.

73.-(1) Where the basic rate for any year of assessment is increased for Scottish taxpayers by a resolution of the Parliament, it shall be the duty of the Board to pay amounts into the Scottish Consolidated Fund in accordance with this section.

    (2) The amounts of the payments to be made by the Board under this section, and the times at which they are to be made, shall be determined by the Board and notified to the Scottish Ministers as soon as reasonably practicable after the passing of the resolution providing for the increase to which they relate.

    (3) Any determination made by the Board under subsection (2) for any year of assessment shall be such as appears to the Board to be necessary for securing that, in the course of that year, amounts are paid into the Scottish Consolidated Fund which are equal in total to the amount estimated by the Board to represent the proportion of the income tax receipts for that year that is properly

attributable to a resolution of the Parliament.

(4) For the purposes of this section the Board shall make and maintain arrangements as to-

(a) the manner of estimating the proportion of the income tax receipts for a year of assessment that is properly attributable to a resolution of the Parliament,

(b) the circumstances and manner in which an estimate of that proportion or of those receipts may be revised before or in the course of the year of assessment to which it relates,

(c) the manner of determining the amount of each payment to be made in respect of any such estimate, and

(d) the times at which, and manner in which, those amounts are to be paid by the Board into the Scottish Consolidated Fund.

(5) Arrangements under subsection (4) may include provision for the making of adjustments to the amounts paid by the Board where any estimate made for the purposes of this section in respect of any year of assessment (whether the current year or a previous year) turns out to have been inaccurate.

(6) Before making or modifying any arrangements under subsection (4) or (5), the Board shall consult with the Scottish Ministers.

(7) In this section "income tax receipts", in relation to any year of assessment, means so much as is referable to income tax charged for that year of any sums which, disregarding both-

(a) subsection (8), and

(b) any regulations or direction made or given by the Treasury,

are sums that have to be paid into the Consolidated Fund under section 10 of the Exchequer and Audit Departments Act 1866 (gross revenues of Board's department to be paid into that Fund after the making of specified deductions).

(8) Sums required by the Board for making payments under this section shall be paid out of the gross revenues of the Board's department; and, accordingly, those sums shall be treated as included in the amounts to be deducted from those revenues before they are paid into the Consolidated Fund under section 10 of the Exchequer and Audit Departments Act 1866.

Effect of tax reduction for Scottish taxpayers.

74.-(1) Where the basic rate for any year of assessment is reduced for Scottish taxpayers by a resolution of the Parliament, payments to the Board in accordance with this section shall be charged on the Scottish Consolidated Fund.

(2) The amounts of the payments to be made out of the Scottish Consolidated Fund under this section, and the times at which they are to be made, shall be determined by the Board and notified to the Scottish Ministers as soon as reasonably practicable after the passing of the resolution providing for the reduction to which they relate.

(3) Any determination made by the Board under subsection (2) for any year of assessment shall be such as appears to the Board to be necessary for securing that in the course of that year amounts are paid to the Board which are equal in total to the amount estimated by the Board to represent the shortfall in

income tax receipts for that year that is properly attributable to a resolution of the Parliament.

(4) For the purposes of this section the Board shall make and maintain arrangements as to-

(a) the manner of estimating the shortfall in income tax receipts for any year of assessment that is properly attributable to a resolution of the Parliament,

(b) the circumstances and manner in which an estimate of that shortfall may be revised before or in the course of the year of assessment to which it relates,

(c) the manner of determining the amount of each payment to be made in respect of any such estimate, and

(d) the times at which, and manner in which, those amounts are to be paid to the Board.

(5) Arrangements under subsection (4) may include provision for the making of adjustments to the amounts paid to the Board where any estimate made for the purposes of this section in respect of any year of assessment (whether the current year or a previous year) turns out to have been inaccurate.

(6) Before making or modifying any arrangements under subsection (4) or (5), the Board shall consult with the Scottish Ministers.

(7) In this section "income tax receipts" has the same meaning as in section 73.

(8) The sums paid to the Board under this section shall be treated for the purposes of section 10 of the Exchequer and Audit Departments Act 1866 (payment, after the making of the specified deductions, of gross revenues into the Consolidated Fund) as comprised in their department's gross revenues.

Supplemental powers to modify enactments.

75.-(1) The Treasury may by order make such modifications of any enactment as they consider necessary or expedient in consequence of-

(a) the fact that the Parliament has, or is to have, the power to pass a tax-varying resolution, or

(b) the fact (where it is the case) that the Parliament has passed such a resolution.

(2) The Treasury may by order make provision-

(a) excluding the operation of section 69(2) in relation to any enactment, and

(b) making any such other modifications of any enactment as they consider necessary or expedient in connection with, or for the purposes of, any such exclusion.

(3) Without prejudice to the generality of the powers conferred by the preceding provisions of this section, an order under this section may provide that, where any tax-varying resolution relating to any year of assessment is passed, that resolution does not require any change in the amounts repayable or deductible under section 203 of the Income and Corporation Taxes Act 1988 (PAYE) between-

(a) the beginning of that year, and

(b) such day falling after the passing of the resolution as may be specified in the order.

(4) An order under this section may, to the extent that the Treasury consider it to be appropriate, take effect retrospectively from the beginning of the year of assessment in which it is made.

(5) In this section-

"enactment" includes an enactment passed or made at any time after the passing of this Act but does not include an enactment contained in this Part, and

"tax-varying resolution" has the same meaning as in section 70.

PART V

MISCELLANEOUS AND GENERAL

Remuneration of members of the Parliament and Executive

Remuneration of members of the Parliament and Executive.

76.-(1) The Parliament shall make provision for the payment of salaries to members of the Parliament and members of the Scottish Executive.

(2) The Parliament may make provision for the payment of allowances to members of the Parliament or members of the Scottish Executive.

(3) The Parliament may make provision for the payment of pensions, gratuities or allowances to, or in respect of, any person who-

(a) has ceased to be a member of the Parliament or the Scottish Executive, or

(b) has ceased to hold such office or other place in connection with the Parliament or the Scottish Executive as the Parliament may determine but continues to be a member of the Parliament or the Scottish Executive.

(4) Such provision may, in particular, include provision for-

(a) contributions or payments towards provision for such pensions, gratuities or allowances,

(b) the establishment and administration (whether by the Parliamentary corporation or otherwise) of one or more pension schemes.

(5) In this section "provision" includes provision-

(a) by an Act of the Scottish Parliament, or

(b) by a resolution of the Parliament addressed to the Parliamentary corporation;

and references to a member of the Scottish Executive include a junior Scottish Minister.

Limits on salaries of members of the Parliament.

77.-(1) The Parliament shall ensure that the amount of salary payable to a member of the Parliament in accordance with section 76 is reduced if any salary is payable to him-

(a) pursuant to a resolution (or combination of resolutions) of either House of Parliament relating to the remuneration of members of that House, or

(b) under section 1 of the European Parliament (Pay and Pensions) Act 1979 (remuneration of United Kingdom MEPs).

(2) The Parliament shall ensure that the amount of salary is reduced-

(a) to a particular proportion of what it would otherwise be or to a particular amount, or

(b) by the amount of any salary payable to the member as mentioned in subsection (1)(a) or (b), by a particular proportion of that amount or by some other particular amount.

Remuneration: supplementary.

78.-(1) The Parliament shall ensure that information concerning sums paid as salaries, allowances, pensions or gratuities of the kind mentioned in section 76 is published for each financial year.

(2) No payment of salary or allowances of the kind mentioned in section 76(1) or (2) shall be made to a person who is required by section 79 to take an oath unless he has done so.

(3) Subsection (2) does not affect any entitlement to payments in respect of the period before the person concerned took the oath once he has done so.

(4) For the purposes of sections 76 and 77, a person who is a member of the Parliament immediately before the Parliament is dissolved shall be treated-

(a) if he continues to hold office by virtue of section 18(2) or paragraph 1 of Schedule 2, as if he were such a member until the end of the day on which he ceases to hold such office, and

(b) if he does not fall within paragraph (a) but is nominated as a candidate at the subsequent general election, as if he were such a member until the end of the day on which the election is held.

(5) Different provision may be made under section 76 or 77 for different cases.

Other provision about members of the Parliament etc.

Oaths.

79.-(1) A person who is returned as a member of the Parliament shall take the oath of allegiance (whether or not he has taken the oath after being returned on a previous occasion or otherwise than as a member of the Parliament).

(2) He shall do so at a meeting of the Parliament and shall not take part in any other proceedings of the Parliament until he has done so.

(3) If he has not done so within the period of two months beginning with the day on which he was returned, or such longer period as the Parliament may have allowed before the end of that period, he shall cease to be a member of the Parliament (so that his seat is vacant).

(4) Each member of the Scottish Executive shall on appointment-

(a) take the official oath in the form provided by the Promissory Oaths Act 1868, and

(b) take the oath of allegiance.

(5) Each junior Scottish Minister shall on appointment take the oath of allegiance.

(6) Subsections (4) and (5) do not require a member of the Parliament to take the oath of allegiance again if he has already done so in compliance with his duty as a member.

(7) In this section, references to taking the oath of allegiance are to taking it in the form provided by the Promissory Oaths Act 1868.

Exemption from jury service.

80.-(1) In Part III of Schedule 1 to the Juries Act 1974 (persons excusable as of right from jury service) after the entries under the heading "Parliament" there is inserted-

"Scottish Parliament and Scottish Executive

Members of the Scottish Parliament.
Members of the Scottish Executive.
Junior Scottish Ministers".

(2) In Part III of Schedule 1 to the Law Reform (Miscellaneous Provisions) (Scotland) Act 1980 (persons excusable as of right from jury service), after the entries in Group A, there is inserted-

"GROUP AB

Scottish Parliament and Scottish Executive

(a) members of the Scottish Parliament;
(b) members of the Scottish Executive; and
(c) junior Scottish Ministers".

Arrangements at Westminster

Scottish representation at Westminster.

81.-(1) Schedule 2 to the Parliamentary Constituencies Act 1986 (rules for redistribution of seats) is amended as follows.

(2) Rule 1(2) (Scotland to have not less than 71 constituencies) is omitted.

(3) After rule 3 there is inserted-

" 3A. A constituency which includes the Orkney Islands or the Shetland Islands shall not include the whole or any part of a local government area other than the Orkney Islands and the Shetland Islands";

and in rule 4, for "3" there is substituted "3A".

(4) In applying rule 5 (electoral quotas for each part of the United Kingdom) to Scotland for the purposes of the first report of the Boundary Commission for Scotland to be submitted under section 3(1) of that Act after the commencement of this subsection, "electoral quota" means the number which, on the enumeration date in relation to that report, is the electoral quota for England.

(5) Paragraph 7 (Commissions do not have to give full effect to all rules), after "rules" there is inserted "(except rule 3A)".

The Advocate General for Scotland.

82.-(1) In Schedule 2 to the House of Commons Disqualification Act 1975 (Ministerial offices) and Part III of Schedule 1 to the Ministerial and other Salaries Act 1975 (salaries of the Law Officers), after the entry for the Solicitor General there is inserted-

" Advocate General for Scotland".

(2) The validity of anything done in relation to the Advocate General is not affected by a vacancy in that office.

(3) If that office is vacant or the Advocate General is for any reason unable to act, his functions shall be exercisable by such other Minister of the Crown as the Prime Minister may determine in writing.

Cross-border public bodies

Cross-border public bodies: initial status.

83.-(1) Sections 49, 105, 106 and 107 shall not apply in relation to any function which is specifically exercisable in relation to a cross-border public body.

(2) A Minister of the Crown shall consult the Scottish Ministers before he exercises, in relation to a cross-border public body, any specific function which is conferred by a pre-commencement enactment and-

(a) which relates to the appointment or removal of members or officers, or particular descriptions of members or officers, of the cross-border public body concerned, or

(b) whose exercise might otherwise affect devolved matters concerning Scotland.

(3) Any cross-border public body or other person which is required by a pre-commencement enactment to lay any report relating to a cross-border public body before Parliament or either House of Parliament shall also lay the report before the Scottish Parliament.

(4) Subsections (2) and (3) are subject to any subordinate legislation made under section 84.

(5) In this Act "cross-border public body" means any body or tribunal-

(a) established by an enactment, and

(b) specified in subordinate legislation under this section,

which, in addition to other functions, has functions exercisable in or as regards Scotland which do not relate to reserved matters.

(6) In this section "report" includes accounts and any statement.

Power to adapt cross-border public bodies.

84.-(1) Subordinate legislation may make provision in relation to a cross-border public body-

(a) enabling powers to be exercised or requiring duties to be performed by the Scottish Ministers instead of by a Minister of the Crown, or by the one or by the other, or by both jointly or by either with the agreement of or after consultation with the other,

(b) requiring or authorising the appointment of additional members,

(c) apportioning any assets or liabilities,

(d) imposing, or enabling the imposition of, any limits or other restrictions in addition to or in substitution for existing limits or restrictions,

(e) providing for sums to be charged on or payable out of, or paid into, the Scottish Consolidated Fund (instead of or in addition to payments into or out of the Consolidated Fund or the National Loans Fund or out of money provided by Parliament),

(f) requiring payments, with or without interest, to a Minister of the Crown or into the Consolidated Fund or National Loans Fund.

(2) Subordinate legislation under this section may, in particular, make provision in relation to the keeping, auditing and certification of accounts and the making of reports.

(3) No subordinate legislation shall be made under this section unless the

cross-border public body concerned has been consulted.

Power to transfer property of cross-border public bodies.
85.-(1) This section applies if an Act of the Scottish Parliament provides for any functions of a cross-border public body to be no longer exercisable in or as regards Scotland.
(2) Subordinate legislation may provide-
(a) for the transfer of any property to which this section applies, or
(b) for any person to have such rights or interests in relation to any property to which this section applies as the person making the legislation considers appropriate (whether in connection with a transfer or otherwise).
(3) This section applies to property belonging to the cross-border public body concerned which appears to the person making the legislation-
(a) to be held or used wholly or partly for or in connection with the exercise of any of the functions concerned, or
(b) not to be within paragraph (a) but, when last held or used for or in connection with the exercise of any function, to have been so held or used for or in connection with the exercise of any of the functions concerned.
(4) Subordinate legislation may provide for the transfer of any liabilities-
(a) to which the cross-border public body concerned is subject, and
(b) which appear to the person making the legislation to have been incurred wholly or partly for or in connection with the exercise of any of the functions concerned.
(5) No subordinate legislation shall be made under this section unless the cross-border public body concerned has been consulted.

Miscellaneous

Maladministration.
86.-(1) The Parliament shall make provision for the investigation of relevant complaints made to its members in respect of any action taken by or on behalf of-
(a) a member of the Scottish Executive in the exercise of functions conferred on the Scottish Ministers, or
(b) the Registrar General of Births, Deaths and Marriages for Scotland, the Keeper of the Registers of Scotland or the Keeper of the Records of Scotland.
(2) For the purposes of subsection (1), a complaint is a relevant complaint if it is a complaint of a kind which could be investigated under the Parliamentary Commissioner Act 1967 if it were made to a member of the House of Commons in respect of a government department or other authority to which that Act applies.
(3) In making provision of the kind required by subsection (1), the Parliament shall have regard (among other things) to the Act of 1967.
(4) Sections 49, 105, 106 and 107 shall not apply in relation to functions

conferred by or under the Act of 1967.

(5) In this section-

"action" includes failure to act (and related expressions shall be read accordingly),

"provision" means provision by an Act of the Scottish Parliament;

and the references to the Act of 1967 are to that Act as it has effect on the commencement of this section.

Agency arrangements.

87.-(1) Arrangements may be made between the Scottish Ministers or the Lord Advocate and any relevant authority for the provision of administrative, professional or technical services by one of them for the other.

(2) In this section "relevant authority" means-

(a) any Minister of the Crown or government department,

(b) any holder of a public office, or

(c) any public body.

Private legislation.

88.-(1) This section applies where a pre-commencement enactment makes provision which has the effect of-

(a) requiring any order to be confirmed by Act of Parliament, or

(b) requiring any order (within the meaning of the Statutory Orders (Special Procedure) Act 1945) to be subject to special parliamentary procedure,

and power to make, confirm or approve the order in question is exercisable by the Scottish Ministers by virtue of section 49.

(2) The provision shall have effect, so far as it relates to the exercise of the power to make, confirm or approve the order by virtue of section 49, as if it required the order-

(a) to be confirmed by an Act of the Scottish Parliament, or

(b) (as the case may be) to be subject to such special procedure as may be provided by or under such an Act.

(3) Section 49 shall not apply in relation to the Private Legislation Procedure (Scotland) Act 1936.

Appointment and removal of judges.

89.-(1) It shall continue to be for the Prime Minister to recommend to Her Majesty the appointment of a person as Lord President of the Court of Session or Lord Justice Clerk.

(2) The Prime Minister shall not recommend to Her Majesty the appointment of any person who has not been nominated by the First Minister for such appointment.

(3) It is for the First Minister to recommend to Her Majesty the appointment of a person as-

(a) a judge of the Court of Session (other than the Lord President or the Lord Justice Clerk), or

(b) a sheriff principal or a sheriff.

(4) A judge of the Court of Session may be removed from office by Her Majesty on the recommendation of the First Minister.

(5) The First Minister shall make such a recommendation if (and only if) the Parliament resolves that the judge in question should be removed from office and the number of members voting in favour of the resolution is not less than two-thirds of the total number of seats for members of the Parliament.

Provision of information to the Treasury.

90.-(1) The Treasury may require the Scottish Ministers to provide, within such period as the Treasury may reasonably specify, such information, in such form and prepared in such manner, as the Treasury may reasonably specify.

(2) If the information is not in their possession or under their control, their duty under subsection (1) is to take all reasonable steps to comply with the requirement.

Judicial Scrutiny

Devolution issues.

91. Schedule 6 (which makes provision in relation to devolution issues) shall have effect.

Legislative power to remedy ultra vires acts.

92. Subordinate legislation may make such provision as the person making the legislation considers necessary or expedient in consequence of-
   (a) any provision which purports to be made by or under any Act of the Scottish Parliament but is not, or may not be, so made, or
   (b) any purported exercise by a member of the Scottish Executive of his functions which is not, or may not be, an exercise or a proper exercise of those functions.

Powers of courts or tribunals to vary retrospective decisions.

93.-(1) This section applies where any court or tribunal decides that—
   (a) an Act of the Scottish Parliament or any provision of such an Act is not within the legislative competence of the Parliament, or
   (b) a member of the Scottish Executive does not have the power to make, confirm or approve a provision of subordinate legislation that he has purported to make, confirm or approve.
(2) The court or tribunal may make an order—
   (a) removing or limiting any retrospective effect of the decision, or
   (b) suspending the effect of the decision for any period and on any conditions to allow the defect to be corrected.
(3) In deciding whether to make an order under this section, the court or tribunal shall (among other things) have regard to the extent to which persons who are not parties to the proceedings would otherwise be adversely affected.
(4) Where a court or tribunal is considering whether to make an order under this section, it shall order intimation of that fact to be given to the Lord

Advocate unless he is a party to the proceedings or has been given intimation under Schedule 6 of any devolution issue which has arisen in the proceedings.

(5) Where the Lord Advocate is given intimation under subsection (4), he may take part as a party in the proceedings so far as they relate to the making of the order.

(6) Paragraphs 36 and 37 of Schedule 6 apply with necessary modifications for the purposes of subsections (4) and (5) as they apply for the purposes of that Schedule.

(7) In this section "intimation" includes notice.

The Judicial Committee.

94.-(1) Any decision of the Judicial Committee in proceedings under this Act shall be stated in open court and shall be binding in all legal proceedings (other than proceedings before the Committee).

(2) No member of the Judicial Committee shall sit and act as a member of the Committee in proceedings under this Act unless he holds or has held—

(a) the office of a Lord of Appeal in Ordinary, or

(b) high judicial office as defined in section 25 of the Appellate Jurisdiction Act 1876 (ignoring for this purpose section 5 of the Appellate Jurisdiction Act 1887).

(3) Her Majesty may by Order in Council—

(a) confer on the Judicial Committee in relation to proceedings under this Act such powers as Her Majesty considers necessary or expedient,

(b) apply the Judicial Committee Act 1833 in relation to proceedings under this Act with exceptions or modifications,

(c) make rules for regulating the procedure in relation to proceedings under this Act before the Judicial Committee.

(4) In this section "proceedings under this Act" means proceedings on a question referred to the Judicial Committee under section 32 or proceedings under Schedule 6.

Supplementary powers

Power to make provision consequential on Acts of the Scottish Parliament.

95. Subordinate legislation may make such provision as the person making the legislation considers necessary or expedient in consequence of any provision made by or under any Act of the Scottish Parliament.

Power to make provision consequential on this Act.

96. Subordinate legislation may make .such modifications in any pre commencement enactment as appear to the person making the legislation necessary or expedient in consequence of this Act.

Power to adapt certain Ministerial and other functions.

97.-(1) Subordinate legislation may make such provision as the person making the legislation considers appropriate for the purpose of enabling or otherwise facilitating the transfer to the Scottish Ministers by virtue of section 49 or 59 of a function exercisable by a Minister of the Crown.

(2) Subordinate legislation under subsection (1) may, in particular, provide for any function, of a Minister of the Crown which is not exercisable separately in or as regards Scotland to be so exercisable.

(3) Subordinate legislation may, for the purposes of this Act, provide for any function of a government department—

(a) which is not exercisable separately in or as regards Scotland so far as it relates to devolved matters to be so exercisable, or

(b) which is so exercisable but is subject to a requirement which relates (wholly or partly) to reserved matters or to matters which do not concern Scotland to be exercisable free from that requirement so far as it so relates.

(4) The reference in subsection (1) to the transfer of a function to the Scottish Ministers shall be read as including the sharing of a function with the Scottish Ministers.

Scottish taxpayers for social security etc. purposes.

98.-(1) The Secretary of State may by order provide for individuals to be treated for the purposes of any of the matters that are reserved matters by virtue of Head 6 of Schedule 5 as if they were, or were not, Scottish taxpayers .

(2) The Secretary of State may by order provide in relation to any year of assessment that, for those purposes, the basic rate in relation to the income of Scottish taxpayers shall be treated as being such rate as is specified in the order (instead of the rate increased or reduced for that year by virtue of any resolution of the Parliament in pursuance of section 69 passed after the beginning of the year).

(3) An order under this section may apply in respect of any individuals whether Scotland is the part of the United Kingdom with which they have the closest connection or not.

(4) In this section "Scottish taxpayer" has the same meaning as in Part IV.

Regulation of Tweed and Esk fisheries.

99.-(1) Her Majesty may by Order in Council make provision for regulating fishing tor salmon. trout. eels and freshwater fish in the River Tweed and the River Esk.

(2) In this section—

"eels", "freshwater fish", "salmon" and "trout" have the same meanings as in the Salmon and Freshwater Fisheries Act 1975,

"the River Tweed" has the same meaning as in section 39 of that Act,

"the River Esk" means the river of that name which, tor part of its length, constitutes the border between England and Scotland and includes its banks and tributary streams.

PART VI
SUPPLEMENTARY
Subordinate legislation

Subordinate legislation: general.

100.-(1) Any power to make subordinate legislation conferred by this Act shall. in relation to its exercise by a Minister of the Crown or a member of the Scottish Executive, be exercisable by statutory instrument.

(2) Subordinate legislation under this Act may make different provision for different purposes.

(3) Subordinate legislation under this Act may make—

(a) such supplementary, incidental or consequential provision, and

(b) such transitory, transitional or saving provision,

as the person making the legislation considers necessary or expedient.

(4) Subordinate legislation under this Act may make provision for the delegation of functions.

(5) Subordinate legislation under any of the following provisions may . modify any enactment (including this Act except Schedule 5), instrument or lo other document: sections 59, 84, 92, 94(3)(a) or (b), 95 to 99 and paragraph 7 of Schedule 2.

(6) Subordinate legislation under sections 29, 54(4), 92 or 95 may make provision having retrospective effect.

(7) Subordinate legislation under this Act may make provision for sums to be payable out of the Scottish Consolidated Fund or charged on the Fund.

(8) Subordinate legislation under this Act made by Her Majesty in Council or by a Minister of the Crown may make provision for the payment of sums out of money provided by Parliament or for sums to be charged on and paid out of the Consolidated Fund.

Subordinate legislation: procedure.

101.-(1) A statutory instrument containing subordinate legislation under any of the following provisions shall be an affirmative instrument in relation to both Houses of Parliament: sections 2(1), 11(1), 29, 97, 98(1), 99 and 111(2).

(2) A statutory instrument containing subordinate legislation under section 64(3) or 75 (other than an order which makes only such provision as is mentioned in section 75(3)) shall be an affirmative instrument in relation to the House of Commons.

(3) A statutory instrument containing subordinate legislation under section 14, 29 or 99 shall be an affirmative instrument in relation to the Parliament.

(4) A Minister of the Crown shall not make any subordinate legislation under this Act—

(a) where the instrument containing the legislation will be an affirmative instrument in relation to both Houses of Parliament unless a draft has been laid before, and approved by resolution of, each House of Parliament,

(b) where the instrument containing the legislation will be an affirmative instrument in relation to the House of Commons unless a draft has been laid before, and approved by resolution of, that House,

(c) where the instrument containing the legislation will be an affirmative instrument in relation to the Parliament unless a draft has been laid before, and approved by resolution of, the Parliament.

(5) No recommendation shall be made to Her Majesty in Council to make any subordinate legislation under this Act—

(a) where the instrument containing the legislation will be an instrument which is an affirmative instrument in relation to both Houses of Parliament unless a draft has been laid before, and approved by resolution of, each House of Parliament,

(b) where the instrument containing the legislation will be an instrument which is an affirmative instrument in relation to the Parliament unless a draft has been laid before, and approved by resolution of, the Parliament.

(6) A statutory instrument containing subordinate legislation under any of the following provisions shall, unless it is an affirmative instrument in relation to both Houses of Parliament, be subject to annulment in pursuance of a resolution of either House of Parliament: sections 33, 54(1), (2) and (4), 56, 58 to 60, 83 to 85, 92, 94(3)(a) or (b), 95, 96, 98(2) and 103(8) and paragraph 2 of Schedule 2.

(7) A statutory instrument containing—

(a) an order under section 61 (5), or

(b) an order which makes such provision as is mentioned in section 75(3), shall, unless it is an affirmative instrument in relation to the House of Commons, be subject to annulment in pursuance of a resolution of that House.

(8) A statutory instrument containing subordinate legislation under any of the following provisions shall, unless it is an affirmative instrument in relation to the Parliament, be subject to annulment in pursuance of a resolution of the Parliament: sections 17(5), 36,59,84 and 85 and paragraph 7 of Schedule 2.

(9) Subsection (6) does not apply to a statutory instrument containing an order merely revoking an order under section 54(1).

Subordinate legislation under open powers.

102.-(1) Any power to make subordinate legislation conferred by this Act shall, if no other provision is made as to the person by whom the power is exercisable, be exercisable by Her Majesty by Order in Council or by a Minister of the Crown by order.

(2) A power to which subsection (I) applies is referred to below as an open power.

(3) A statutory instrument containing subordinate legislation under an open power which, apart from this subsection, would be subject to annulment in pursuance of a resolution of either House of Parliament or of the House of Commons or of the Parliament is not so subject if a draft has been laid before and approved by either House or the House of Commons or the Parliament (as the case may be).

(4) An Order in Council under an open power may revoke, amend or re-

enact an order, as well as an Order in Council, under the power; and an order under an open power may revoke, amend or re-enact an Order in Council, as well as an order, under the power.

(5) A statutory instrument containing an Order in Council or order under an open power which revokes, amends or re-enacts subordinate legislation under an open power may be subject to a different procedure under section 101 or this section from the procedure to which the instrument containing the original legislation was subject.

Transfer of property: supplementary.

103.-(1) This section applies in relation to subordinate legislation under section 56, 58, 60 or 85 or paragraph 2 of Schedule 2.

(2) Any such subordinate legislation may, in particular, provide for—

(a) the creation of rights or interests, or the imposition of liabilities or conditions, in relation to property transferred, or rights or interests acquired, under the legislation,

(b) any property, liabilities or conditions to be determined under the legislation.

(3) Subordinate legislation to which this section applies shall have effect in relation to any property or liabilities to which it applies despite any provision (of whatever nature) which would otherwise prevent, penalise or restrict the transfer of the property or liabilities.

(4) A right of pre-emption, right of irritancy, right of return or other similar right shall not operate or become exercisable as a result of any transfer of property by virtue of any subordinate legislation to which this section applies.

(5) Any such right shall have effect in the case of any such transfer as if the transferee were the same person in law as the transferor and as if no transfer of the property had taken place.

(6) Such compensation as is just shall be paid to any person in respect of any such right which would, apart from subsection (4), have operated in favour of, or become exercisable by, that person but which, in consequence of the operation of that subsection, cannot subsequently operate in his favour or (as the case may be) become exercisable by him.

(7) Any compensation payable by virtue of subsection (6) shall be paid by the transferor or by the transferee or by both.

(8) Subordinate legislation under this subsection may provide for the determination of any disputes as to whether and, if so, how much, compensation is payable by virtue of subsection (6) and as to the person to whom or by whom it shall be paid.

(9) Subsections (3) to (8) apply in relation to the creation of rights or interests, or the doing of anything else, in relation to property as they apply in relation to a transfer of property; and references to the transferor and transferee shall be read accordingly.

(10) In this section "right of return" means any right under a provision for the return or reversion of property in specified circumstances.

General modification of enactments

Ministers of the Crown.

104. So far as may be necessary for the purpose or in consequence of the exercise by a member of the Scottish Executive of any function exercisable by virtue of section 49, any pre-commencement enactment or other document shall be read as if references to a Minister of the Crown were or included references to the Scottish Ministers.

Subordinate instruments.

105.-(1) Subsection (2) applies in relation to the exercise by a member of the Scottish Executive by virtue of section 49 of a function to make, confirm or approve subordinate legislation.

(2) If a pre-commencement enactment makes provision—

(a) for any instrument or the draft of any instrument made in the exercise of such a function to be laid before Parliament or either House of Parliament,

(b) for the annulment or approval of any such instrument or draft by or in pursuance of a resolution of either or both Houses of Parliament, or

(c) prohibiting the making of such an instrument without that approval,

the provision shall have effect, so far as it relates to the exercise of the function by virtue of section 49, as if any reference in it to Parliament or either House of Parliament were a reference to the Scottish Parliament.

(3) Subsection (2) shall also apply in relation to the exercise, as regards Scotland and so far as it does not relate to reserved matters, of a function to make, confirm or approve subordinate legislation conferred on a person other than a Minister of the Crown by a pre-commencement enactment.

(4) If a pre-commencement enactment applies the Statutory Instruments Act 1946 as if a function of the kind mentioned in subsection (3) were exercisable by a Minister of the Crown, that Act shall apply, in relation to the exercise of the function as regards Scotland and so far as it does not relate to reserved matters, as if the function were exercisable by the Scottish Ministers.

(5) This section does not apply to any retained functions of the Lord Advocate.

Consolidated Fund, etc.

106.-(1) In this section-

"Scottish functions" means functions so far as they are exercisable in or as regards Scotland by any person (other than a Minister of the Crown by virtue of section 52 or 53),

but does not include functions relating to reserved matters.

(2) Subject to subsections (3) and (4), a provision of a pre-commencement enactment which-

(a) requires or authorises the payment of any sum out of the Consolidated Fund or money provided by Parliament, or

(b) requires or authorises the payment of any sum into the Consolidated Fund, shall cease to have effect in relation to any Scottish functions.

(3) A provision of a pre-commencement enactment which-

(a) charges any sum on the Consolidated Fund,

(b) requires the payment of any sum out of the Consolidated Fund without further appropriation, or

(c) requires or authorises the payment of any sum into the Consolidated Fund by a person other than a Minister of the Crown,

shall have effect in relation to any Scottish functions as if it provided for the sum to be charged on the Scottish Consolidated Fund or required it to be paid out of that Fund without further approval or required or authorised it to be paid into that Fund (as the case may be).

(4) A provision of a pre-commencement enactment which authorises any sums to be applied as money provided by Parliament instead of being paid into the Consolidated Fund shall have effect in relation to any Scottish functions as if it authorised those sums to be applied as if they had been paid out of the Scottish Consolidated Fund in accordance with rules under section 62(1)(c) instead of being paid into that Fund.

(5) Where a power to lend money under a pre-commencement enactment is exercisable by the Scottish Ministers, subsection (6) applies to any sums which, for the purpose or as the result of the exercise of the power, would be required (apart from that subsection)-

(a) to be issued by the Treasury out of the National Loans Fund, or

(b) to be paid into that Fund.

(6) Those sums shall instead-

(a) be paid out of the Scottish Consolidated Fund without further approval, or

(b) be paid into that Fund,

(as the case may be).

(7) A provision of a pre-commencement enactment which-

(a) requires any account to be examined, certified and reported on by, or to be open to the inspection of, the Comptroller and Auditor General, or

(b) requires him to have access to any other document for carrying out any such examination,

shall have effect in relation to any Scottish functions as if the references to the Comptroller and Auditor General were to the persons exercising the functions mentioned in section 66(2).

Requirements to lay reports etc. before Parliament.

107.-(1) This section applies where-

(a) a pre-commencement enactment makes provision for any report to be laid before Parliament or either House of Parliament, and

(b) the report concerns Scottish functions.

(2) If the report only concerns Scottish functions, it shall be laid instead before the Scottish Parliament.

(3) In any other case, it shall be laid before the Scottish Parliament as well as before Parliament or (as the case may be) either House of Parliament.

(4) In this section-

"report" includes accounts and any statement, and

"Scottish functions" has the same meaning as in section 106.

Crown land.

108.-(1) In any provision about the application of any pre-commencement enactment to Crown land-

> (a) references to a Minister of the Crown or government department shall be read as including the Scottish Ministers and the Lord Advocate, and
>
> (b) references to a Minister of the Crown or government department having the management of the land shall be read as including any member of the Scottish Executive having the management of the land.

(2) In this section, "Crown land" has the meaning given by section 242 of the Town and Country Planning (Scotland) Act 1997.

Stamp duty.

109. In section 55 of the Finance Act 1987 (Crown exemption from stamp duty) references to a Minister of the Crown shall be read as including the Scottish Ministers, the Lord Advocate and the Parliamentary corporation.

Amendments, repeals etc.

Amendments, repeals, etc.

110.-(1) Schedule 7 (which makes modifications of enactments) shall have effect.

(2) The enactments mentioned in Schedule 8 are repealed to the extent specified in that Schedule.

Final provisions

Interpretation.

111.-(1) In this Act-

> "body" includes unincorporated association,
>
> "constituencies" and "regions", in relation to the Parliament, mean the constituencies and regions provided for by Schedule 1,
>
> "constituency member" means a member of the Parliament for a constituency,
>
> "the Convention rights" has the same meaning as in the Human Rights Act 1998,
>
> "document" means anything in which information is recorded in any form (and references to producing a document are to be read accordingly),
>
> "enactment" includes an Act of the Scottish Parliament, an enactment of the Parliament of Northern Ireland, a Measure of the Northern Ireland Assembly, an Order in Council under section 1(3) of the Northern Ireland (Temporary Provisions) Act 1972 or paragraph 1 of Schedule 1 to the Northern Ireland Act 1974, a Royal Warrant and an enactment comprised in subordinate legislation,
>
> "financial year" means a year ending with 31st March,

"functions" includes powers and duties, and "confer", in relation to functions, includes impose,

"the Human Rights Convention" means the Convention for the Protection of Human Rights and Fundamental Freedoms, agreed by the Council of Europe at Rome on 4th November 1950 as it has effect for the time being in relation to the United Kingdom,

"Minister of the Crown" includes the Treasury,

"modify" includes amend or repeal,

"the Parliament" means the Scottish Parliament,

"parliamentary", in relation to constituencies, elections and electors, is to be taken to refer to the Parliament of the United Kingdom,

"the principal appointed day" means the day appointed by an order under section 114 which is designated by the order as the principal appointed day,

"proceedings", in relation to the Parliament, includes proceedings of any committee or sub-committee,

"property" includes rights and interests of any description,

"regional member" means a member of the Parliament for a region,

"Scotland" includes so much of the internal waters and territorial sea of the United Kingdom as are adjacent to Scotland,

"statutory functions" means functions conferred by virtue of any enactment, including this Act,

"subordinate legislation" has the same meaning as in the Interpretation Act 1978 and also includes an instrument made under an Act of the Scottish Parliament.

(2) Her Majesty may by Order in Council determine, or make provision for determining, for the purposes of this Act any boundary between waters which are to be treated as internal waters or territorial sea of the United Kingdom adjacent to Scotland and those which are not.

(3) References in this Act to Scots private law are to the following areas of the civil law of Scotland-

(a) the law of persons (including natural persons, legal persons and unincorporated bodies),

(b) the law of obligations (including voluntary and conventional obligations, obligations of restitution and obligations of reparation),

(c) the law of property (including heritable and moveable property, trusts and succession), and

(d) the law of actions (including remedies, evidence, procedure, diligence, recognition and enforcement of court orders, prescription and limitation and arbitration).

(4) References in this Act to Scots criminal law include criminal offences, evidence, procedure and penalties and the treatment of offenders.

(5) References in this Act and in any other enactment to the Scottish Administration include references to the Registrar General of Births, Deaths and Marriages for Scotland, the Keeper of the Registers of Scotland and the Keeper of the Records of Scotland.

(6) In this Act-

(a) all those rights, powers, liabilities, obligations and restrictions from time to time created or arising by or under the Community Treaties, and

(b) all those remedies and procedures from time to time provided for by or under the Community Treaties,

are referred to as "Community law".

(7) In this Act, "international obligations" means any international obligations of the United Kingdom other than obligations-

(a) under Community law, or

(b) not to do acts incompatible with any of the Convention rights.

(8) In this Act, "by virtue of" includes "by" and "under".

Index of defined expressions.

112. In this Act, the expressions listed in the left-hand column have the meaning given by, or are to be interpreted in accordance with, the provisions listed in the right-hand column.

Expression	*Provision of this Act*
Act of the Scottish Parliament	Section 27(1)
Advocate General	Section 31(6)
Body	Section 111(1)
By virtue of	Section 111(8)
Clerk, and Assistant Clerk	Section 19 and paragraph 3 of Schedule 2
Community law	Section 111(6)
Constituencies and constituency member	Section 111(1)
The Convention rights	Section 111(1)
Cross-border public body	Section 83(5)
Devolved matters	Section 29(4)
Document	Section 111(1)
Enactment	Section 111(1)
Financial year	Section 111(1)
Functions	Section 111(1)
The Human Rights Convention	Section 111(1)
International obligations	Section 111(7)
Judicial Committee	Section 31(6)
Legislative competence	Section 28
Minister of the Crown	Section 111(1)
Modify	Section 111(1)
The Parliament	Section 111(1)
"parliamentary" (in relation to constituencies, elections and electors)	Section 111(1)
The Parliamentary corporation	Section 20(1)

Expression	Provision of this Act
Pre-commencement enactment	Section 49(3)
Presiding Officer	Section 18
Principal appointed day	Section 111(1)
Proceedings	Section 111(1)
Property	Section 111(1)
Regional list (in relation to a party)	Section 44(4)
Regions and regional member	Section 111(1)
Regional returning officer	Section 11(5)
Regional vote	Section 5(2)
Registered political party	Section 4(8)
Reserved matters	Schedule 5
Retained functions (in relation to the Lord Advocate)	Section 48(6)
Scotland	Section 111(1) and (2)
Scots criminal law	Section 111(4)
Scots private law	Section 111(3)
Scottish Administration	Section 111(5)
Scottish Ministers	Section 41(2)
Scottish Seal	Section 2(6)
Staff of the Parliament	Paragraph 3 of Schedule 2
Statutory functions	Section 111(1)
Subordinate legislation	Section 111(1)

Expenses.

113.-(1) There shall be paid out of money provided by Parliament-

(a) any expenditure incurred by a Minister of the Crown by virtue of this Act, and

(b) any increase attributable to this Act in the sums payable out of money so provided under any other enactment.

(2) There shall be paid into the Consolidated Fund any sums received by a Minister of the Crown by virtue of this Act which are not payable into the National Loans Fund.

Commencement.

114.-(1) The preceding provisions of this Act (and the Schedules relating to them) shall come into force on such day as the Secretary of State may by order appoint.

(2) Different days may be appointed under this section for different purposes.

Extent.

115. Section 24 extends only to Scotland.

Short title.
116. This Act may be cited as the Scotland Act 1998.

SCHEDULES
SCHEDULE 1
CONSTITUENCIES, REGIONS AND REGIONAL MEMBERS
General

1. The constituencies for the purposes of this Act are-

    (a) the Orkney Islands,

    (b) the Shetland Islands, and

    (c) the parliamentary constituencies in Scotland, except a parliamentary constituency including either of those islands.

2.-(1) There shall be eight regions for the purposes of this Act.

    (2) Those regions shall be the eight European Parliamentary constituencies which were provided for by the European Parliamentary Constituencies (Scotland) Order 1996.

    (3) Seven regional members shall be returned for each region.

    (4) Sub-paragraphs (2) and (3) are subject to any Order in Council under the Parliamentary Constituencies Act 1986 (referred to in this Schedule as the 1986 Act), as that Act is extended by this Schedule.

Reports of Boundary Commission

3.-(1) This paragraph applies where the Boundary Commission for Scotland (referred to in this Schedule as the Commission) submit a report to the Secretary of State under section 3(1) or 3(3) of the 1986 Act recommending any alteration in any parliamentary constituencies.

    (2) In the report the Commission shall recommend any alteration-

    (a) in any of the regions, or

    (b) in the number of regional members to be returned for any of the regions,

which, in their opinion, is required to be made in order to give effect to the rules in paragraph 7.

    (3) If in the case of a report under section 3(1) or 3(3) of that Act the Commission do not make any recommendation within sub-paragraph (2), they shall in the report state that, in their opinion, no such alteration is required.

    (4) A report making a recommendation for an alteration in any region shall state-

    (a) the name by which the Commission recommend that the region should be known, and

    (b) the number of regional members to be returned for the region.

    (5) The Commission shall lay any report recommending any alteration in parliamentary constituencies before the Parliament.

4. - (1) An Order in Council under section 4 of the 1986 Act which has the effect of making any alteration in any constituency of the Parliament, or makes any alteration within paragraph 3(2), may come into force for the purposes of any election for membership of the Parliament on a different day from the day on which it comes into force for the purposes of any parliamentary election;

and paragraph 1(c) shall be read accordingly.

(2) The coming into force of such an Order, so far as it has the effect of making any alteration in any constituency of the Parliament or makes any alteration within paragraph 3(2), shall not affect the return of any member of the Parliament, or its constitution, until the Parliament is dissolved.

Notices

5.-(1) Where the Commission have provisionally determined to make recommendations affecting any region, they shall publish in at least one newspaper circulating in the region a notice stating-

    (a) the effect of the proposed recommendations and (except in a case where they propose to recommend that no alteration within paragraph 3(2) be made) that a copy of the recommendations is open to inspection at a specified place or places within the region, and

    (b) that representations with respect to the proposed recommendations may be made to the Commission within one month after the publication of the notice;

and the Commission shall take into consideration any representations duly made in accordance with any such notice.

(2) Where the Commission revise any proposed recommendations after publishing notice of them under sub-paragraph (1), the Commission shall comply again with that sub-paragraph in relation to the revised recommendations, as if no earlier notice had been published.

Local inquiries

6.-(1) The Commission may, if they think fit, cause a local inquiry to be held in respect of any region.

(2) If, on the publication of a notice under paragraph 5(1) of a recommendation for any alteration within paragraph 3(2), the Commission receive any representation objecting to the proposed recommendation-

    (a) from an interested authority, or

    (b) from a body of electors numbering 500 or more,

the Commission shall not make the recommendation unless a local inquiry has been held in respect of the region since the publication of the notice.

(3) If a local inquiry was held in respect of the region before the publication of the notice under paragraph 5(1), sub-paragraph (2) shall not apply if the Commission, after considering the matters discussed at the local inquiry, the nature of the representations received on the publication of the notice and any other relevant circumstances, are of the opinion that a further local inquiry would not be justified.

(4) In this paragraph, in relation to any recommendation-

"interested authority" means the council for an area which is wholly or partly included in the region affected by the recommendation, and

"elector" means an elector for the purposes of an election for membership of the Parliament in any constituency included in the region.

(5) Sections 210(4) and (5) of the Local Government (Scotland) Act 1973

(attendance of witnesses at inquiries) shall apply in relation to any local inquiry held under this paragraph.

The rules

7.-(1) The rules referred to in paragraph 3 are:

    1. A constituency shall fall wholly within a region.

    2. The regional electorate of any region shall be as near the regional electorate of each of the other regions as is reasonably practicable having regard, where appropriate, to special geographical considerations.

    3. So far as reasonably practicable, the ratio which the number of regional member seats bears to the number of constituency member seats shall be 56 to 73.

    4. The number of regional member seats for a region shall be-

        (a)   one eighth of the total number of regional member seats, or

        (b)   (if that total number is not exactly divisible by eight) either one eighth of the highest number which is less than that total number and exactly divisible by eight or the number produced by adding one to one eighth of that highest number (as provided by sub-paragraphs (2) to (4)).

(2) If the total number of regional member seats is not exactly divisible by eight, the Commission shall calculate the difference between-

    (a) the total number of regional member seats, and

    (b) the highest number which is less than that total number and exactly divisible by eight,

and that is the number of residual seats to be allocated by the Commission.

(3) The Commission shall not allocate more than one residual seat for a region.

(4) The Commission shall divide the regional electorate for each region by the aggregate of-

    (a) the number of constituencies in the region, and

    (b) one eighth of the highest number which is less than the total number of regional member seats and exactly divisible by eight,

and, in allocating the residual seat or seats for a region or regions, shall have regard to the desirability of allocating the residual seat or seats to the region or regions for which that calculation produces the highest number or numbers.

8.-(1) For the purposes of any report of the Commission in relation to a region, the regional electorate is the number of persons-

    (a) whose names appear on the enumeration date on the registers of local government electors, and

    (b) who are registered at addresses within a constituency included in the region.

(2) In sub-paragraph (1), "the enumeration date" means the date on which the notice about the report is published in accordance with section 5(1) of the 1986 Act.

SCHEDULE 2
SCOTTISH PARLIAMENTARY CORPORATE BODY
Membership

1. A person appointed under section 20(2)(b) shall hold office until another member of the Parliament is appointed in his place, unless he previously resigns or ceases to be a member of the Parliament otherwise than by virtue of a dissolution.

Property

2.-(1) The corporation may hold property.

(2) Subordinate legislation may provide-

(a) for the transfer to the corporation of any property to which this sub-paragraph applies, or

(b) for the corporation to have such rights or interests in relation to any property to which this sub-paragraph applies as the person making the legislation considers appropriate (whether in connection with a transfer or otherwise).

(3) Sub-paragraph (2) applies to any property belonging to a Minister of the Crown which appears to the person making the subordinate legislation to be property which is or may be required wholly or partly for the purposes of the corporation's functions.

(4) Subordinate legislation under sub-paragraph (2) in relation to any property may provide for the transfer to the corporation of any liabilities relating to the property to which a Minister of the Crown is subject and which subsist immediately before the subordinate legislation comes into force.

Staff

3.-(1) The corporation shall appoint Assistant Clerks and may appoint other staff.

(2) The Clerk and other persons appointed by the corporation are referred to in this Act as the staff of the Parliament.

(3) It is for the corporation to determine the terms and conditions of appointment of the staff of the Parliament, including arrangements for the payment of pensions, gratuities or allowances to, or in respect of, any person who has ceased to be a member of the staff of the Parliament.

(4) Accordingly, the corporation may-

(a) make contributions or payments towards provision for such pensions, gratuities or allowances,

(b) establish and administer one or more pension schemes.

Powers

4.-(1) Subject to sub-paragraph (3), the corporation may do anything which appears to it to be necessary or expedient for the purpose of or in connection with the discharge of its functions.

(2) That includes, in particular-

(a) entering into contracts,

(b) investing sums not immediately required in relation to the discharge of its functions, and

(c) accepting gifts.

(3) The corporation may borrow sums in sterling by way of overdraft or otherwise for the purpose of meeting a temporary excess of expenditure over sums otherwise available to meet that expenditure.

(4) The corporation may borrow money only under sub-paragraph (3) and may borrow under that sub-paragraph only in accordance with the special or general approval of the Parliament.

Delegation

5. The corporation may delegate any of its functions to the Presiding Officer or the Clerk.

Proceedings and business

6.-(1) The validity of any proceedings of the corporation shall not be affected by any vacancy among the members, or by any defect in the appointment, or qualification for membership, of any member.

(2) The corporation may determine its own procedure.

(3) The Presiding Officer shall preside at meetings of the corporation, but the corporation may appoint another of its members to preside if the office of Presiding Officer is vacant or the Presiding Officer is for any reason unable to act.

Crown status

7.-(1) Her Majesty may by Order in Council provide for the corporation to be treated to any extent as a Crown body for the purposes of any enactment.

(2) In particular, the Order may for the purposes of any enactment provide-

(a) for employment under the corporation to be treated as employment under the corporation as a Crown body,

(b) for land held, used or managed by the corporation, or operations carried out by or on behalf of the corporation, to be treated (as the case may be) as land held, used or managed, or operations carried out by or on behalf of, the corporation as a Crown body.

(3) For the purposes of this paragraph, "Crown body" means a body which is the servant or agent of the Crown, and includes a government department.

SCHEDULE 3
STANDING ORDERS - FURTHER PROVISION
Preservation of order

1.-(1) The standing orders shall include provision for preserving order in the proceedings of the Parliament, including provision for preventing conduct which would constitute a criminal offence or contempt of court.

(2) Such provision may provide for excluding a member of the Parliament from proceedings.

Proceedings to be in public

2.-(1) The standing orders shall include provision requiring the proceedings of the Parliament to be held in public, except in such circumstances as the standing orders may provide.

(2) The standing orders may include provision as to the conditions to be complied with by any member of the public attending the proceedings, including provision for excluding from the proceedings any member of the public who does not comply with those conditions.

Reporting and publishing proceedings

3. The standing orders shall include provision for reporting the proceedings of the Parliament and for publishing the reports.

Committees

4.-(1) Standing orders which provide for the appointment of committees may include provision for those committees to have power to appoint sub-committees.

(2) The standing orders shall include provision for ensuring that, in appointing members to committees and sub-committees, regard is had to the balance of parties in the Parliament.

(3) The standing orders may include provision for excluding from the proceedings of a committee or sub-committee a member of the Parliament who is not a member of the committee or sub-committee.

Crown interests

5. The standing orders shall include provision for ensuring that a Bill containing provisions which would, if the Bill were a Bill for an Act of Parliament, require the consent of Her Majesty, the Prince and Steward of Scotland or the Duke of Cornwall shall not pass unless such consent has been signified to the Parliament.

SCHEDULE 4
PROVISIONS OF ACT NOT PROTECTED FROM MODIFICATION

1. Section 28(2)(b) does not prevent an Act of the Scottish Parliament modifying sections 20(5) and (6) and 23(7).

2.-(1) Section 28(2)(b) does not prevent an Act of the Scottish Parliament modifying any enactment so far as the enactment is modified by-
    (a) sections 88 and 104 to 108, or
    (b) the following paragraphs of Schedule 7: 5, 6, 8 and 16 to 18.
    (2) Sub-paragraph (1) does not apply to section 106(3), as it has effect in relation to any provision of an Act of Parliament relating to judicial salaries, or to section 106(6).

3.-(1) Section 28(2)(b) does not prevent an Act of the Scottish Parliament modifying any provision of this Act (other than section 106) which-
    (a) charges any sum on the Scottish Consolidated Fund,
    (b) requires any sum to be paid out of that Fund without further approval, or
    (c) requires or authorises the payment of any sum into that Fund.
    (2) Sub-paragraph (1) does not apply to sections 61(7), 63(2), 67(5), 73 and 74.

4. Section 28(2)(b) does not prevent an Act of the Scottish Parliament-
    (a) establishing a new fund, in addition to the Scottish Consolidated Fund, out of which loans may be made by the Scottish Ministers, and
    (b) making any amendments of Part III which are necessary or expedient for the purpose or in consequence of the establishment of the new fund.

5.-(1) Section 28(2)(b) does not prevent an Act of the Scottish Parliament modifying any reference in this Act mentioned in sub-paragraph (2) if such a modification is otherwise within the legislative competence of the Parliament.
    (2) Those references are the references to-
the Court of Session,
the High Court of Justiciary,
the Lands Tribunal for Scotland,
the Scottish Land Court,
sheriff principals and sheriffs,
the Keeper of the Registers of Scotland,
the Keeper of the Records of Scotland,
the Registrar General of Births, Deaths and Marriages for Scotland,
the Register of Sasines,
the Land Register of Scotland,
local government elections and registers of local government electors, and
the enactments mentioned in sections 37(2), 38(2), 80(2) and 99(2) and paragraph 6(5) of Schedule 1.

SCHEDULE 5
RESERVED MATTERS
PART I
GENERAL RESERVATIONS
The Constitution

1. The constitution, including the Crown, the succession to the Crown and a regency and the Parliament of the United Kingdom, are reserved matters.

2.-(1) Subject to sub-paragraph (2), paragraph 1 does not reserve those of Her Majesty's prerogative and other executive functions which are exercisable on Her behalf by a Minister of the Crown or other person, including functions conferred on any Minister of the Crown or other person by any enactment.

(2) Paragraph 1 does reserve-

(a) the functions of the Lord Lyon King of Arms so far as relating to the granting of arms,

(b) honours and dignities apart from the functions of the Lord Lyon King of Arms,

(c) the Crown Estate Commissioners.

3.-(1) Subject to sub-paragraph (3), paragraph 1 does not reserve property belonging to Her Majesty in right of the Crown or belonging to a government department or held in trust for Her Majesty for the purposes of a government department.

(2) Paragraph 1 does not reserve the ultimate superiority of the Crown or the superiority of the Prince and Steward of Scotland.

(3) Paragraph 1 does reserve-

(a) the hereditary revenues of the Crown,

(b) the royal arms and standard.

4.-(1) Subject to sub-paragraph (2), paragraph 1 does not reserve property held by Her Majesty in Her private capacity.

(2) Paragraph 1 does reserve the subject-matter of the Crown Private Estates Acts 1800 to 1873.

5. Paragraph 1 does not reserve-

(a) the conferral of powers on Her Majesty to make Orders in Council and the procedure of the Parliament in relation to such Orders,

(b) the use of the Scottish Seal,

(c) acquisition of land for the purposes of the Scottish Administration.

Foreign affairs, EU etc.

6.-(1) International relations, including relations with territories outside the United Kingdom, the European Union and its institutions and other international organisations, regulation of international trade, and international development assistance and co-operation are reserved matters.

(2) Sub-paragraph (1) does not reserve-

(a) observing and implementing international obligations, obligations under the Human Rights Convention and obligations under Community law,

(b) assisting Ministers of the Crown in relation to any matter to which that sub-paragraph applies.

Public service

7.-(1) The Civil Service of the State is a reserved matter.

(2) Sub-paragraph (1) does not reserve the subject-matter of-

(a) Part I of the Sheriff Courts and Legal Officers (Scotland) Act 1927 (appointment of sheriff clerks and procurators fiscal, etc.),

(b) Part III of the Administration of Justice (Scotland) Act 1933 (officers of the High Court of Justiciary and of the Court of Session).

Defence

8.-(1) The following are reserved matters-

(a) the defence of the realm,

(b) the naval, military or air forces of the Crown, including reserve forces,

(c) visiting forces,

(d) international headquarters and defence organisations,

(e) trading with the enemy and enemy property.

(2) Sub-paragraph (1) does not reserve-

(a) civil defence,

(b) the conferral of enforcement powers in relation to sea fishing.

Treason

9. Treason (including constructive treason), treason felony and misprision of treason are reserved matters.

PART II
SPECIFIC RESERVATIONS
Preliminary

1. The matters to which any of the Sections in this Part apply are reserved matters for the purposes of this Act.

2. A Section applies to any matter described or referred to in the entry under the heading "reservation", when read with any other entries in that Section.

3. The other entries in a Section relate only to that Section, unless otherwise indicated (so that an entry under the heading "exceptions from reservation" does not generally affect any other Section).

Reservations
HEAD 1 - FINANCIAL AND ECONOMIC MATTERS
SECTION 1 - FISCAL, ECONOMIC AND MONETARY POLICY
Reservation

Fiscal, economic and monetary policy, including the issue and circulation

of money, taxes and excise duties, government borrowing and lending, control over United Kingdom public expenditure, the exchange rate and the Bank of England.

Exception from reservation

Local taxes to fund local authority expenditure (for example, council tax and non-domestic rates).

Scots private law

In spite of section 28(4), interest on sums due in respect of taxes or excise duties and refunds of such taxes or duties is not within the legislative competence of the Parliament.

SECTION 2 - THE CURRENCY

Reservation

Coinage, legal tender and bank notes.

SECTION 3 - FINANCIAL SERVICES

Reservation

Financial services, including investment business, banking and deposit-taking, collective investment schemes and insurance.

Exceptions from reservation

The subject-matter of section 1 of the Banking and Financial Dealings Act 1971 (bank holidays).

SECTION 4 - FINANCIAL MARKETS

Reservation

Financial markets, including listing and public offers of securities and investments, transfer of securities and insider dealing.

SECTION 5 - MONEY LAUNDERING

Reservation

The subject-matter of the Money Laundering Regulations 1993, but in relation to any type of business.

HEAD 2 - HOME AFFAIRS
SECTION 1 - MISUSE OF DRUGS

Reservation

The subject-matter of-

(a) the Misuse of Drugs Act 1971,
(b) sections 12 to 14 of the Criminal Justice (International Co-operation) Act 1990 (substances useful for manufacture of controlled drugs), and
(c) Part V of the Criminal Law (Consolidation) (Scotland) Act 1995 (drug trafficking) and, so far as relating to drug trafficking, the Proceeds of Crime (Scotland) Act 1995.

SECTION 2 - DATA PROTECTION

Reservation

The subject matter of-

(a) the Data Protection Act 1984, and

(b) Council Directive 95/46/EC (protection of individuals with regard to the processing of personal data and on the free movement of such data).

SECTION 3 - ELECTIONS

Reservation

The subject matter of-

(a) the European Parliamentary Elections Act 1978,

(b) the Representation of the People Act 1983 and the Representation of the People Act 1985, and

(c) the Parliamentary Constituencies Act 1986.

Exception from reservation

Local government elections, except the franchise.

SECTION 4 - FIREARMS

Reservation

The subject-matter of the Firearms Acts 1968 to 1997.

SECTION 5 - ENTERTAINMENT

Reservation

The subject-matter of-

(a) the Hypnotism Act 1952,

(b) sections 12 to 14 of the Theatres Act 1968 (licensing of premises),

(c) the Video Recordings Act 1984, and

(d) sections 1 to 16 of the Cinemas Act 1985 (control of exhibitions).

The classification of films for public exhibition by reference to their suitability for viewing by persons generally or above a particular age, with or without any advice as to the desirability of parental guidance.

SECTION 6 - IMMIGRATION AND NATIONALITY

Reservation

Nationality; immigration, including asylum and the status and capacity of persons in the United Kingdom who are not British citizens; free movement of persons within the European Economic Area; issue of travel documents.

SECTION 7 - SCIENTIFIC PROCEDURES ON LIVE ANIMALS

Reservation

The subject-matter of the Animals (Scientific Procedures) Act 1986.

SECTION 8 - NATIONAL SECURITY, INTERCEPTION OF COMMUNICATIONS, OFFICIAL SECRETS AND TERRORISM

Reservation

National security.

The subject-matter of the Interception of Communications Act 1985, except so far as relating to the prevention or detection of serious crime (within the meaning of that Act).

The Security Service, the Secret Intelligence Service and the Government Communications Headquarters.

The subject-matter of-

(a) the Official Secrets Acts 1911 and 1920, and

(b) the Official Secrets Act 1989, except so far as relating to any information, document or other article protected against disclosure by section 4(2) (crime) and not by any other provision of sections 1 to 4.

Special powers, and other special provisions, for dealing with terrorism.

SECTION 9 - BETTING, GAMING AND LOTTERIES

Reservation

Betting, gaming and lotteries.

SECTION 10 - EMERGENCY POWERS

Reservation

Emergency powers.

SECTION 11 - EXTRADITION

Reservation

Extradition.

SECTION 12 - LIEUTENANCIES

Reservation

The subject-matter of the Lieutenancies Act 1997.

HEAD 3 - TRADE AND INDUSTRY
SECTION 1 - BUSINESS ASSOCIATIONS

Reservation

The creation, operation, regulation and dissolution of types of business association.

Exceptions from reservation

The creation, operation, regulation and dissolution of-

(a) particular public bodies, or public bodies of a particular type, established by or under any enactment,

(b) charities.

Interpretation

"Business association" means any person (other than an individual) established for the purpose of carrying on any kind of business, whether or not for profit; and "business" includes the provision of benefits to the members of an association.

SECTION 2 - INSOLVENCY

Reservation

In relation to business associations-

(a) the modes of, the grounds for and the general legal effect of winding up, and the persons who may initiate winding up,

(b) liability to contribute to assets on winding up,

(c) powers of courts in relation to proceedings for winding up, other than the power to sist proceedings,

(d) arrangements with creditors, and

(e) procedures giving protection from creditors.

Preferred or preferential debts for the purposes of the Bankruptcy (Scotland) Act 1985, the Insolvency Act 1986, and any other enactment relating to the sequestration of the estate of any person or to the winding up of business associations, the preference of such debts against other such debts and the extent of their preference over other types of debt.

Regulation of insolvency practitioners.

Co-operation of insolvency courts.

Exceptions from reservation

In relation to business associations-

(a) the process of winding up, including the person having responsibility for the conduct of a winding up or any part of it, and his conduct of it or of that part,

(b) the effect of winding up on diligence, and

(c) avoidance and adjustment of prior transactions on winding up.

Floating charges and receivers, except in relation to preferential debts, regulation of insolvency practitioners and co-operation of insolvency courts.

Interpretation

"Business association" has the meaning given in Section 1 of this Head, but does not include any person whose estate may be sequestrated under the Bankruptcy (Scotland) Act 1985 or any public body established by or under an enactment.

"Winding up", in relation to business associations, includes winding up of solvent, as well as insolvent, business associations.

SECTION 3 - COMPETITION

Reservation

Regulation of anti-competitive practices and agreements; abuse of dominant position; monopolies and mergers.

Exceptions from reservation
Regulation of particular practices in the legal profession for the purpose of regulating that profession or the provision of legal services.

Interpretation
"The legal profession" means advocates, solicitors and qualified conveyancers and executry practitioners within the meaning of Part II of the Law Reform (Miscellaneous Provisions) (Scotland) Act 1990.

SECTION 4 - INTELLECTUAL PROPERTY
Reservation
Intellectual property.

Exception from reservation
The subject-matter of Part I of the Plant Varieties and Seeds Act 1964 (plant breeders' rights).

SECTION 5 - IMPORT AND EXPORT CONTROL
Reservation
The subject-matter of the Import, Export and Customs Powers (Defence) Act 1939.
Prohibition and regulation of the import and export of endangered species of animals and plants.

Exceptions from reservation
Prohibition and regulation of movement into and out of Scotland of-
(a) food, animals, animal products, plants and plant products for the purposes of protecting human, animal or plant health, animal welfare or the environment or observing or implementing obligations under the Common Agricultural Policy, and
(b) animal feeding stuffs, fertilisers and pesticides for the purposes of protecting human, animal or plant health or the environment.

SECTION 6 - CONSUMER PROTECTION
Reservation
Regulation of-
(a) the sale and supply of goods and services to consumers,
(b) guarantees in relation to such goods and services,
(c) hire purchase. including the subject-matter of Part III of the Hire Purchase Act 1964,
(d) trade descriptions, except in relation to food,
(e) misleading and comparative advertising, except regulation specifically in relation to food, tobacco and tobacco products,
(f) price indications,
(g) trading stamps,
(h) the conduct of estate agency business,

(i) auctions and mock auctions of goods and services, and

(j) hall-marking and gun barrel proofing.

Safety of, and liability for, services supplied to consumers.

The subject-matter of—

(a) the Hearing Aid Council Act 1968,

(b) the Unsolicited Goods and Services Acts 1971 and 1975,

(c) Parts I to III and XI of the Fair Trading Act 1973,

(d) the Consumer Credit Act 1974,

(e) the Timeshare Act 1992,

(f) the Package Travel, Holidays and Tours Regulations 1992, and

(g) the Commercial Agents (Council Directive) Regulations 1993.

Exception from reservation

The subject-matter of section 16 of the Food Safety Act 1990 (food safety and consumer protection).

SECTION 7 - PRODUCT STANDARDS SAFETY AND LIABILITY
Reservation

Technical standards and requirements in relation to products in pursuance of an obligation under Community law.

Product safety and liability.

Product labelling.

Exceptions from reservation

Food, agricultural and horticultural produce, fish and fish products, seeds, animal feeding stuffs, fertilisers and pesticides.

In relation to food safety, materials which come into contact with food.

SECTION 8 - WEIGHTS AND MEASURES
Reservation

Units and standards of weight and measurement.

Regulation of trade so far as involving weighing, measuring and quantities.

SECTION 9 - TELECOMMUNICATIONS AND WIRELESS TELEGRA-PHY
Reservation

Telecommunications and wireless telegraphy.

Internet services.

Electronic encryption.

The subject-matter of Part 11 of the Wireless Telegraphy Act 1949 (electro-magnetic disturbance).

Exception from reservation

The subject-matter of the Interception of Communications Act 1985 so far as relating to the prevention or detection of serious crime (within the meaning of that Act).

SECTION 10 - POST OFFICE, POSTS AND POSTAL SERVICES
Reservation
The Post Office, posts (including postage stamps, postal orders and postal packets) and regulation of postal services.

Exception from reservation
The subject-matter of the Interception of Communications Act 1985 so far as relating to the prevention or detection of serious crime (within the meaning of that Act).

SECTION 11 - RESEARCH COUNCILS
Reservation
Research Councils within the meaning of the Science and Technology Act 1965.
The subject-matter of section 5 of that Act (funding of scientific research) so far as relating to Research Councils.

SECTION 12 - DESIGNATION OF ASSISTED AREAS
Reservation
The subject-matter of section I of the Industrial Development Act 1982.

SECTION 13 - PROTECTION OF TRADING AND ECONOMIC INTER-
ESTS
Reservation
The subject-matter of—
(a) section 2 of the Emergency Laws (Re-enactments and Repeals) Act 1964 (Treasury power in relation to action damaging to economic position of United Kingdom),
(b) Part 11 of the Industry Act 1975 (powers in relation to transfer of control of important manufacturing undertakings), and
(c) the Protection of Trading Interests Act 1980.

HEAD 4 - ENERGY
SECTION 1 - ELECTRICITY
Reservation
Regulation of the generation. transmission, distribution and supply of electricity. The subject-matter of Part 11 of the Electricity Act 1989.

SECTION 2 - OIL AND GAS
Reservation
Oil and gas, including—
(a) the ownership of, exploration for and exploitation of deposits of oil and natural gas,
(b) offshore installations and pipelines,
(c) the subject-matter of the Pipe-lines Act 1962 (including section 5 (deemed planning permission)) so far as relating to pipelines within the

meaning of section 65 of that Act,

(d) the application of Scots law and the jurisdiction of the Scottish courts in relation to offshore activities,

(e) pollution relating to oil and gas exploration and exploitation, but only outside controlled waters (within the meaning of section 30A(I) of the Control of Pollution Act 1974),

(f) restrictions on navigation, fishing and other activities in connection with offshore activities, and

(g) liquefaction of natural gas and the conveyance, shipping and supply of gas through pipes.

Exceptions from reservation

The subject-matter of the Offshore Petroleum Development (Scotland) Act 1975, other than sections 3 to 7.

The manufacture of gas.

The conveyance, shipping and supply of gas other than through pipes.

SECTION 3 - COAL
Reservation

Coal, including its ownership and exploitation, deep and opencast coal mining and coal mining subsidence.

Exceptions from reservation

Sections 53 (environmental duties in connection with planning) and 54 (obligation to restore land affected by coal-mining operations) of the Coal Industry Act 1994.

SECTION 4 - NUCLEAR ENERGY
Reservation

Nuclear energy and nuclear installations, including—

(a) nuclear safety, security and safeguards, and

(b) liability for nuclear occurrences.

Exception from reservation

The subject-matter of—

(a) Part I of the Environmental Protection Act 1990, and

(b) the Radioactive Substances Act 1993.

SECTION 5 - ENERGY CONSERVATION
Reservation

The subject-matter of the Energy Act 1976, other than section 9.

Exception from reservation

The encouragement of energy efficiency other than by prohibition or regulation.

HEAD 5 - TRANSPORT
SECTION 1 - ROAD TRANSPORT

Reservation

The subject-matter of—

(a) the Motor Vehicles (International Circulation) Act 1952,

(b) the Public Passenger Vehicles Act 1981 and the Transport Act 1985, so far as relating to public service vehicle operator licensing,

(c) section 17 (traffic regulation on special roads), section 25 (pedestrian crossings), Part V (traffic signs) and Part VI (speed limits) of the Road Traffic Regulation Act 1984,

(d) the Road Traffic Act 1988 and the Road Traffic Offenders Act 1988,

(e) the Vehicle Excise and Registration Act 1994,

(f) the Road Traffic (New Drivers) Act 1995, and

(g) the Goods Vehicles (Licensing of Operators) Act 1995.

Regulation of proper hours or periods of work by persons engaged in the carriage of passengers or goods by road.

The conditions under which international road transport services for passengers or goods may be undertaken.

Regulation of the instruction of drivers of motor vehicles.

Grants to operators of bus services so as to defray any duty charged on fuel.

Exceptions from reservation

Sections 39 and 40 (road safety information and training) and 157 to 159 (payments for treatment of traffic casualties) of the Road Traffic Act 1988.

SECTION 2 - RAIL TRANSPORT

Reservation

Provision and regulation of railway services.

Rail transport security.

The subject-matter of the Channel Tunnel Act 1987.

The subject-matter of the Railway Heritage Act 1996.

Exceptions from reservation

Grants so far as relating to railway services; but this exception does not apply in relation to—

(a) the subject-matter of section 63 of the Railways Act 1993 (government financial assistance where railway administration orders made),

(b) "railway services" as defined in section 82(1)(b) of the Railways Act 1993 (carriage of goods by railway), or

(c) the subject-matter of section 136 of the Railways Act 1993 (grants and subsidies) .

Interpretation

"Railway services" has the meaning given by section 82 of the Railways Act 1993 (excluding the wider meaning of "railway" given by section 81(2) of that Act).

SECTION 3 - MARINE TRANSPORT

Reservation

The subject-matter of-

(a) the Coastguard Act 1925,

(b) the Carriage of Goods by Sea Act 1971,

(c) the Merchant Shipping (Liner Conferences) Act 1982,

(d) the Aviation and Maritime Security Act 1990, other than Part I (Aviation Security),

(e) the Carriage of Goods by Sea Act 1992,

(f) the Merchant Shipping Act 1995,

(g) the Shipping and Trading Interests (Protection) Act 1995, and

(h) section 24 (implementation of international agreements relating to protection of wrecks), section 26 (piracy) and sections 27 and 28 (international bodies concerned with maritime matters) of the Merchant Shipping and Maritime Security Act 1997.

Navigational rights and freedoms.

Financial assistance for shipping services which start or finish or both outside Scotland.

Exceptions from reservation

Ports, harbours, piers and marine works, except in relation to the matters reserved in (d) above.

Regulation of works which may obstruct or endanger navigation.

The subject-matter of the Highlands and Islands Shipping Services Act 1960 in relation to financial assistance for bulk freight services.

Scots private law

In spite of section 28(4), provisions modifying Scots private law as it applies to the subject-matter of the Carriage of Goods by Sea Act 1992 are not within the legislative competence of the Parliament.

Interpretation

"Marine works" has the same meaning as in section 57(1) of the Harbours Act 15 1964.

SECTION 4 - AIR TRANSPORT

Reservation

Regulation of aviation and air transport, including the subject-matter of—

(a) the Carriage by Air Act 1961,

(b) the Carriage by Air (Supplementary Provisions) Act 1962,

(c) the Carriage by Air and Road Act 1979 so far as relating to carriage by air,

(d) the Civil Aviation Act 1982,

(e) the Aviation Security Act 1982,

(f) the Airports Act 1986, and

(g) sections 1 (endangering safety at aerodromes) and 48 (powers in relation to certain aircraft) of the Aviation and Maritime Security Act 1990,
and arrangements to compensate or repatriate passengers in the event of an air
transport operator's insolvency.

Exceptions from reservation

The subject-matter of the following sections of the Civil Aviation Act 1982—
(a) section 25 (Secretary of State's power to provide aerodromes),
(b) section 30 (provision of aerodromes and facilities at aerodromes by
local authorities),
(c) section 34 (financial assistance for certain aerodromes),
(d) section 35 (facilities for consultation at certain aerodromes),
(e) section 36 (health control at Secretary of State's aerodromes and aerodromes of Civil Aviation Authority), and
(f) sections 41 to 50 (powers in relation to land exercisable in connection
with civil aviation) where land is acquired for the purpose of airport 40
development or expansion.

The subject-matter of Part II (transfer of airport undertakings of local authorities), sections 63 and 64 (airport byelaws) and 66 (functions of operators
of designated airports as respects abandoned vehicles) of the Airports Act 1986.

SECTION 5 - OTHER MATTERS

Reservation

Transport of radioactive material.

Standards for public passenger transport for disabled persons, including
the subject-matter of—
(a) section 125(7) and (8) of the Transport Act 1985 (Secretary of State's
guidance and consultation with the Disabled Persons Transport Advisory Committee), and
(b) Part V of the Disability Discrimination Act 1995 (public transport).
Regulation of the carriage of dangerous goods.

Interpretation

"Radioactive material" has the same meaning as in section 1(1) of the Radioactive Material (Road Transport) Act 1991.

HEAD 6 - SOCIAL SECURITY
SECTION 1 - SOCIAL SECURITY SCHEMES

Reservation

Schemes supported from central or local funds which provide assistance
for social security purposes to or in respect of individuals by way of benefits.
Requiring persons to—
(a) establish and administer schemes providing assistance for social security purposes to or in respect of individuals, or
(b) make payments to or in respect of such schemes,
and to keep records and supply information in connection with such schemes.

The circumstances in which a person is liable to maintain himself or another for the purposes of the enactments relating to social security and the Child Support Acts 1991 to 1995.

The subject-matter of the Vaccine Damage Payment Scheme.

Illustrations of reservation

National Insurance; Social Fund; administration and funding of housing benefit and council tax benefit by local authorities; recovery of benefits for accident, injury or disease from persons paying damages; sharing information between government departments for the purposes of the enactments relating to social security; making decisions for the purposes of schemes mentioned in the reservation and appeals against such decisions.

Exceptions from reservation

The subject-matter of section 22 of the National Assistance Act 1948 (charges for local authority accommodation), Part 11 of the Social Work (Scotland) Act 1968 (social welfare services), section 50 of the Children Act 1975 (payments towards maintenance of children), sections 22 (promotion of welfare of children in need), 29 and 40 30 (advice and assistance for young persons formerly looked after by local authorities) of the Children (Scotland) Act 1995 and the Community Care (Direct Payments) Act 1996.

Interpretation

"Benefits" includes pensions, allowances, grants, loans and any other form of financial assistance.

Providing assistance for social security purposes to or in respect of individuals includes (among other things) providing assistance to or in respect of individuals—

(a) who qualify by reason of old age, survivorship, disability, sickness, incapacity, injury, unemployment, maternity or the care of children or others needing care,

(b) who qualify by reason of low income, or

(c) in relation to their housing costs or liabilities for local taxes (for example, council tax and non-domestic rates).

SECTION 2 - CHILD SUPPORT
Reservation
The subject-matter of the Child Support Acts 1991 to 1995.

SECTION 3 - OCCUPATIONAL AND PERSONAL PENSIONS
Reservation
Occupational pension schemes and personal pension schemes.

Where pension payable to or in respect of any class of persons under a public service pension scheme is covered by this reservation, so are enactments making provision in their case—

(a) for compensation for loss of office or employment, for their office or employment being affected by constitutional changes, or circumstances arising from such changes, in any territory or territories or for loss or diminution of emoluments, or

(b) for benefits in respect of death or incapacity resulting from injury or disease.

Illustrations of reservation

The Pensions (Increase) Act 1971.

Schemes for the payment of pensions which are listed in Schedule 2 to that Act; schemes under section 26 of the Fire Services Act 1947, the Superannuation Act 1972, the Overseas Pensions Act 1973 or section I of the Police Pensions Act 1976.

The Pensions Acts.

Exceptions from reservation

Provision tor the payment, in accordance with the Pensions Acts, of pensions—

(a) in pursuance of section 76, or

(b) to or in respect of any person who has ceased to be a member of the staff of the Parliament.

Authorising or requiring any public body with functions relating to devolved . matters to provide tor pensions for its members or staff in accordance with the Pensions Acts.

Scots private law

In spite of section 28(4)—

(a) the obligations of the trustees or managers of an occupational or personal pension scheme in cases where liabilities under orders made in matrimonial proceedings, or agreements made between the parties to a marriage, are to be satisfied out of assets of the scheme, and

(b) other provisions of the law about occupational or personal pension schemes which regulates the trustees or managers of such schemes,

are not within the legislative competence of the Parliament.

Interpretation

"The Pensions Acts" means the Pension Schemes Act 1993 and Part I of the Pensions Act 1995.

"Occupational pension scheme" and "personal pension scheme" have the 5 meanings given by section I of the Pension Schemes Act 1993, but as if the reference to employed earners in the definition of personal pension scheme were to any earners.

"Pension" includes gratuities and allowances.

"Public service pension scheme" includes any scheme within the definition of public service pension scheme in section I of the Pension Schemes Act 1993, but as if the references to a Minister of the Crown included the Scottish Ministers.

SECTION 4 - WAR PENSIONS

Reservation

Schemes for the payment of pensions for or in respect of persons who have a 15 disablement or have died in consequence of service as members of the armed forces of the Crown.

The subject-matter of any scheme under the Personal Injuries (Emergency Provisions) Act 1939, sections 3 to 5 and 7 of the Pensions (Navy, Army, Air Force and Mercantile Marine) Act 1939 or section I of the Polish Resettlement Act 1947.

Illustrations of reservation

The provision of pensions under the Naval, Military and Air Forces Etc. (Disablement and Death) Service Pensions Order 1983.

Interpretation

"Pension" includes grants, allowances, supplements and gratuities.

HEAD 7 - REGULATION OF THE PROFESSIONS
SECTION 1 - ARCHITECTS

Reservation

Regulation of the profession of architect.

SECTION 2 - HEALTH PROFESSIONS

Reservation

Regulation of the health professions.

Exceptions from reservation

The subject-matter of—

(a) section 21 of the National Health Service (Scotland) Act 1978 (require-ment of suitable experience for medical practitioners), and

(b) section 25 of that Act (arrangements for the provision of general dental services), so far as it relates to vocational training and disciplinary pro-ceedings.

Interpretation

"The health professions" means the professions regulated by the Pharmacy Act 1954, the Professions Supplementary to Medicine Act 1960, the Veteri-nary Surgeons Act 1966, the Medical Act 1983, the Dentists Act 1984, the Opticians Act 1989, the Osteopaths Act 1993, the Chiropractors Act 1994, and the Nurses, Midwives and Health Visitors Act 1997.

SECTION 3 - AUDITORS

Reservation

Regulation of the profession of auditor.

HEAD 8 - EMPLOYMENT
SECTION 1 - EMPLOYMENT AND INDUSTRIAL RELATIONS
Reservation

Employment rights and duties and industrial relations, including the subject matter of—

(a) the Employers' Liability (Compulsory Insurance) Act 1969,

(b) the Employment Agencies Act 1973,

(c) the Pneumoconiosis etc. (Workers' Compensation) Act 1979,

(d) the Transfer of Undertakings (Protection of Employment) Regulations

(e) the Trade Union and Labour Relations (Consolidation) Act 1992,

(f) the Industrial Tribunals Act 1996, and

(g) the Employment Rights Act 1996.

Exception from reservation

The subject-matter of the Agricultural Wages (Scotland) Act 1949.

SECTION 2 - HEALTH AND SAFETY
Reservation

The subject-matter of the following Parts of the Health and Safety at Work etc. Act 1974—

(a) Part I (health, safety and welfare in connection with work, and control of dangerous substances) as extended or applied by section 36 of the Consumer Protection Act 1987, section 1 and 2 of the Offshore Safety Act 1992 and section 117 of the Railways Act 1993, and

(b) Part II (the Employment Medical Advisory Service).

Exception from reservation

Public safety in relation to matters which are not reserved.

SECTION 3 - JOB SEARCH AND SUPPORT
Reservation

Provision of advice and support, including financial support, for the purposes of assisting persons to select, obtain training for, obtain and retain employment or for the purposes of assisting persons to obtain suitable employees.

Exceptions from reservation

Provision of schemes, by bodies carrying on activities only within Scotland, for the giving of such advice and support.

The subject-matter of sections 8 to 10A of the Employment and Training Act 1973 (careers services).

HEAD 9 - HEALTH AND MEDICINES
SECTION 1 - ABORTION
Reservation

Abortion.

SECTION 2 - XENOTRANSPLANTATION
Reservation

Xenotransplantation.

SECTION 3 - EMBRYOLOGY, SURROGACY AND GENETICS
Reservation

Surrogacy arrangements, within the meaning of the Surrogacy Arrangements Act 1985, including the subject-matter of that Act.

The subject-matter of the Human Fertilisation and Embryology Act 1990. Human genetics.

SECTION 4 - MEDICINES AND POISONS
Reservation

The subject-matter of—
(a) the Medicines Act 1968 and the Medicines for Human Use (Marketing Authorisations Etc.) Regulations 1994,
(b) the Poisons Act 1972, and
(c) the Biological Standards Act 1975.

Regulation of prices charged for medicines supplied for the purposes of the health service established under section I of the National Health Service (Scotland) Act 1978.

SECTION 5 - WELFARE FOODS
Reservation

Schemes made by regulations under section 13 of the Social Security Act 1988 (schemes for distribution of welfare foods).

HEAD 10 - MEDIA AND CULTURE
SECTION 1 - BROADCASTING
Reservation

The subject-matter of the Broadcasting Act 1990 and the Broadcasting Act 1996.

The British Broadcasting Corporation.

SECTION 2 - PUBLIC LENDING RIGHT

Reservation

The subject-matter of the Public Lending Right Act 1979.

SECTION 3 - GOVERNMENT INDEMNITY SCHEME

Reservation

The subject-matter of sections 16 and 16A of the National Heritage Act 1980 (public indemnities tor objects on loan to museums, art galleries, etc.).

SECTION 4 - PROPERTY ACCEPTED IN SATISFACTION OF TAX

Reservation

The subject-matter of sections 8 and 9 of the National Heritage Act 1980 (payments to Inland Revenue in respect of property accepted in satisfaction of tax, and disposal of such property).

HEAD 11 - MISCELLANEOUS
SECTION 1 - JUDICIAL REMUNERATION

Reservation

Determination of the remuneration of—

(a) judges of the Court of Session,

(b) sheriffs principal and sheriffs,

(c) members of the Lands Tribunal for Scotland, and

(d) the Chairman of the Scottish Land Court.

SECTION 2 - EQUAL OPPORTUNITIES

Reservation

Equal opportunities, including the subject-matter of—

(a) the Equal Pay Act 1970,

(b) the Sex Discrimination Act 1975,

(c) the Race Relations Act 1976, and

(d) the Disability Discrimination Act 1995.

Exceptions from reservation

The encouragement of the observance of the equal opportunity requirements.

Imposing duties on public bodies with functions relating to devolved matters to 30 make arrangements with a view to securing that their functions are carried out with due regard to the need to meet the equal opportunity requirements.

Interpretation

"Equal opportunities" means the prevention, elimination or regulation of discrimination between persons on grounds of sex or marital status, on racial grounds, or on grounds of disability or of other personal attributes, including beliefs or opinions, such as religious beliefs or political opinions.

"Equal opportunity requirements" means the requirements of the law for the time being relating to equal opportunities.

SECTION 3 - CONTROL OF WEAPONS

Reservation

Control of nuclear, biological and chemical weapons and other weapons of mass destruction .

SECTION 4 - ORDNANCE SURVEY

Reservation

The subject-matter of the Ordnance Survey Act 1841.

SECTION 5 - TIME

Reservation

Timescales, time zones and the subject-matter of the Summer Time Act 1972.

The calendar; units of time; the date of Easter.

Exceptions from reservation

The computation of periods of time.

The subject-matter of—

(a) section I of the Banking and Financial Dealings Act 1971 (bank holidays), and

(b) the Term and Quarter Days (Scotland) Act 1990.

SECTION 6 - OUTER SPACE

Reservation

Regulation of activities in outer space.

PART III
INTERPRETATION

1. References in this Schedule to any enactment-

    (a) are to be read as references to that enactment as it has effect on the principal appointed day or, if it ceased to have effect on an earlier day, as it had effect immediately before that earlier day, and

    (b) include references to that enactment as amended, but do not include references to that enactment as extended or applied, by any other enactment.

    2. Paragraph 1 is subject to any express provision to the contrary.

SCHEDULE 6
DEVOLUTION ISSUES
PART I
PRELIMINARY

1. In this Schedule "devolution issue" means a question-

(a) whether an Act of the Scottish Parliament or any provision of an Act of the Scottish Parliament is within the legislative competence of the Parliament,

(b) whether subordinate legislation which a member of the Scottish Executive has purported to make or is proposing to make, or any provision of such legislation, would be within the legislative competence of the Parliament if it were included in an Act of the Scottish Parliament,

(c) whether a matter in relation to which a member of the Scottish Executive has purported to exercise or proposes to exercise a function (other than a function to make subordinate legislation) is a reserved matter,

(d) whether a purported or proposed exercise of a function (other than a function to make subordinate legislation) by a member of the Scottish Executive is, or would be, incompatible with any of the Convention rights or with Community law,

(e) whether a failure to act by a member of the Scottish Executive is incompatible with any of the Convention rights or with Community law, or

(f) whether a matter in relation to which a Minister of the Crown has purported to exercise or proposes to exercise a function is a devolved matter.

2. A devolution issue shall not be taken to arise in any proceedings merely because of any contention of a party to the proceedings which appears to the court or tribunal before which the proceedings take place to be frivolous or vexatious.

PART II
PROCEEDINGS IN SCOTLAND
Application of Part II

3. This Part of this Schedule applies in relation to devolution issues in proceedings in Scotland.

Institution of proceedings

4. - (1) Proceedings for the determination of a devolution issue may be instituted by the Advocate General or the Lord Advocate.

(2) The Lord Advocate may defend any such proceedings instituted by the Advocate General.

(3) This paragraph is without prejudice to any power to institute or defend proceedings exercisable apart from this paragraph by any person.

Intimation of devolution issue

5. A court or tribunal shall order intimation of any devolution issue which

arises in any proceedings before it to be given to the Advocate General and the Lord Advocate (unless the person to whom the intimation would be given is a party to the proceedings).

6. A person to whom intimation is given in pursuance of paragraph 5 may take part as a party in the proceedings, so far as they relate to a devolution issue.

Reference of devolution issue to higher court
7. A court, other than the House of Lords or any court consisting of three or more judges of the Court of Session, may refer any devolution issue which arises in proceedings (other than criminal proceedings) before it to the Inner House of the Court of Session.

8. A tribunal from which there is no appeal shall refer any devolution issue which arises in proceedings before it to the Inner House of the Court of Session; and any other tribunal may make such a reference.

9. A court, other than any court consisting of two or more judges of the High Court of Justiciary, may refer any devolution issue which arises in criminal proceedings before it to the High Court of Justiciary.

References from superior courts to Judicial Committee
10. Any court consisting of three or more judges of the Court of Session may refer any devolution issue which arises in proceedings before it (otherwise than on a reference under paragraph 7 or 8) to the Judicial Committee.

11. Any court consisting of two or more judges of the High Court of Justiciary may refer any devolution issue which arises in proceedings before it (otherwise than on a reference under paragraph 9) to the Judicial Committee.

Appeals from superior courts to Judicial Committee
12. An appeal against a determination of a devolution issue by the Inner House of the Court of Session on a reference under paragraph 7 or 8 shall lie to the Judicial Committee.

13. An appeal against a determination of a devolution issue by-
    (a) a court of two or more judges of the High Court of Justiciary (whether in the ordinary course of proceedings or on a reference under paragraph 9), or
    (b) a court of three or more judges of the Court of Session from which there is no appeal to the House of Lords,
shall lie to the Judicial Committee, but only with leave of the court concerned or, failing such leave, with special leave of the Judicial Committee.

PART III
PROCEEDINGS IN ENGLAND AND WALES
Application of Part III

14. This Part of this Schedule applies in relation to devolution issues in proceedings in England and Wales.

Institution of proceedings

15.-(1) Proceedings for the determination of a devolution issue may be instituted by the Attorney General.

(2) The Lord Advocate may defend any such proceedings.

(3) This paragraph is without prejudice to any power to institute or defend proceedings exercisable apart from this paragraph by any person.

Notice of devolution issue

16. A court or tribunal shall order notice of any devolution issue which arises in any proceedings before it to be given to the Attorney General and the Lord Advocate (unless the person to whom the notice would be given is a party to the proceedings).

17. A person to whom notice is given in pursuance of paragraph 16 may take part as a party in the proceedings, so far as they relate to a devolution issue.

Reference of devolution issue to High Court or Court of Appeal

18. A magistrates' court may refer any devolution issue which arises in proceedings (other than criminal proceedings) before it to the High Court.

19.-(1) A court may refer any devolution issue which arises in proceedings (other than criminal proceedings) before it to the Court of Appeal.

(2) Sub-paragraph (1) does not apply to-

(a) a magistrates' court, the Court of Appeal or the House of Lords, or

(b) the High Court if the devolution issue arises in proceedings on a reference under paragraph 18.

20. A tribunal from which there is no appeal shall refer any devolution issue which arises in proceedings before it to the Court of Appeal; and any other tribunal may make such a reference.

21. A court, other than the House of Lords or the Court of Appeal, may refer any devolution issue which arises in criminal proceedings before it to-

(a) the High Court (if the proceedings are summary proceedings), or

(b) the Court of Appeal (if the proceedings are proceedings on indictment).

References from Court of Appeal to Judicial Committee

22. The Court of Appeal may refer any devolution issue which arises in proceedings before it (otherwise than on a reference under paragraph 19, 20 or 21) to the Judicial Committee.

Appeals from superior courts to Judicial Committee

23. An appeal against a determination of a devolution issue by the High Court or the Court of Appeal on a reference under paragraph 18, 19, 20 or 21 shall lie to the Judicial Committee, but only with leave of the High Court or (as the case may be) the Court of Appeal or, failing such leave, with special leave of the Judicial Committee.

PART IV
PROCEEDINGS IN NORTHERN IRELAND
Application of Part IV

24. This Part of this Schedule applies in relation to devolution issues in proceedings in Northern Ireland.

Institution of proceedings

25.-(1) Proceedings for the determination of a devolution issue may be instituted by the Attorney General for Northern Ireland.

(2) The Lord Advocate may defend any such proceedings.

(3) This paragraph is without prejudice to any power to institute or defend proceedings exercisable apart from this paragraph by any person.

Notice of devolution issue

26. A court or tribunal shall order notice of any devolution issue which arises in any proceedings before it to be given to the Attorney General for Northern Ireland and the Lord Advocate (unless the person to whom the notice would be given is a party to the proceedings).

27. A person to whom notice is given in pursuance of paragraph 26 may take part as a party in the proceedings, so far as they relate to a devolution issue.

Reference of devolution issue to Court of Appeal

28. A court, other than the House of Lords or the Court of Appeal in Northern Ireland, may refer any devolution issue which arises in any proceedings before it to the Court of Appeal in Northern Ireland.

29. A tribunal from which there is no appeal shall refer any devolution issue which arises in any proceedings before it to the Court of Appeal in Northern Ireland; and any other tribunal may make such a reference.

References from Court of Appeal to Judicial Committee

30. The Court of Appeal in Northern Ireland may refer any devolution issue which arises in proceedings before it (otherwise than on a reference under paragraph 28 or 29) to the Judicial Committee.

Appeals from Court of Appeal to Judicial Committee

31. An appeal against a determination of a devolution issue by the Court of Appeal in Northern Ireland on a reference under paragraph 28 or 29 shall lie to

the Judicial Committee, but only with leave of the Court of Appeal in Northern Ireland or, failing such leave, with special leave of the Judicial Committee.

PART V
GENERAL
Proceedings in the House of Lords

32. Any devolution issue which arises in judicial proceedings in the House of Lords shall be referred to the Judicial Committee unless the House considers it more appropriate, having regard to all the circumstances, that it should determine the issue.

Direct references to Judicial Committee

33. The Lord Advocate, the Advocate General, the Attorney General or the Attorney General for Northern Ireland may require any court or tribunal to refer to the Judicial Committee any devolution issue which has arisen in proceedings before it to which he is a party.

34. The Lord Advocate, the Attorney General, the Advocate General or the Attorney General for Northern Ireland may refer to the Judicial Committee any devolution issue which is not the subject of proceedings.

35.-(1) This paragraph applies where a reference is made under paragraph 34 in relation to a devolution issue which relates to the proposed exercise of a function by a member of the Scottish Executive.

(2) The person making the reference shall notify a member of the Scottish Executive of that fact.

(3) No member of the Scottish Executive shall exercise the function in the manner proposed during the period beginning with the receipt of the notification under sub-paragraph (2) and ending with the reference being decided or otherwise disposed of.

(4) Proceedings relating to any possible failure by a member of the Scottish Executive to comply with sub-paragraph (3) may be instituted by the Advocate General.

(5) Sub-paragraph (4) is without prejudice to any power to institute proceedings exercisable apart from that sub-paragraph by any person.

Expenses

36.-(1) A court or tribunal before which any proceedings take place may take account of any additional expense of the kind mentioned in sub-paragraph (3) in deciding any question as to costs or expenses.

(2) In deciding any such question, the court or tribunal may award the whole or part of the additional expense as costs or (as the case may be) expenses to the party who incurred it (whatever the decision on the devolution issue).

(3) The additional expense is any additional expense which the court or tribunal considers that any party to the proceedings has incurred as a result of the participation of any person in pursuance of paragraph 6, 17 or 27.

Procedure of courts and tribunals

37. Any power to make provision for regulating the procedure before any court or tribunal shall include power to make provision for the purposes of this Schedule including, in particular, provision-

 (a) for prescribing the stage in the proceedings at which a devolution issue is to be raised or referred,

 (b) for the sisting or staying of proceedings for the purpose of any proceedings under this Schedule, and

 (c) for determining the manner in which and the time within which any intimation or notice is to be given.

Interpretation

38. Any duty or power conferred by this Schedule to refer a devolution issue to a court shall be construed as a duty or (as the case may be) power to refer the issue to the court for decision.

SCHEDULE 7
MODIFICATIONS OF ENACTMENTS
Crown Suits (Scotland) Act 1857 (c.44)
1.-(1) The Crown Suits (Scotland) Act 1857 is amended as follows.

(2) In section 1 (Crown suits may be brought by or against Lord Advocate)-

(a) after "Crown" there is inserted "(including the Scottish Administration)",
and

(b) for "Her Majesty's Advocate for the time being" there is substituted
"the appropriate Law Officer".

(3) In section 2 (authority of Crown required)-

(a) for "Her Majesty's Advocate" there is substituted "the appropriate Law
Officer", and

(b) after "Majesty" there is inserted "of the Scottish Administration".

(4) In section 3 (absence of authority cannot be founded upon), for "Her
Majesty's Advocate" there is substituted "the appropriate Law Officer".

(5) After section 4 there is inserted-

"Meaning of "the appropriate Law Officer".

4A. In this Act "the appropriate Law Officer" means-

(a) the Lord Advocate, where the action, suit or proceeding
is on behalf of or against any part of the Scottish Administration, and

(b) the Advocate General for Scotland, in any other case."

(6) In section 5 (change of Lord Advocate not to affect proceedings)-

(a) for "Her Majesty's Advocate" there is substituted "the Lord Advocate
or the Advocate General for Scotland", and

(b) for "the office of Her Majesty's Advocate" there is substituted "that
office".

Private Legislation Procedure (Scotland) Act 1936 (c.52)
2. In section 1 of the Private Legislation Procedure (Scotland) Act 1936 (application for provisional order: notices), after subsection (4) there is added-

"(5) This section shall not apply where any public authority or any persons desire to obtain parliamentary powers the conferring of which is wholly
within the legislative competence of the Scottish Parliament."

Crown Proceedings Act 1947 (c.44)
3.-(1) The Crown Proceedings Act 1947 is amended as follows.

(2) In the proviso to section 44 (remit from sheriff court to Court of Session
on Lord Advocate's certificate)-

(a) for "Lord Advocate" there is substituted "appropriate Law Officer",
and

(b) at the end there is inserted-

"In this proviso, "the appropriate Law Officer" means-

(a) the Lord Advocate, where the proceedings are against the
Scottish Administration, and

(b) the Advocate General for Scotland, in any other case."

(3) In section 50 (application to Scotland of section 35), subsection (2) of section 35 as substituted for Scotland is amended as follows-

(a) in paragraph (d)-

 (i) after "Crown" there is inserted "in right of Her Majesty's Government in the United Kingdom",

 (ii) for "Lord Advocate" there is substituted "Advocate General for Scotland", and

 (iii) after "department", in the second place where it appears, there is inserted-

> "(i) shall not be entitled to avail itself of any set-off or counterclaim if the subject matter thereof relates to the Scottish Administration, and
>
> (ii) ", and

(b) after that paragraph there is inserted-

> "(e)the Scottish Administration, in any proceedings against it or against the Lord Advocate on its behalf, shall not be entitled to avail itself of any set-off or counterclaim if the subject matter thereof relates to the Crown in right of Her Majesty's Government in the United Kingdom,
>
> (f) the Scottish Administration, in any proceedings against it or against the Lord Advocate on its behalf, shall not be entitled to avail itself of any set-off or counterclaim if the subject-matter thereof does not relate to the same part of the Administration as the proceedings."

(4) In section 51(2) (application to Scotland of section 38), in paragraph (ii), after "Lord Advocate" there is inserted "or the Advocate General for Scotland".

Lands Tribunal Act 1949 (c. 42)

4. In section 2 of the Lands Tribunal Act 1949 (members etc. of Lands Tribunal for Scotland), after subsection (9) there is inserted-

> "(10) In the application of this section to the Lands Tribunal for Scotland-
>
> (a) in subsection (8) the words "remuneration and" are omitted, and
>
> (b) after that subsection there is inserted-
>
> > '(8A) The remuneration of members of the Lands Tribunal shall be charged on the Scottish Consolidated Fund'."

Defamation Act 1952 (c.66)

5. In section 10 of the Defamation Act 1952 (limitation on privilege at elections), after "local government authority" there is inserted "to the Scottish Parliament".

Defamation Act (Northern Ireland) 1955 (c.11 (N.I.))

6. In section 10(2) of the Defamation Act (Northern Ireland) 1955 (limitation on privilege at elections), after "Parliament of the United Kingdom" there is

inserted "or to the Scottish Parliament".

European Communities Act 1972 (c. 68)

7.-(1) The European Communities Act 1972 is amended as follows.

(2) In section 2 (general implementation of Treaties)-

(a) references to a statutory power or duty include a power or duty conferred by an Act of the Scottish Parliament or an instrument made under such an Act, and

(b) references to an enactment include an enactment within the meaning of
this Act.

(3) Section 106 of this Act does not apply to the words from the beginning
of section 2(3) to "such Community obligation".

(4) In relation to regulations made by the Scottish Ministers, or an Order in
Council made on the recommendation of the First Minister, under section 2-

(a) in subsection (2), "designated" in the first sentence, and the second
sentence, shall be disregarded,

(b) "Act of Parliament" in subsection (4) shall be read as referring to an
Act of the Scottish Parliament, and

(c) paragraph 2(2) of Schedule 2 shall have effect as if the references to
each, or either, House of Parliament were to the Scottish Parliament.

Interpretation Act 1978 (c. 30)

8.-(1) The Interpretation Act 1978 is amended as follows.

(2) In section 20 (references to other enactments), after subsection (2) there
is inserted-

"(3) In this section "enactment" includes an enactment comprised in an
Act of the Scottish Parliament."

(3) In section 21 (interpretation etc.), after subsection (1) there is inserted-

"(1A) In sections 15 to 18, "Act" includes an Act of the Scottish Parliament.

(1B) In the application of those sections to an Act which is not an Act of
the Scottish Parliament-

(a) "enactment" includes an enactment comprised in an Act of the Scottish Parliament, and

(b) "subordinate legislation" includes an instrument made under an Act
of the Scottish Parliament."

Mental Health Act 1983 (c.20)

9. In section 141 of the Mental Health Act 1983, after subsection (7), there is
added-

"(8) This section also has effect in relation to members of the Scottish
Parliament but as if-

(a) any references to the House of Commons or the Speaker were references to the Scottish Parliament or (as the case may be) the Presiding Officer,

(b) the words from "and thereupon" in subsection (6) to the end of the

The Scotland Bill

subsection were omitted, and

(c) the reference in subsection (7) to sums defrayed out of moneys provided by Parliament were a reference to sums payable out of the Scottish Consolidated Fund."

National Audit Act 1983 (c. 44)

10. Sections 6 and 7 of the National Audit Act 1983 (value for money studies) shall not apply in relation to-

(a) the Scottish Administration or any part of it, or

(b) any other person who only exercises functions in or as regards Scotland none of which relate to reserved matters.

Insolvency Act 1986 (c.45)

11. In section 427(5) of the Insolvency Act 1986 (Parliamentary disqualification)-

(a) after "Commons", where it first appears, there is inserted "or member of the Scottish Parliament",

(b) the words "or, as the case may be, to" are omitted, and

(c) after "Commons", where it appears for the second time, there is inserted "or, as the case may be, the Presiding Officer of the Scottish Parliament."

Public Order Act 1986 (c.64)

12. In section 26(1) of the Public Order Act 1986 (savings for reports of parliamentary proceedings), after "Parliament" there is inserted "or in the Scottish Parliament".

Copyright, Designs and Patents Act 1988 (c. 48)

13.-(1) The Copyright, Designs and Patents Act 1988 is amended as follows.

(2) In section 12(9) (duration of copyright in literary, dramatic, musical or artistic works), for "166" there is substituted "166A".

(3) In section 153(2) (qualification for copyright protection), for "166" there is substituted "166A".

(4) In section 163(6) (Crown copyright), for "and 166" there is substituted "to 166A".

(5) In section 164(1) (Crown copyright in Acts of Parliament etc.), after "Parliament" there is inserted "Act of the Scottish Parliament".

(6) After section 166 there is inserted-

"Copyright in Bills of the Scottish Parliament.

166A.-(1) Copyright in every Bill introduced into the Scottish Parliament belongs to the Scottish Parliamentary Corporate Body.

(2) Copyright under this section subsists from the time when the text of the Bill is handed in to the Parliament for introduction-

(a) until the Bill receives Royal Assent, or

(b) if the Bill does not receive Royal Assent, until it is with-

212

drawn or rejected or no further parliamentary proceedings may be taken in respect of it.

(3) References in this Part to Parliamentary copyright (except in section 165) include copyright under this section; and, except as mentioned above, the provisions of this Part apply in relation to copyright under this section as to other Parliamentary copyright.

(4) No other copyright, or right in the nature of copyright, subsists in a Bill after copyright has once subsisted under this section; but without prejudice to the subsequent operation of this section in relation to a Bill which, not having received Royal Assent, is later reintroduced into the Parliament."

(7) In section 178 (minor definitions), in the definition of "parliamentary proceedings", after "Assembly" there is inserted "of the Scottish Parliament".

(8) In section 179 (index of defined expressions), in column 2 of the entry for "Parliamentary copyright", for "and 166(6)" there is substituted "166(6) and 166A(3)".

European Communities (Amendment) Act 1993 (c. 32)
14. In section 6 of the European Communities (Amendment) Act 1993 (persons who may be proposed for membership of the Committee of the Regions), after "he is" there is inserted "a member of the Scottish Parliament".

Value Added Tax Act 1994 (c. 23)
15. In section 41 of the Value Added Tax Act 1994 (application to the Crown), in subsection (6), after "includes" there is inserted "the Scottish Administration".

Requirements of Writing (Scotland) Act 1995 (c. 7)
16. In section 12(1) of the Requirements of Writing (Scotland) Act 1995 (interpretation)-
 (a) in the definition of "Minister", after "1975" there is inserted "and also includes a member of the Scottish Executive", and
 (b) in paragraph (a) of the definition of "officer", after "Department" there is inserted "or, as the case may be, as a member of the staff of the Scottish Ministers or the Lord Advocate".

Criminal Procedure (Scotland) Act 1995 (c.46)
17. After section 288 of the Criminal Procedure (Scotland) Act 1995 there is inserted-
 "Advocate General"
 Rights of appeal for Advocate General: devolution issues.
 288A.-(1) This section applies where-
  (a) a person is acquitted or convicted of a charge (whether on indictment or in summary proceedings), and
  (b) the Advocate General for Scotland was a party to the pro-

ceedings in pursuance of paragraph 6 of Schedule 6 to the Scotland Act 1998 (devolution issues).

(2) The Advocate General for Scotland may refer any devolution issue which has arisen in the proceedings to the High Court for their opinion; and the Clerk of Justiciary shall send to the person acquitted or convicted and to any solicitor who acted for that person at the trial, a copy of the reference and intimation of the date fixed by the Court for a hearing.

(3) The person may, not later than seven days before the date so fixed, intimate in writing to the Clerk of Justiciary and to the Advocate General for Scotland either-

(a) that he elects to appear personally at the hearing, or

(b) that he elects to be represented by counsel at the hearing, but, except by leave of the Court on cause shown, and without prejudice to his right to attend, he shall not appear or be represented at the hearing other than by and in conformity with an election under this subsection.

(4) Where there is no intimation under subsection (3)(b), the High Court shall appoint counsel to act at the hearing as amicus curiae.

(5) The costs of representation elected under subsection (3)(b) or of an appointment under subsection (4) shall, after being taxed by the Auditor of the Court of Session, be paid by the Advocate General for Scotland out of money provided by Parliament.

(6) The opinion on the point referred under subsection (2) shall not affect the acquittal or (as the case may be) conviction in the trial.

(7) In this section "devolution issue" has the same meaning as in Schedule 6 to the Scotland Act 1998.

Defamation Act 1996 (c.31)

18.-(1) The Defamation Act 1996 is amended as follows.

(2) In section 17(1) (interpretation), in the definition of "statutory provision" after "1978", there is inserted-

"(aa)a provision contained in an Act of the Scottish Parliament or in an instrument made under such an Act,"

(3) In paragraph 11(1)(c) of Schedule 1 (qualified privilege), after "Minister of the Crown" there is inserted "a member of the Scottish Executive".

SCHEDULE 8
REPEALS

Chapter	Short title	Extent of repeal
1975 c. 24.	The House of Commons Disqualification Act 1975	In Schedule 2, the entries for the Lord Advocate and the Solicitor General for Scotland.
1975 c. 27.	The Ministerial and other Salaries Act 1975.	In Part III of Schedule 1, the entries for the Lord Advocate and the Solicitor General for Scotland.
1986 c. 45.	The Insolvency Act 1986.	In section 427(5), the words "or, as the case may be, to".
1986 c. 56.	The Parliamentary Constituencies Act 1986.	In Schedule 2, rule 1(2).

TABLE OF BILL PROVISIONS